User Involvement and Participation in Social Care

of related interest

Innovative Education and Training for Care Professionals
A Provider's Guide
Edited by Rachel Pierce and Jenny Weinstein
ISBN 1 85302 613 5

Ethical Practice and the Abuse of Power in Social Responsibility
Leave No Stone Unturned
Edited by Helen Payne and Brian Littlechild
ISBN 1 85302 743 X

The Changing Role of Social Care
Edited by Bob Hudson
ISBN 1 85302 752 9

Advocacy Skills for Health and Social Care Professionals
Neil Bateman
ISBN 1 85302 865 7

Mediation in Context
Marian Liebmann
ISBN 1 85302 894 0

Good Practice in Risk Assessment and Risk Management 1
Edited by Jackie Pritchard and Hazel Kemshall
ISBN 1 85302 338 8

Good Practice in Risk Assessment 2
Key Themes for Protection, Rights and Responsibilities
Edited by Hazel Kemshall and Jacki Pritchard
ISBN 1 85302 441 4

User Involvement and Participation in Social Care

Research Informing Practice

*Edited by Hazel Kemshall
and Rosemary Littlechild*

Jessica Kingsley Publishers
London and Philadelphia

The right of the contributors to be identified as authors of this work has been asserted by them in accordance with the Copyright, Designs and Patents Act 1988.

First published in the United Kingdom in 2000 by
Jessica Kingsley Publishers Ltd,
116 Pentonville Road, London
N1 9JB, England
and
325 Chestnut Street,
Philadelphia, PA 19106, USA.

www.jkp.com

3 1254 03523 0081

Library of Congress Cataloging in Publication Data
A CIP catalog record for this book is available from the Library of Congress

British Library Cataloguing in Publication Data
A CIP catalogue record for this book is available from the British Library

ISBN 1 85302 777 4

Printed and Bound in Great Britain by
Athenaeum Press, Gateshead, Tyne and Wear

Contents

INTRODUCTION   7
*Hazel Kemshall, De Montfort University
and Rosemary Littlechild, Birmingham University*

1. Participation and Involvement in Social Care :
   An Overview   9
   Suzy Braye, Staffordshire University

2. Just Inquiry? Research and Evaluation for Service Users   29
   Ian Shaw, Cardiff University

3. Totem not Token: Groupwork as a Vehicle for User Participation   45
   Dave Ward, De Montfort University

4. Action Research for the Development of Children's
   Services in Ukraine   65
   Jennie Fleming, Centre for Social Action, De Montfort University

5. Family Involvement in Child Protection:
   The Use of Family Group Conferences   83
   Kate Morris, Birmingham University and Carmel Shepherd, Guardian ad Litem

6. Politics into Practice: The Production of a Disabled Person's Guide to
   Accessing Community Care Assessments   97
   Kathryn Ellis, Luton University and Kirstein Rummery, Manchester University

7. Breaking the Ice: Developing Strategies for Collaborative Working
   with Carers of Older People with Mental Health Problems   111
   Helen Rogers, Birmingham University

8. Listening to Children: Meeting the Needs of Young Carers   129
   *Chris Dearden, Loughborough University
   and Saul Becker, Loughborough University*

9. Older People as 'Participating Patients'   143
   *Rosemary Littlechild, Birmingham University
   and Jon Glasby, Birmingham University*

10. Working with Sickle Cell/Thalassaemia Support Groups   159
    Simon Dyson, De Montfort University

11. 'Framing our Own Questions': Empowering Patients
    and Primary Health Care Workers in the Planning
    of Primary Health Care Services   175
    Angus McCabe, Birmingham University and Liz Ross, Birmingham University

12. Policies of Neglect: Female Offenders and the Probation Service   193
    Judith Rumgay, London School of Economics

13. User Involvement, Community Care and Disability Research   215
    Kathryn Ellis, Luton University

14. Research Informing Practice: Some Concluding Remarks   233
    Hazel Kemshall, De Montfort University
    and Rosemary Littlechild, Birmingham University

    THE CONTRIBUTORS   243

    SUBJECT INDEX   247

    AUTHOR INDEX   253

Introduction

Hazel Kemshall and Rosemary Littlechild

User participation has become a key issue in much current social work and social policy literature. Many of these texts have focused upon themes such as consumerism, citizens' rights and the role of service users in the planning and delivery of social care services. Participation and user involvement in such settings has often been restricted to the micro-level of client influence upon the activities of front-line workers, with little effect on policy making or agency decision making at senior management level. Shaw (1997) has described this as the 'rhetoric of participation'.

In addition to the interest shown by policy makers, managers and practitioners, researchers have also recently acknowledged the relevance of the concepts of participation and user involvement to research enterprises (Everitt and Hardiker 1996; Fuller and Petch 1995). Research has the potential to objectify and stigmatise on the one hand, or to promote user participation and involvement on the other. In the action-based research commissioned most often by managers and funding agencies, it is crucial that the research enterprise can mirror the goals of participation and involvement which it is seeking to promote. Through a range of substantive topic areas including health care, child care services, physical disability and criminal justice, this book will explore various methodologies which have attempted to engage participants and promote a sense of mutuality in the research process.

The book is primarily concerned with the following key themes:

- research methodologies which promote 'just inquiry' (for example, those adopted by some feminist research or those which actively promote empowerment and social justice, such as social action)

- research methodologies which mirror goals of participation and involvement

- commitment to mutuality between researchers and respondents (for example, the active inclusion of service users in research design and dissemination)

- ways in which service users can be engaged in research, and their possible level of involvement
- techniques for informing respondents about the findings of the research
- involvement of service users in decisions about the outcome of the research
- the role of participants in evaluating the research process.

This book presents 14 chapters written by researchers and practitioners currently working in the field of evaluative research. Chapter 1 gives a critical overview of the concepts of participation and involvement, identifying the ingredients for achieving changes in practice. Chapter 2 addresses the range of research and evaluation strategies that can promote user participation and involvement in research. Chapter 3 presents an account of research informed by a social action perspective and of the contribution of such an approach to user involvement and participation.

Chapters 4–12 draw upon empirically based studies in the areas of health, social care and criminal justice. These studies have not been chosen for their unqualified success in promoting service-user participation and involvement, but for the lessons learnt from undertaking them. The chapters illustrate a diversity of research strategies designed to engage service users, demonstrating differing approaches and levels of commitment to participation and involvement. As a collection they illustrate, in a range of settings, both the difficulty and complexity of engaging service users in the research process. Key lessons can be drawn from these empirically based studies of the practical application of user participation and involvement.

Chapter 13 critically examines current debates about disabled people's involvement in community care and social research. The final chapter explores the limitations and potential for contemporary social research to contribute to the participation agenda, drawing together some good-practice guidelines for researchers wanting to conduct participatory research, and identifying some key issues for research teaching and training.

References

Everitt, A. and Hardiker, P. (1996) *Evaluating for Good Practice.* Basingstoke: Macmillan.

Fuller, R. and Petch, A. (1995) *Practitioner Research: The Reflexive Social Worker.* Buckingham: Open University Press.

Shaw, I. (1997) 'Engaging the User: Participation, Empowerment, and the Rhetoric of Quality.' In A. Pithouse and H. Williamson (eds) *Engaging the User in Welfare Services.* Birmingham: Venture Press.

CHAPTER 1

Participation and Involvement in Social Care

An Overview

Suzy Braye

Introduction

Participation and involvement, along with their companion concepts partnership and empowerment, have become defining features of the social care landscape. Whether in disability, older people's and mental health provision, or in services for children and their families, the practice of service planners and providers is, in principle at least, open to scrutiny and influence by service users. This emphasis reflects a broader focus in society on the participatory rights and responsibilities of citizenship and participatory democracy, which aspires to put government in touch with the people, and promotes the social inclusion of those traditionally marginalised within the power structures of society.

Yet this is a contested territory. The literature of social work and social care abounds with attempts to define and classify the range of concepts and the words used to describe them. Three things are clear. First, the language of participation is complex: the same term means different things to different people, and the same concept may be known by a number of different terms. Second, the apparent consensus that participation is a good thing masks major differences of ideology between different interest groups. Third, ends and means are confused; participation is presented both as a means to an end and as an end in itself, and at times the purpose and the process appear indivisible.

This chapter will not attempt to propose any definitive versions of the terms, although they will be explored. The terminology is less important than the intention behind the actions it describes. The fundamental contest in this territory is between rhetoric and reality. Talking and writing about participation and involvement, even understanding the concepts at a theoretical level, does not necessarily make them happen. What makes a difference in practice is the will and commitment in the hearts of those with power to meet the challenge and demands of those excluded, to change the nature of the relationship between them.

This chapter will explore a series of questions. First, attention will be given to the opportunities that exist for participation in differing aspects of social care, addressing the question, *participation in what?* Second, the reasons for promoting participation will be explored, identifying the differing mandates and the issues they are intended to address; in effect, *why participation?* Third, the concept itself will be examined and set alongside related concepts, identifying the range of terminologies and understandings and clarifying the question, *what models of participation?* Fourth, it is important to look at some of the counter-challenges, factors which prevent or work against participation; in effect, *why not participation?* Lastly, some of the mechanisms of participation will be identified, exploring the question *how participation?*

Participation in What?

There are a number of arenas in social care in which participation by service users has developed.

The first of these is the involvement of an individual service user, or prospective service user, in their own use of service. Commonly, use of service is preceded by an assessment of need, undertaken by the agency responsible for arranging a service if one is necessary. This is a statutory duty for social services. Assessment will be followed by care planning, which will identify the objectives to be achieved by providing a service, its core components and details of how it will be delivered. Usually plans will be reviewed periodically to determine whether the objectives are being achieved and what changes may be necessary. Care plans might be linked to a range of different services, such as support at home, day services or residential provision, that would be offered with a view to promoting independence, enhancing skills and abilities, or ensuring protection. All of these processes – assessment, care planning and review – may, to varying degrees, involve the individuals concerned in at least discussion and consultation about what is decided at any point. In some cases more extensive levels of participation are apparent. Local authorities may make financial resources available to service users once assessment has established their need for community care services, to enable people to make their own practical arrangements independently of the authority.

Participation may be a feature even where service use does not arise voluntarily on the part of the service user, as where compulsory action to manage risk is a possibility. Family group conferences, for example, where family networks take the initiative in planning responses to meet both their own needs and the concerns of professionals, have been attempted in child care services (Marsh and Crow 1998; see chapter 5 of this book).

The second arena for participation and involvement is that of strategic planning for service provision and development. The focus here moves from individual use of service to the general features of provision. Users may be involved in planning meetings, in advisory or management groups, or in monitoring, inspection and review mechanisms. Their role may be to offer a perspective on the service informed by their own personal experience and expertise, or to act as a representative of a user organisation or group which has an interest in the type of services in question. Alternatively, service planners may liaise with and consult a range of organisations or groups of service users, in effect developing a planning consultative network rather than a single planning forum. Consultation on service plans, which local authorities must produce for their locality in respect of both community care and children's services, is commonly undertaken through a range of such mechanisms – events, workshops, meetings, surveys – designed to elicit the views of users and to take these into account in future planning.

The focus in the participatory arenas described above is upon the service as experienced by users, and seeks either to improve service quality by enhancing responsiveness to expressed need or preference, or to enhance users' control over design, management, delivery and review (Barnes and Wistow 1994a). These are the most commonly found forms of participation and involvement (Evans 1998).

A third arena for participation in social care delivery is through the development of user-led services – organisations which are independent of the local authority but play a role in the mixed economy of welfare, providing, for example, community care services alongside other independent agencies. They have often developed as a response to users' dissatisfaction with existing statutory service models, and their desire for radical change (Morris 1994). They demonstrate a degree of flexibility, choice, involvement and accountability to users that is sought but not attained in statutory sector organisations or even in traditional voluntary sector agencies.

Fourth, an emerging arena for participation is that of research into social care and welfare provision. This involvement takes place at a number of levels. At the most basic level, the views and experiences of people who use social care services have increasingly been seen as valid contributions to the building of knowledge and understanding about need for, and use of, welfare services. Reliance on positivist research paradigms, which seek to establish cause and effect in programmes and outcomes through processes of scientific inquiry, is not relevant to many of the processes of social care. More interpretivist approaches have sought to engage with the subjective meanings attached to the experiences of those using welfare provision. The outcomes as perceived by users, and users' views on how outcomes have been achieved, are as important to elucidate as tangible, quantifiable change, or the achievement of programme policy objectives. Thus service-user perspectives on services have increasingly been sought by researchers and evaluators. Beyond this, however, lies a more radical, emancipatory research paradigm that challenges the traditional model of a small group of powerful experts studying a larger number of relatively powerless research subjects (Oliver 1992). Such a model seeks dialogue about whether and why research is done at all, what issues are explored, the formulation of research design, the collection and interpretation of data, and the ownership and dissemination of findings. Service users may actively participate as researchers. There is a shift in the balance of power between researcher and researched, in terms both of involvement in the processes of research and, more fundamentally, of what is valued as knowledge, and how knowledge is created (Everitt *et al.* 1992).

Service users have also participated, as both consultants and trainers, in the training of staff working in social care services. Such involvement has become a key feature of some professional qualifying courses in social work and of some in-service training programmes in service agencies (Crepaz-Keay, Binns and Wilson 1997; NHSTD 1993).

A further arena for participation is that of promoting the involvement of service users in their broader social context. In some fields of social care provision the service may be seen as the means to a much broader goal of social participation in, for example, employment or education, promoting the achievement of community presence (O'Brien 1986) by people who have been devalued, stigmatised and segregated and thus excluded from such participation. Social care staff increasingly work outside segregated units located in designated buildings, accompanying, facilitating and supporting people's use of mainstream facilities.

A final arena for participation goes beyond the focus on users of services and targets the wider community. In the moves to involve service users in the ways described above, there has been an artificial boundary placed around those whose needs bring them into contact with service provision organisations. Their status in the dialogue is determined by reference to their use of service rather than by reference to notions of citizenship or community membership. At a rhetorical level, contemporary political agendas seek to address the marginalisation of social services and their users: 'social services are not just about a small number of social casualties, they are an important part of the fabric of a caring society' (DoH 1998, p.1). Proposals for democratic reform (DETR 1998) seek to engage a wider constituency of people in dialogue about traditionally marginalised services, in effect to enhance the participation of people as citizens rather than as service users.

This leads to a related question, *participation by whom?* Participation in social care provision will reflect the patterns of dominance, inequality and exclusion that are inherent in the structures of wider society. Users of social care provision have needs which arise from and in turn reinforce their exclusion from the sources of power in mainstream society. In addition, the impacts of exclusion reflect differing sources of inequality, such as race, gender and class, and differing mechanisms of oppression. Patterns of participation are similarly influenced by these dynamics, and must be understood by reference to the structural context in which they occur. Everitt *et al.* (1992) term this a critical understanding of participation, one which attends not just to participation but to who participates and who does not, to how people are prevented from participating and thus which views are not heard.

Why Participation?

What, then, are the driving forces behind the development of participatory approaches in social care? The mandates arise from a number of directions, and reflect differing ideologies and motivations.

Legal and policy mandates

The principle of involvement is integral to the core legal mandates for social care services. Statutory guidance on both the Children Act 1989 and the NHS and Community Care Act 1990 is peppered with references to the need to inform, consult and involve people who use services. In provision for adults, for example: 'the individual service user and normally, with his or her agreement, any carers, should be involved throughout the assessment and care management process. They should feel that the process is aimed at meeting their wishes' (DoH 1990, p.25). The Community Care (Direct Payments) Act 1996 goes further, enabling local authorities to allocate money rather than services, thus enhancing service users' control over arrangements made. Accessible information should be available: 'to enable users and carers to exercise genuine choice and participation in the assessment of their care needs and in the making of arrangements for meeting these needs' (DoH 1990, p.26). This reinforces the duty under the Disabled Persons (Services, Consultation and Representation) Act 1986 to provide information about services. There is recognition of inequality in the relationship, but 'the present imbalance can be corrected by sharing information more openly and by encouraging users and carers...to take a full part in decision-making' (DoH 1991a, p.14). The Mental Health Act 1983 Code of Practice (DoH 1999) promotes the principle of involvement in the formulation and delivery of care and treatment, again with emphasis on access to information and explanation from professionals. Community care plans required under the NHS and Community Care Act 1990 must address how information will be made available to potential users of services, how consumer choice will be managed and what it will involve (DoH 1990). The range of organisations with which consultation about the plan must take place includes voluntary organisations representing users and carers, and guidance is given on consulting about options rather than decisions already made, and on finding ways to incorporate differing perspectives (DoH 1992). Guidance also emphasises the need for action to combat the marginalisation of black and minority ethnic groups, and gendered assumptions about caring (DoH 1991a).

Complaints procedures are intended to provide mechanisms for representation and redress, and to establish a participatory dialogue for problem resolution (DoH 1991b).

The emphasis in official guidance is upon information, consultation and *post hoc* redress, and it is clear that these alone do not constitute involvement or participation. There is evidence that many groups remain marginalised from these processes: disabled people (Bewley and Glendinning 1994), people with sensory impairment (Lovelock and Powell 1995), black and minority ethnic groups (SSI 1998). Older people remain least likely of all to have influence in decision making, and are seldom seen as partners in planning (Crosby 1998; Harding 1999; Littlechild and Blakeney 1996). Such is the state of communication between local authorities and service users that independent advocacy and mediation have been necessary to secure even basic information about access to community care services (Coombs and Sedgwick 1998). Legal remedies for redress are far from providing greater accountability to service users (Braye and Preston-Shoot 1999).

In services for children and families, 'the development of a working partnership with parents is usually the most effective route to providing supplementary or substitute care for children' (DoH 1989, p.8). Corby (1996) notes the significant shift in thinking about the role and rights of families that followed events in Cleveland in the late 1980s. Here local child protection services had taken a highly interventionist stance in relation to suspicions of child sexual abuse in a large number of families, and were subsequently criticised for so doing. The cornerstones of partnership with families, contained in the Children Act 1989 and statutory guidance, are information, consultation, written agreements, reviews of services, access to complaints procedures and advocacy. Similarly emphasised are the views of children themselves, although the requirement to give 'due consideration' to their and their parents' views is not accompanied by clarity about how much weight should be attached to each. The influence of legal judgement in the case of Gillick v. West Norfolk and Wisbech Area Health Authority [1986] AC112, which established a child's right to make his or her own decisions when of sufficient understanding and intelligence to be capable of doing so, is apparent within the Act. It has since, however, been eroded by further judgements indicating that children's views may be overruled (Re R (A Minor)(Wardship: Consent to Treatment)[1991]; Re W (A Minor)(Medical Treatment: Court's Jurisdiction)[1992]).

More recent emphasis in children's services has shifted attention from child protection to family support, seeking early intervention to address barriers to effective parenting (DoH 1995a). State family policy seeks to remove the stigma of receiving support, and it is intended that improved access to integrated mainstream services will enhance parenting capability (Home Office 1998). Statutory services are expected to become more responsive to the expressed support-needs of parents, breaking the pattern of low expectations associated with their image of compulsion and removal.

The legal mandates for participation and involvement may be criticised as partial, contradictory and ineffectual. The participation of children is an important example here. Guidance on the Children Act 1989 (DoH 1991c) calls for partnership with parents, but only consultation with children. Many of the developments in participatory practice in child care have concerned parental involvement in processes of investigation, assessment, decision making and review in child protection, working to the agenda set by *Working Together* (DoH 1991d). Thoburn, Lewis and Shemmings (1995), in studying case-conference processes, noted a large number of initiatives promoting parental involvement, but little change in children's participation. Biss (1995) is critical of the emphasis on partnership with parents when pursued uncritically as a dominant goal, because of its assumption that children are rightly the possessions of their parents.

The United Nations Convention on the Rights of the Child, ratified by the UK government in 1991 as the Children Act was implemented, is a strong statement of principle on participation. Article 12 encodes the right of children to express views freely and for those views to be given due weight; Article 13 confers the right to freedom of expression, to seek, receive and impart information and ideas; Article 23 promotes the right to active participation in the community. Yet there remains widespread ignorance about the Convention, and a lack of co-ordinated activity to develop its practical implementation (Willow 1998). Morris (1998a) contends that social services departments, constructed on medical model ideologies of *caring for* vulnerable people, have innate difficulties with the notion of rights. Children's exclusion from participatory rights, and their objectification as either dependents or victims, have led to calls for a co-ordinating body at national level to develop a strategy for children's visibility in government, and to promote their active participation in society (Hodgkin 1998). Some progress may be made through proposals for children's rights officers to be located in regional Commissions for Care Standards designed to strengthen the quality monitoring of social care services (DoH 1998).

An important development in the legal mandate is the incorporation into UK law of the European Convention on Human Rights and Fundamental Freedoms, brought about by the Human Rights Act 1998. This will have an important contribution to make to rights-based provision, potentially empowering service users to question and challenge agency and professional decisions that are not made with their participation.

Professional mandates

Parallel to legal and policy mandates for participation are those arising from within the social care profession, and in particular from social work. There are two distinct strands here.

Traditional social work values draw heavily upon principles of respect for persons and self-determination. People who use social care services are to be valued for their unique individuality and respected in their exercise of autonomy. Professional codes commonly urge practitioners to value people's capabilities and to promote choice and independence as routes to personal fulfilment. Such an approach is influenced by principles of natural justice: the right to have a say, to know what is said by others, to be involved in decisions that affect one's life. Social work also espouses a more radical value base, recognising the limitations of a traditional, individualised focus, and drawing on the premise that people's life chances are determined by their position in society's structure. This is characterised by division along lines of race, gender and class, with further major differentiation on grounds of age, disability, sexuality, health status, religion and ethnic origin, and profound inequality in the power within these groupings to gain and sustain access to privilege and advantage (Braye and Preston-Shoot 1995). Thus there is a need for a positive stance on tackling non-personal barriers to fulfilment, and a focus on collective experience and action.

The combination of the traditional and radical value bases has important implications for participatory practice. At the heart of the professional mandate is a will to understand oppression and a commitment to counter it through practice which is participative and empowering, whether the focus is upon the professional/agency/user relationship or their joint efforts to address barriers elsewhere. Hugman (1991, p.216) terms this a more 'democratic profession-alism'.

A second strand to the professional mandate is driven less by principle than by pragmatism. This is the recognition that in many arenas of professional practice the goals of intervention are enhanced by participation, or indeed that participation is essential to their achievement. It is not possible, for example, to protect children whilst they are living with their families, or to improve their health and development, without involving their parents or carers in that aim. This requires openness to participation irrespective of values and ideology. Government guidance supports this approach: for example, in child protection the emphasis on partnership is linked to recognition of the unique importance of adult family members in children's lives, and of their role as a source of information and in contributing to ensuring children's welfare (DoH 1995b). In mental health services, care-programme approaches have been found to be more effective if users are involved in the planning and implementation of the programme (Carpenter and Sbaraini 1997).

The professional mandate is constructed inevitably upon an assumption of professional power in the processes of social care. Professional status is derived from a number of sources of power which fundamentally remain unchallenged by professionally led initiatives to increase service-user participation. A more radical mandate is one which is driven by the people who use services themselves, or by those who might have need of services but find their interests not well served by existing structures.

User mandates

The service-user mandates for participation also contain two strands. Where people are receiving or using services as individuals, there are demands for greater levels of involvement and participation in decision making, and for a greater emphasis on people's rights as consumers. This might amount to self-definition of need, representation and self-advocacy, services based on entitlement, and choice about or control of services (Morris 1998b).

At a deeper level, however, many people who use services are not merely wanting greater involvement in the service relationship. They also fundamentally challenge the dominant paradigms upon which provision is based and the models used for understanding need and entitlement. Implicit within social care provision is the assumption that needs arise from factors pertaining to individuals: from the physical processes of ageing, genetic factors, medical conditions, impairment or functional loss, lack of skills, or from psychological responses to immediate environmental stresses. Care is provided to do things for people that they are prevented from doing for themselves, or to enhance their personal coping. Alternative models, such as the social model of disability, or survivors' perspectives in mental health, focus instead upon how the experience of disability, older age, or distress is socially constructed. The experience is to be understood by reference to factors within the social structure and environment, such as harrassment, prejudice, isolation and inaccessibility, that form social, economic and environmental barriers to aspiration (Morris 1998b).

The mental health user movement shows evidence of both these perspectives. Peck and Barker (1997), in tracing its development since the mid-1980s, distinguish between demands from service users as consumers, and their demands as survivors. Both are contrasted with traditional views of service users as patients. Bowl (1996) similarly distinguishes between challenges to the professional dominance of both interpretations of and responses to distress. Barnes and Wistow (1994a) identify a range of ways in which service users have sought to exercise control over services, mentioning examples of all the arenas for action reviewed in the earlier part of this chapter. They point to a wide range of motivations also, but the common theme is one of challenge to the balance of power, within the service system and beyond it. The goals are summarised succinctly by Peck and Barker (1997): fight it (campaigning to change services), fix it (giving advice to planners and providers), escape it (providing somewhere safe to run to) and replace it (setting up user-run alternatives).

What Models of Participation?

Emerging from the differing influences and mandates underpinning participation are two broad ideological themes which assist in making conceptual sense of the complexity. They permit classification first by reference to the purpose of partici- pation, and second by reference to the degree or level of participation achieved.

Purposes of participation

In relation to purpose, there is a broad distinction to be drawn between a consumerist model of participation and a democratic model (Beresford and Croft 1993). Consumerism in social care accompanies the ideology of welfare markets, in which needs and services are commodities to be traded, and regulated through supply and demand. Consumers, in theory, choose from a range of services, influ- encing both price and quality through their purchasing power. The core princi- ples of commercial consumerism – accessibility, information, choice, redress and representation – are embedded in many of the policy and practice requirements for social care. Involvement and participation in decisions affecting people's lives is fundamental to this notion, but its purpose is to influence individual consump- tion of service. Services may become more responsive, flexible and relevant, but remain essentially owned and controlled by the agency or professionals involved.

The notion of consumerism is an uneasy foundation for public welfare when profound inequalities exist in the distribution of resources. It does little to tackle social exclusion, meet need as opposed to want, enact collective agendas or promote citizenship. There are in addition a range of factors which constrain and limit its relevance: eligibility criteria, agency defensiveness, resource shortage, commissioning and contracting practice, and professional control of the avenues for representation and redress (Braye and Preston-Shoot 1995). Its limitation as a concept is particularly apparent where actual or implied coercion is a feature of the service: 'to me, the administration of a large dose of major tranquilliser, and the physical manhandling that accompanied it, remain a sharp reminder that I have neither the respect, power nor legal protection of any consumer' (Plumb 1987, p.6). Many service users are in the position described so graphically by Barker and Peck (1987, p.1): 'survivors of the mental health system are no more consumers of services than cockroaches are consumers of Rentokil.'

A democratic model of participation, by contrast, is about participation with the purpose of achieving greater influence and control. This may relate to service provision, but operates at the level of policy making, resource allocation, organisation and management, as a means of changing the experience for users collectively rather than individually. It is likely also to work to a wider agenda, seeking improvements not just in service provision but in all aspects of social experience: 'people want more say in their lives, not just in services' (Beresford 1993, p.17). The goals will thus reside in the wider avenues of citizenship in which oppression and exclusion are experienced. They will be chosen and expressed by people themselves, rather than enacting professional agendas for meeting need. People have a right to be heard, to participate, to exercise choice, to define problems and action (Mullender and Ward 1991). Within this model there is a strong emphasis on collective rather than individual action, and upon a developmental model of welfare in which the state has a positive role in reducing social inequalities (Everitt et al. 1992). The focus is upon participatory rights rather than welfare needs.

These models of participation are conceptually distinct and at a theoretical level appear opposed. Forbes and Sashidharan (1997), for example, propose a fundamental contradiction between the consumerist and what they term a liberationist perspective. In practice, however, the two can exist side by side. Wistow and Barnes (1993, p.350) note that 'the general commitment to consumerism often conceals the different brands which are being marketed', and observe in practice how people with very differing motivations can work together on projects to improve participation (Barnes and Wistow 1994b). Because the models can and do co-exist, however, they risk overlap and confusion. Whilst both demand change to the *status quo*, the consumerist model often has a stronger presence – it is more tangible and may appear easier to achieve – thus giving the illusion of participation without the substance: 'participation is reduced from people's right to participate fully in society...to being involved in the running of welfare services they might prefer not to receive' (Beresford 1993, p.18). Bowl (1996) draws attention to this fudging of interests as one of the distinguishing characteristics of user involvement. Again in practice he found widespread disparities and confusion about the appropriateness and purpose of participation.

It is possible to identify a third purpose of participation, which may be termed a therapeutic model: the notion that participation has some intrinsic value because it is good for people. Barnes and Wistow (1994b) call this enabling people to get things off their chest, this process being as important as any outcome. This is a strand running through policy guidance (e.g. DoH 1995b), which emphasises the dignity and respect to be sought within the relationship between user and provider, without any attempt to change the balance of power within it. Bowl (1996), in observing generalised staff resistance to participation, found professionals more accepting of its therapeutic purpose than any other.

Degrees or levels of participation

The second broad theme to assist understanding at a conceptual level is that of varying levels of participation and involvement, each marked by differing degrees of power sharing or equality between the parties. At a simple level, a distinction is drawn between full and partial participation: full participation is a process where power to determine the outcome of decisions is shared equally between the parties; in partial participation the parties influence each other, but the final power rests with one only (Pateman 1970). The word partnership is sometimes used to describe forms of participation that involve power sharing, as distinct from those which do not (Jackson, Fisher and Ward 1996; Tunnard 1991).

The range of participatory opportunities is sometimes presented as a scale or ladder, the most commonly quoted example being Arnstein's (1969) model, comprising (in descending order of power sharing): citizen control, delegated power, partnership, placation, consultation, informing, therapy, manipulation. Others have adapted this for specific service applications; for example, Thoburn *et al.* (1995), in analysing participation in child protection, delete citizen control but add further subtle distinctions lower down the ladder. They contend, however, that individual case variables are influential upon the level achieved, and that the nature of the statutory role does not necessarily preclude the achievement of partnership in some cases. This mirrors recognition in official guidance (DoH 1995b) that there are different models of participatory practice appropriate to different situations, although ultimately the decision about how far up the ladder the level should be set is seen as residing with the professionals.

The contested notion of empowerment

There is thus no common language of participation, and the boundaries between the different levels may be difficult both to define and to observe in practice. One of the most sought-after and elusive definitions is for the concept of empowerment – a term found in most commentaries on participation, acting as a 'pill for all seasons' (Rees 1991, p.4). One core distinction in the definitions is whether empowerment is seen as an active or a passive process. Thomas and Pierson (1995, p.134) capture this duality, defining empowerment as 'how people may gain collective control over their lives, so as to achieve their interests, and a method by which social workers seek to enhance the power of people who lack it'. Adams (1990, p.1) emphasises self-help, defining empowerment as an active process of 'becoming powerful'. Beresford and Croft (1993, p.50) by contrast imply that it may also be something people can do for others: 'making it possible for people to exercise power and have more control over their lives', with a view ultimately to changing the power balance in the relationship. Payne (1997, p.266) identifies a similar transfer – empowerment 'seeks to help clients gain power of decision and action over their own lives'. Plumb (1991), however, is critical of empowerment as a process under professional control, feeling that when professionals talk of empowerment, survivors' own power struggles are being overlooked.

In government policy, empowerment is linked to the consumerist agenda:

> the rationale for this reorganisation (of services) is the empowerment of users and carers. Instead of users and carers being subordinate to the wishes of service-providers, the roles will be progressively adjusted. In this way, users and carers will be enabled to exercise the same power as consumers of other services. (DoH 1991a, p.7)

Rees (1991) identifies how this use by the political right wing arises from a belief in the merits of economic independence at all costs, with citizens having a right to fend for themselves and participate as free agents in the marketplace. He argues that by contrast the spirit and objectives of empowerment must incorporate an understanding of ways in which people's interests are defined by a system which in fact works against them, and a vision of how this might change. This then becomes a key challenge for social care professionals. People become service users because they have needs they are not able to meet for themselves, since both the marketplace and the hierarchies of representative democracy have failed to secure their interests. Participation in services, and empowerment in that relationship, may be a compensatory mechanism, but need to progress further if people's broader exclusion from citizenship is to be addressed.

Social care professional texts commonly recognise this challenge, and often see empowerment in the social care relationship as a preliminary focus – its aims being to build capacity, to equip people with personal resources of self-esteem and confidence, and to share knowledge and skills. Removing the personal blocks is thus a stepping stone to the wider objective of tackling inequities in the distribution of power and resources in society. Thompson (1997) exemplifies this approach, identifying that emancipatory practice has two components: life politics, where empowerment lies in identifying and addressing barriers to self-actualisation, and emancipatory politics, where it addresses barriers to equality and social justice.

Why not Participation?

In the face of such strong mandates and such a wealth of opportunity for promoting participation in social care, why has greater progress not been made? What are the blocks and barriers to participation? There are two main areas of difficulty: the politics of organisations and the politics of professions.

Organisational politics

One development linked to marketisation of the care sector is the espousal by public sector agencies of the ethos and practices of private sector management. Exworthy and Halford (1999) and Johnson (1999), for example, comment on the widespread emergence of new public management, or new managerialism, in the 1990s, which replaces management by 'bureau-professionals' with entrepreneurial business practices designed to secure economy, efficiency and effectiveness.

Managerialist influences include an emphasis on tight, centralised control to set mission and broad strategy, accompanied by a degree of delegated autonomy for operational managers, but within strict performance targets. It might be argued that there is little room within this structure for shared control with other stakeholders. Although in theory the organisation's mission might incorporate the agendas raised through consultation, the reality is that many organisations have investment in a range of services which are difficult to disaggregate without serious damage to the economic rationality of service operations.

Organisational politics are characterised by strong conflict between managerial and professional aims and values. Flynn (1999) considers that there are fundamental differences in values and practices between professionals and the new managers. Managers' orientation is towards corporate success, and thus employee effort must be aligned with the organisation's mission, in sharp contrast to the individual-client orientation of professional staff. In pursuit of organisational objectives, managerialism prioritises explicit standards and quantifiable performance measurement, efficiency in resource allocation and increased managerial control over the workforce. Thus procedurally led, rule-bound practice takes precedence over professional objectives, whether these have been determined in partnership with service users or not. The imposition of strict eligibility criteria and mechanistic procedures for assessment and review adds up to a trend which marginalises professional values and removes from practitioners the potential to promote empowering practice with service users. Resource shortage plays a key role also in limiting the range of choice and flexibility available. Despite overwhelming preferences expressed, for example, by older people to remain in their own homes with supportive services (Harding 1999), legal backing exists for resources to be taken into account when determining how needs will be met (R v. Gloucestershire County Council, ex parte Barry [1997] 2 All ER 1), and can lead to residential placements on cost grounds. An associated trend is the necessity to focus services on needs which fall highest up the eligibility scale. Thus situations of risk and safety secure a response, whereas lower eligibility needs for quality of life improvement are neglected. In this situation, many people are in effect excluded from entering into dialogue with the organisation, because they never reach the first base of achieving status as a service user.

Professional politics

The politics of professionalism set another range of barriers to the achievement of participation. They flow from the patterns of power ownership upon which professional status is constructed, achieving role security from the use of specialist expertise and function. Professionals may be defensive and resistant to challenge, through uncertainty and fear of what lies beyond attempts to share power. They may find justification in stereotypical views of users' competence to participate. Many groups have been disqualified from self-advocacy, or their representations ignored, through stigmatising and devaluing assumptions about the capacity of old age, childhood, mental ill-health or learning disability. Some groups experience multiple exclusion: disabled children, for example are not seen as bona fide participants (Beresford 1997), images of disability adding to those of childood to question the reliability of their information.

A further justification for professionals lies in the conflicting imperatives that drive their work. Balancing rights to autonomy against need for protection, for example, or determining the balance to be struck between risk management and empowerment, is integral to the professional task (Braye and Preston-Shoot 1997). The politics of negotiation between legal, policy and procedural mandates, alongside perspectives informed by professional values, are already complex enough to provide familiar refuge from the even more challenging and unsettling agenda of participation. To move on from this position involves, as Biggs (1997) identifies, fundamental changes to professional and user identities, and enhanced permeability of the boundary between them. The uncertainty engendered by this task is, he suggests, as likely to produce rigidity and resistance as it is to produce fluidity and progress.

The sum result of both the organisational and professional politics described above is a range of unsatisfactory initiatives. Service users have become accustomed to being invited to participation that is tokenistic, where agendas, dominated by professional or agency jargon, are confined to existing services or predetermined decisions, in which their experience is denied or minimised, and their representativeness challenged, without training or recompense for their involvement. They have become used to influencing processes without influencing outcomes, to having their participation 'managed'.

Initiatives for Change

The analysis above has demonstrated the complexity of the participation agenda in social care. What, then, might be key initiatives for making a difference in practice?

There have been many attempts to list the characteristics and qualities of participatory practice. Contributions from a wide range of user literature stress the following dimensions:

- clarity about what level of involvement is being offered
- involvement from the start of new initiatives, in decision-making arenas
- tangible goals for involvement
- involvement by choice, not compulsion
- inclusion of diverse and marginalised perspectives, such as those of black and minority ethnic groups
- inclusion of both individual and collective perspectives
- provision of time, information, resources and training
- openness to advocacy
- clear channels of representation and complaint
- open agendas
- accessible structures for dialogue.

Beresford and Croft (1993) have summarised these features as access to the organisation and support to use it. It is increasingly apparent, though, that piecemeal initiatives in isolation may have limited impact, and that organisations and users together must take a strategic approach. This will involve setting clear aims and objectives for participation, building on capability and strength but also targeting barriers and areas of weakness within the organisation to make it more receptive to the opportunities for participation that are created. Identifying specific action steps, along with the resources of time, money and responsibility for achieving them, and monitoring progress, will all be important. Public service agencies increasingly work and manage their business in this way, and participation must be identified on the agenda until it is integral to all an organisation does. This does not mean that action is confined to the strategic levels in the organisation. High-level backing is important, but implementation of strategy will make demands at all levels, with team targets for participation initiatives in specific service areas as important as those corporately identified.

Nor does strategy setting mean a loss of individual professional responsibility for the participation agenda. The only part of an organisation that many service users come into contact with is their individual worker or service team. Much rides on the quality of this encounter, and the extent to which the parties are able to develop a relationship in which professional expertise is put at the disposal of the service user's agenda. Each individual professional must own this commitment in order to formulate the will to engage participatively within their own sphere of influence (Braye and Preston-Shoot 1993).

More fundamentally, however, professionals and organisations must question their core assumptions about the needs and rights of people who become service users, and espouse a model which recognises the impact of social environments upon both individual and collective experience. This extends the focus and aims of such relationships beyond the provision of social care services, however responsive and participatory, and looks jointly to influencing the broader infrastructure that supports exclusion.

It is clear that successful initiatives are possible. There is much to be learnt from empirically based studies of the practical application of participation and involvement, such as those that follow in this volume. It is important to reflect on and take pride in achievements, as well as to recognise what remains to be done.

References

Adams, R. (1990) *Self-Help, Social Work and Empowerment.* London: Macmillan.

Arnstein, S. (1969) 'A Ladder of Citizen Participation.' *Journal of the American Institute of Planners* 35, 4, 216–224.

Barker, I. and Peck, E. (1987) *Power in Strange Places.* London: Good Practices in Mental Health.

Barnes, M. and Wistow, G. (1994a) 'Learning to Hear Voices: Listening to Users of Mental Health Services.' *Journal of Mental Health 3*, 525–540.

Barnes, M. and Wistow, G. (1994b) 'Achieving a Strategy for User Involvement in Community Care.' *Health and Social Care in the Community 2*, 347–356.

Beresford, B. (1997) *Personal Accounts: Involving Disabled Children in Research.* London: Social Policy Research Unit/The Stationery Office.

Beresford, P. (1993) 'A Programme for Change: Current Issues in User Involvement and Empowerment.' In P. Beresford and T. Harding (eds) *A Challenge to Change: Practical Experiences of Building User-Led Services.* London: NISW.

Beresford, P. and Croft, S. (1993) *Citizen Involvement: A Practical Guide for Change.* London: Macmillan.

Bewley, C. and Glendinning, C. (1994) *Involving Disabled People in Community Care Planning.* York: Joseph Rowntree Foundation.

Biggs, S. (1997) 'User Voice, Interprofessionalism and Postmodernity.' *Journal of Interprofessional Care 11*, 2, 195–203.

Biss, D. (1995) 'Weighing up the Limitations of Partnership Policies in Child Protection: Commentary on Thoburn, Lewis and Shemmings.' *Child Abuse Review 4*, 172–175.

Bowl, R. (1996) 'Legislating for User Involvement in the UK: Mental Health Services and the NHS and Community Care Act 1990.' *International Journal of Social Psychiatry 42*, 3, 165–180.

Braye, S. and Preston-Shoot, M. (1993) 'Empowerment and Partnership in Mental Health: Towards a Different Relationship.' *Journal of Social Work Practice 7*, 2, 115–128.

Braye, S. and Preston-Shoot, M. (1995) *Empowering Practice in Social Care.* Buckingham: Open University Press.

Braye, S. and Preston-Shoot, M. (1997) *Practising Social Work Law.* Second edition. London: Macmillan.

Braye, S. and Preston-Shoot, M. (1999) 'Accountability, Administrative Law and Social Work Practice: Redressing or Reinforcing the Power Balance?' *Journal of Social Welfare and Family Law 21*, 3, 235–256.

Carpenter, J. and Sbaraini, S. (1997) *Choice, Information and Dignity: Involving Users and Carers in Care Management in Mental Health.* Bristol: Policy Press.

Coombs, M. and Sedgwick, A. (1998) *Right to Challenge: The Oxfordshire Community Care Rights Project.* Bristol: Policy Press.

Corby, B. (1996) 'Risk Assessment in Child Protection Work.' In H. Kemshall and J. Pritchard (eds) *Good Practice in Risk Assessment and Risk Management I.* London: Jessica Kingsley Publishers.

Crepaz-Keay, D., Binns, C. and Wilson, E. (1997) *Dancing with Angels: Involving Survivors in Mental Health Training.* London: Central Council for Education and Training in Social Work.

Crosby, G. (1998) 'Elderly People.' In P. Neate (ed) *Research Matters: User-Focused Research.* London: Community Care.

DETR (1998) *Modern Local Government: In Touch with the People.* London: Department for the Environment, Transport and the Regions.

Department of Health (1989) *The Care of Children: Principles and Practice in Regulations and Guidance.* London: HMSO.

Department of Health (1990) *Community Care in the Next Decade and Beyond: Policy Guidance.* London: HMSO.

Department of Health (1991a) *Care Management and Assessment: Summary of Practice Guidance.* London: HMSO.

Department of Health (1991b) *The Right to Complain: Practice Guidance on Complaints Procedures in Social Services Departments.* London: HMSO.

Department of Health (1991c) *The Children Act 1989 Guidance and Regulations, Volume 3, Family Placements.* London: HMSO.

Department of Health (1991d) *Working Together: A Guide to Arrangements for Inter-Agency Co-operation for the Protection of Children.* London: HMSO.

Department of Health (1992) *Implementing Community Care: Improving Independent Sector Involvement in Community Care Planning.* London: HMSO.

Department of Health (1995a) *Child Protection – Messages from Research.* London: HMSO.

Department of Health (1995b) *The Challenge of Partnership in Child Protection: Practice Guide.* London: HMSO.

Department of Health (1998) *Modernising Social Services.* London: The Stationery Office.

Department of Health (1999) *Mental Health Act Code of Practice.* London: The Stationery Office.

Evans, C. (1998) 'Personal Social Services Acceptable to Users.' In A. O'Neil and D. Statham (eds) *Shaping Futures: Rights, Welfare and Personal Social Services.* London: NISW/Joseph Rowntree Foundation.

Everitt, A., Hardiker, P., Littlewood, J. and Mullender, A. (1992) *Applied Research for Better Practice.* London: Macmillan.

Exworthy, M. and Halford, S. (1999) 'Professionals and Managers in a Changing Public Sector: Conflict, Compromise or Collaboration?' In M. Exworthy and S. Halford (eds) *Professionals and the New Managerialism in the Public Sector.* Buckingham: Open University Press.

Flynn, R. (1999) 'Managerialism, Professionalism and Quasi-Markets.' In M. Exworthy and S. Halford (eds) *Professionals and the New Managerialism in the Public Sector.* Buckingham: Open University Press.

Forbes, J. and Sashidharan, S. (1997) 'User Involvement in Services – Incorporation or Challenge?' *British Journal of Social Work 27,* 4, 481–498.

Harding, T. (1999) 'Elderly People.' In P. Neate (ed) *Research Matters, April-October.* London: Community Care.

Hodgkin, R. (1998) 'Children's Voices in the Corridors of Power: The Case for a Minister for Children.' In D. Utting (ed) *Children's Services Now and in the Future*. London: National Children's Bureau.

Home Office (1998) *Supporting Families: A Consultation Document*. London: The Home Office.

Hugman, R. (1991) *Power in Caring Professions*. London: Macmillan.

Jackson, S., Fisher, M. and Ward, H. (1996) 'Key Concepts in Looking after Children: Parenting, Partnership and Outcomes.' In S. Jackson and S. Kilroe (eds) *Looking after Children: Good Parenting, Good Outcomes: Reader*. London: HMSO.

Johnson, N. (1999) *Mixed Economies of Welfare: A Comparative Perspective*. London: Prentice Hall Europe.

Littlechild, R. and Blakeney, J. (1996) 'Risk and Older People.' In H. Kemshall and J. Pritchard (eds) *Good Practice in Risk Assessment and Risk Management I*. London: Jessica Kingsley Publishers.

Lovelock, R. and Powell, J. with Craggs, S. (1995) *Shared Territory: Assessing the Social Support Needs of Visually Impaired People*. York: Joseph Rowntree Foundation.

Marsh, P. and Crow, G. (1998) *Family Group Conferences in Child Welfare*. Oxford: Blackwell.

Morris, J. (1994) *The Shape of Things to Come? User-Led Social Services. Social Services Policy Forum Paper No.3*. London: NISW.

Morris, J. (1998a) *Accessing Human Rights: Disabled Children and the Children Act*. Ilford: Barnados.

Morris, J. (1998b) 'The Personal Social Services: Identifying the Problem.' In A. O'Neil and D. Statham (eds) *Shaping Futures: Rights, Welfare and Personal Social Services*. London: NISW/Joseph Rowntree Foundation.

Mullender, A. and Ward, D. (1991) *Self-Directed Groupwork: Users Take Action for Empowerment*. London: Whiting and Birch.

NHSTD (1993) *Training and User Involvement in Mental Health Services*. London: National Health Service Training Directorate in collaboration with Survivors Speak Out, Mindlink and the National Advocacy Network.

O'Brien, J. (1986) 'A Guide to Personal Futures Planning.' In G. Bellamy and B. Wilcox (eds) *The Activities Catalogue: A Community Programming Guide for Youth and Adults with Severe Disabilities*. Baltimore, MD: Paul H. Brookes Publishing Co.

Oliver, M. (1992) 'Changing the Social Relations of Research Production?' *Disability, Handicap and Society 7*, 2, 101–114.

Pateman, C. (1970) *Participation and Democratic Theory*. Cambridge: Cambridge University Press.

Payne, M. (1997) *Modern Social Work Theory*. Second edition. London: Macmillan.

Peck, E. and Barker, I. (1997) 'Users as Partners in Mental Health – Ten Years of Experience.' *Journal of Interprofessional Care 11*, 3, 269–277.

Plumb, A. (1987) 'That Word Consumer.' *Rochdale and District Mind Newsletter 4*, 6–7.

Plumb, A. (1991) 'The Challenge of Self-Advocacy,' unpublished paper, subsequently amended and published (Plumb 1993).

Plumb, A. (1993) 'The Challenge of Self-Advocacy.' *Feminism and Psychology 3*, 2, 169–187.

Rees, S. (1991) *Achieving Power*. Sydney: Allen and Unwin.

SSI (1998) *They Look after Their Own, Don't They? Inspection of Community Care Services for Black and Ethnic Minority Older People*. London: Department of Health.

Thoburn, J., Lewis, A. and Shemmings, D. (1995) *Paternalism or Partnership? Family Involvement in the Child Protection Process*. London: HMSO.

Thomas, M. and Pierson, J. (1995) *Dictionary of Social Work*. London: Collins Educational.

Thompson, N. (1997) *Promoting Equality: Challenging Discrimination and Oppression in the Human Services.* London: Macmillan.

Tunnard, J. (1991) 'Setting the Scene for Partnership.' In Family Rights Group *The Children Act 1989: Working in Partnership with Families: Reader.* London: HMSO.

Willow, C. (1998) 'Listening to Children in Local Government.' In D. Utting (ed) *Children's Services Now and in the Future.* London: National Children's Bureau.

Wistow, G. and Barnes, M. (1993) 'User Involvement in Community Care: Origins, Purposes and Applications.' *Public Administration 71,* 3, 279–299.

CHAPTER 2

Just Inquiry?

Research and Evaluation for Service Users

Ian Shaw

Introduction

How can research and evaluation strategies be used to promote user participation and involvement? The question is still fairly novel, and there is by no means universal agreement that such purposes should be part and parcel of inquiry. Social work research is conventionally assumed to involve a rigorous application of methodology in order to provide answers to policy, practice or conceptual problems. Lincoln and Guba define research as a 'type of disciplined inquiry undertaken to resolve some problem in order to achieve understanding or to facilitate action' (Lincoln and Guba 1986, p.549) Research is viewed as a relatively sophisticated means to a larger end. The problem focus, research design, fieldwork, analysis, reporting and dissemination of results are all seen as the work of experts undertaken for the good of some present or future beneficiaries.

This book starts from a very different point. Social care practitioners have increasingly been challenged by the emergence of forms of inquiry which are seen not as means to some future end but as ends in themselves. This is captured in this book's editorial vision of a research enterprise that mirrors practitioners' goals of participation and involvement. To borrow Stake's apt phrase, social workers have become 'reluctant to separate epistemology from ideology, findings from yearnings' (Stake 1997, p.471). The forms taken by this radical challenge are varied and include:

- participatory reflective inquiry and practice
- participatory inquiry for empowerment
- evaluating as direct practice
- feminist research
- justice-based commitments within research.

There are various strands of *participatory reflective inquiry* which go under names such as co-operative inquiry, action science, action inquiry, and participatory action research, and are associated with the writings of Heron, Reason, Whyte, Schon, Argyris and Eisner. In a familiar passage Schon says:

> both ordinary people and professional practitioners often think about what they are doing, sometimes even while doing it. Stimulated by surprise, they turn thought back on action and on the knowing which is implicit in the action… As [the professional] tries to make sense of it, he [*sic*] also reflects on the understandings which have been implicit in his action, understandings which he surfaces, restructures and embodies in further action.
>
> It is this entire process of reflection-in-action which is central to the 'art' by which practitioners deal well with situations of uncertainty, instability, uniqueness and value conflict. (Schon 1983, p.50)

The strengths of Schon's argument are common to the majority of reflective inquirers:

1. Reflective evaluating is about *tacit knowledge*. It is a disciplined activity in which the sources of understanding and action are not automatically picked off the surface. Skilful action often reveals 'a knowing more than we can say' (Schon 1983, p.51).

2. Reflective evaluating involves *reflexivity* – a testing by reflection. Erikson's injunction is apt. We should be constantly trying to 'force our favourite assumptions to become probable inferences' (Erikson 1959, p.94). Practitioners are not simply users but generators of knowledge.

3. There is an inherent comparability between 'professional' and lay persons' capacities for displaying the elements of reflective inquiry.

Schon's analysis is original and provocative. He is, for example, the only theorist in the field of practitioner and reflective evaluation who has developed a model which is not specific to any one profession. Despite the gendered framework of his observation, the transformative implications of his position become clear when he reflects on the relationship envisaged between professionals and those with whom they work. The relationship

> takes the form of a literally reflective conversation… He attributes to his client, as well as to himself, a capacity to mean, know and plan. He recognises that his meanings may have different meanings for his client than he intends… He recognises an obligation to make his own understandings accessible to his client… [He] tries to discover the limits of his expertise through reflective conversation with the client. (Schon 1983, pp.295–296)

However, in addition to the absence from his analysis of gender and broader power issues, Schon does not seem to envisage any directly participative dimension. His examples focus extensively on the practitioner in discussion with colleagues and supervisors, rather than involving students, children or other service users. Heron and Reason have developed a much more explicitly collaborationist vision of reflective inquiry. Reflective practice in social work has been developed in the work of England (1986), Gould and Taylor (1996) and Fook (1996). Participatory research approaches committed to *empowerment* have taken this a significant step further and have included some degree of emphasis on an explicitly liberationist strategy, an educative dimension through consciousness raising, and an integrated commitment to political action and social transformation. There are four main strands to this commitment. Early appeals for participatory evaluation drew their strength from a redistributive welfare position. For example, Holman pleads for 'research from the underside' because 'the values I hold are such that I long for the end of poverty and the promotion of equality. My interest in research is just this, how can research help the poor?' (Holman 1987, p.669).

Second, there have been efforts to bring Third World development research closer to development practice. Edwards draws on his experience of working in non-governmental organisations when he laments the creation and perpetuation of a series of divorces, the most complete of which 'lies between research output and the subjects of this research – poor people themselves' (p.128). While he is insistent that method has not been the only problem, he nonetheless insists that 'participatory research is the vehicle for understanding and changing the world simultaneously' (Edwards 1989, p.128). In the telling words of a Mexican proverb which he quotes, 'we make the path by walking it'.

Participatory strategies have also followed from some versions of feminist research. For instance, feminist standpoint theory draws on an activist view of evaluation as undertaken for explicitly political purposes, is committed to empowerment, and entails a model of evaluation that works towards the participation of members of oppressed groups in every phase of research activity. Once we concede that the purpose of research includes 'to enact rather than simply state' (Lather 1991, p.123), then the researcher will endeavour to 'maximise the research process as a change-enhancing, reciprocally educative encounter' (Lather 1986, p.72), in which the process is more important than the product. The work of Humphries (e.g. Humphries 1999; Truman, Humphries and Mertens 1999) and Mullender (e.g. Dullea and Mullender 1999) has been at the forefront of feminist approaches to social work inquiry in Britain.

Finally, empowerment approaches to social work research and evaluation have been driven by a training agenda of supporting the development of practitioners committed to combating discrimination and oppression in its various forms. Beresford, Fisher (e.g. Evans and Fisher 1999), Everitt and Hardiker (e.g. Everitt and Hardiker 1996) have each contributed significantly to working out the implications of this agenda for research.

The 1990s have witnessed the emergence of an approach to evaluation that blends aspects of both reflective practice and empowerment evaluation. The underlying premises of this approach are that all professionals should be reflective, enabling and rigorous evaluators-in-practice, and that qualitative methodology offers the basis of such a 'methodological practice' (Fook, Munford and Sanders 1999; Shaw 1996, 1997; Shaw and Lishman 1999; Tanner and Le Riche 1999). In summary, evaluating in practice is committed to a view of evaluative *purpose* which is *for* service users, and to an evaluative *process* which involves:

1. participatory evaluating *with* service users

2. reflecting on tacit knowing-in-practice

3. describing practice in ways that render access to its strengths and weaknesses feasible

4. mutual reflexivity of both practitioner and service user

5. legitimation through falsifying and establishing an empirically supported plausibility.

In essence this entails a view of evaluation as just as much a part of direct practice as assessing, planning, or delivering intervention.

There is a sense in which each of the approaches described so far can claim a commitment to social justice. Hence the implication of the chapter title that no research is merely inquiry, but raises problems and challenges for a just practice. Yet social work research and evaluation have failed to address the issues raised by literature and practice which specifically focus on ideas and ideals of justice. Such issues are almost entirely absent in the North American empirical practice movement, the British practitioner research literature, and the slowly growing literature from America, Britain and Australia on reflective inquiry. They are, of course, present in an axiomatic form in much of the literature on empowerment forms of evaluation, but remain largely uninspected.

We should not regard this as simply one more gap to fill. Whether we recognise it or not, issues of politics and associated questions of justice are present in our day-to-day practice. Weiss argued that political considerations intrude in three ways in evaluation. She is talking about broader policy and programme evaluation, but much of what she says probably applies to social work practice. First, the programmes and policies being evaluated are themselves generated by political decisions.

Second, evaluation entails political considerations because its reports enter the political arena. The nature and processes by which research is used cannot be understood outside a political framework. Third, there are politics implicit in the evaluation process itself. Research tends to accept the broad premises of the programme, and serious research 'gives an aura of legitimacy to the enterprise' (Weiss 1987, p.57). In consequence 'Most evaluations – by accepting a program emphasis on services – tend to ignore the social and institutional structures within which the problems of the target groups are generated and sustained' (p.57).

We cannot be neutral about justice issues. As the evaluation theorist Ernest House remarked some time ago, we 'do not live in a state of methodological grace' (House 1991, p.245).

The successful development of direct practice implications of these commitments is the litmus test of the authenticity of our claims to mutuality, respect and empowerment. Rather than attempt an overview of such developments, I will use the central part of this chapter to give examples of ways in which these commitments may be worked out within social work practice.

Mutuality, Respect and Empowerment in Practice Inquiry

Reflective practice

Hugh England, in his valuable discussion of social work as art, analyses what constitutes a rounded description and appraisal of practice. He perhaps goes too far when he concludes that 'without adequate description there can be no possibility of evaluation' (England 1986, p.155), but his assertion is helpful for good practice because without such description we certainly will not force our favourite assumptions to become probable inferences. He rightly insists that social work practice 'must be subject to a description and analysis which can determine quality' (p.139). It has to be described in such a way that it renders access to and evaluation of its strengths and weaknesses feasible. By making clear the links between 'understanding, action and effect' (p.154), practitioners will be able to conclude whether they have plausibly and adequately helped.

England's concern is not with participatory practice, yet the implications are readily transferable. Whether or not they are able to reach agreement, social workers, service users, carers, and others who are part of the change agent system, need to make explicit the 'inventories of evidential signs they regularly but unwittingly scan' (Erikson 1959, p.82).

A useful application of reflective practice is peer interviewing, either between practitioners or between a service user and someone chosen by the service user. The core strategy involves enabling practitioner and service users to unpick the assumptions they have made regarding whether or not social work intervention went well. Questions that may trigger such reflection include asking one another to describe examples of work undertaken, and to be explicit about what aspects went well or less well. Participants may also ask one another to be clear about *how* one knows that something went well or not, and what evidence was drawn on in the particular instance under review. It may also be worth exploring whether the practitioner or service user believes that other key 'stakeholders' share their views about the quality and outcomes of the work, and if they would have used the same or different criteria in deciding whether the work had gone well.

Participatory inquiry for empowerment

Whitmore's account of an evaluation of a pre-natal programme for single, pregnant mothers illustrates how positive outcomes may on balance be achieved. The evaluation was carried out over several months by four women who had themselves been through the programme, with Whitmore as consultant to the project. There were tensions in the group, and communication failures. One member left and another protested to Whitmore that:

> Our world is different from yours. The fear is that people always want to humiliate you, put you down [for being on welfare]...We have a different lifestyle from you. We just don't trust people the way you do. (Whitmore 1994, p.92)

Whitmore concluded that she could never entirely share the worlds of the women with whom she worked. 'My small words were often their big words. What I assumed was "normal talk", they saw as "professor words"' (p.95). But the strength of the group's final achievements is evidence that participatory evaluation with oppressed groups is not only political rhetoric.

Social workers have sometimes been slow to reflect on models of empowering participatory practice in other occupations. A sensitive and arresting example of participatory research is provided by Miller's account of three years' collaborative research with teachers who had until that time been her postgraduate students. They aimed to 'extend the concept of teacher as researcher into reciprocal and interactive forms' with an emancipatory agenda (Miller 1990, p.ix). The accounts portray the sustained commitments of the group as they 'continue to struggle with ways in which the intentions and forms of emancipatory pedagogy and research both attract and confound us' (Miller and Martens 1990, p.45).

The group worked together for at least six years. They kept transcripts of their meetings, and each group member agreed to keep a journal. They had early misgivings about the term emancipatory research, as a kind of 'authoritative discourse' (Miller 1990, p.16) from someone else. There was a constant struggle 'not to impose the concept of empowerment upon others in the name of liberation' (p.18). The recurring issues they faced included:

- The worry that there might be 'nothing there'

- A constant re-surfacing of 'conceptualisations of knowledge determined by someone else's research' (p.71). The standard separation of research and practice 'confounded our efforts to conceive of research as *praxis*' (p.73)

- The uncertainty, in the words of one member, of 'are we doing this right?'

- No one to talk to outside the group who shared their assumptions about becoming creators rather than transmitters of objective knowledge. The typical school does not encourage or welcome inquiry and reflection on work. The irony of their inquiry was that they were part of an institution that perpetuated the technical rationality model of research and evaluation which they wished to challenge

- 'The halting and undulating nature of our quest to become challengers' (p.70).

The group was unwilling to regard their collaboration as practitioner research. 'We wonder if the label, teacher-as-researcher, in fact contributes in subtle ways to those theoretical and practical distinctions that continue to obscure the ways in which teaching itself is a "quiet form of research"' (p.150). They were also concerned that practitioner research provides little if any challenge to the often hierarchical nature of university-formulated research agendas and interpretations of classroom teachers' work (Miller and Martens, 1990). Such questions offer a challenge to some forms of practitioner research in social work. Most British examples of practitioner research in social work are not participatory and tend to rest on unduly pragmatic approaches to decisions about methodology.

There are ethical risks in participatory inquiry and practice. Feminist work has provided some of the most sensitive accounts of such dilemmas, and of the need to 'protect us from our own passions' (Lather 1986, p.77). For example, Acker and her colleagues, in their study of the relation between women's attempts to move into the labour market and changes in their consciousness, tried three strategies to reduce unequal power and acknowledge the subjectivity of the participants, although they admit they did not solve this problem (Acker, Barry and Esseveld 1983):

1. They encouraged the interviewee to take the lead in deciding what to talk about. This did not always work. The women often wanted to be asked questions. However, the approach did work better for those women with whom they had more than one interview.

2. They established reciprocity, by offering to tell women something of themselves. This was accepted and often invited, and 'we formed friendships with many of the women' (p.428).

   However, we recognized a usually unarticulated tension between friendship and the goal of research. The researcher's goal is always to gather information, thus…attempting to create a more equal relationship can paradoxically become exploitation and use (p.428).

3. They showed their written material to the women. However, they did not do so with all of them. They admit that they shared most with 'those who identified themselves as consciously trying to change'. They were there-

fore the women who 'most shared our worldview', and 'we have to admit some reluctance to share our interpretations with those who, we expected, would be upset by them' (p.428). This raises the issue of whether the evaluator should share interpretations with those whose explanations are radically different from their own. This is the 'tension between the goal of reducing the power differences between the researcher and the researched and the difficulties of carrying this out when there is a lack of agreement on the meaning of experiences' (p.429).

For example, when they asked the women to read their draft manuscript, the latter typically wanted 'more of our own sociological analysis. They wanted us, the researchers, to interpret their experience to them' (p.429). They concluded that 'If we were to fulfil the emancipatory aim for the people we were studying, we had to go beyond the faithful representation of their experience, beyond "letting them talk for themselves"' (Acker *et al.* 1983, p.429).

There are five minimum requirements that must be met if participatory inquiry is to be more than a rhetorical flourish: first, clarify and mutually agree the *purpose of participation*. It is unlikely to work if some participants see it as democratising while others view it as directly challenging to existing power structures (Barnes and Wistow 1992).

Second, be clear with each other regarding the different *kinds of 'users'* who may have an interest. Fisher, for example, suggests that much participatory evaluation is naïve in underplaying the differences between voluntary and 'captive' clients. 'A problem in the new voluntarist language of welfare consumerism is that too little recognition is given to users who are "captive"' (Fisher 1992, p.55).

Third, establish genuine mechanisms for continued collaborative work. Verbal agreements are usually too non-specific, and are liable to chronic decay.

Fourth, seek agreement on the recurrent risks of intrusion and imposition. 'Whether intrusion into your life takes place in the name of "helping" or "researching" the experience, it seems, can feel all too similar if you are on the receiving end' (Davis 1992, p.37).

Finally, agree the harm to be avoided and the benefits to be gained by those who collaborate. In reflecting on an extensive project to involve carers in the processes of planning and review in an English local authority social services department, Barnes and Wistow caution that there are dangers in giving insufficient thought to whether meeting the needs of the service planning system, and meeting the needs of users and carers who become involved in that system, are incompatible.

> Providers should be sensitive to the demands they are placing on people whose lives are already complex and demanding. They should be ready to ensure that people derive some direct benefits from participation, as well as

ensuring that…participation is justified by the outcomes it achieves.(Barnes and Wistow 1994, p.91)

Evaluating in Practice

We noted earlier that the underlying premises of this approach are that all professionals should be reflective, enabling and rigorous evaluators-in-practice, and that qualitative methodology offers the basis of such a 'methodological practice'. Qualitative methodology provides a wide range of methods that can potentially be 'translated' and 'colonised' by professional practitioners (Figure 2.1).

Personal texts and narrative
Life histories
Interviewing
Focus groups
Participant observation
Participatory inquiry
Simulations
Member 'validation'
Cultural reviews

Figure 2.1. Methods for qualitative evaluating in practice

We should avoid naïve versions of this argument. It is *not* the case that social work and any particular forms of research involve the same logic and processes (Shaw 1999). The metaphors of translation and colonisation are inadequate descriptors of the extensive bridging work that 'methodological practice' calls for, but they do caution us against simplistic solutions. We should also note that it is *methodological* practice that is called for rather than any specific *methods*. In research, *method* usually refers to the techniques through which data is collected (e.g. sampling, participant observation, questionnaires). *Methodology* is a broader term, which takes into account the theoretical and value premises that lie behind research, and the social processes through which it is carried out.

Evaluating in practice applies both to direct practice for and with service users, and to indirect practice that seeks to improve services more generally. Focus groups provide one example of the former, and developments in simulations illustrate the latter.

Focus groups have three particular advantages for evaluating in practice. First, the group interaction is itself the data – 'the interaction is the method' (Jarrett 1993, p.198). Kitzinger says in summary that the method 'enables the researcher to examine people's different perspectives as they operate within a social network and to explore how accounts are constructed, expressed, censored, opposed and changed through social interaction' (1994, p.159). Second, focus groups are a form of participatory evaluation. They are valuable when there is a power differential between participants and decision makers, and hence have considerable potential for application within qualitative evaluation. Finally, they introduce a valuable approach to learning the extent of consensus on a particular issue. 'The co-participants act as co-researchers taking the research into new and often unexpected directions and engaging with each other in ways which are both complementary...and argumentative' (Kitzinger 1994, p.166).

The majority of writers in this field have opposed the application of focus groups to anything other than research or formal evaluation purposes. In my view this is an unhelpful generalisation. Focus groups also have a particular contribution to make to practitioner and participatory evaluating. Exercises in problem-setting, project development, anti-discriminatory practice, addressing projects that have become 'stuck', consumer feedback exercises, and evaluating sensitive topics are all ways in which focus groups have something to offer to qualitative evaluating. Gibbs summarises the case for focus groups:

> [They] are particularly useful when there are power differences between the participants and decision makers or professionals, when the everyday use of language and culture of particular groups is of interest, and when one wants to explore the degree of consensus on a given topic. (Gibbs 1997)

Despite the promise of this method, focus groups should be used within their limitations. The current, almost knee-jerk, adoption of group interviews labelled focus groups, regardless of their mode of operation, has been too undiscriminating. Focus groups, for example, always rely on interaction within the group based on topics that are supplied by the facilitator. There is little evidence on the relative benefits of focus groups and interview methods, and there are situations where focus groups should probably not be used. They should not be used if the practitioner's intention is to improve participants' communication or group skills. More generally, they should not be adopted for therapeutic purposes, or when the main purpose is to secure immediate action. If information, understanding or explanation is not central to the group's agenda, then other methods of intervention should be used. It may also be difficult to identify clearly individual messages within the group. There are other practical constraints on focus group work. If personal views cannot readily be expressed in such a context, or if breaches of confidentiality are likely to be a problem, then the method should not be used. When group members know each other particularly well, focus groups are also ill

advised. Finally, bearing in mind the benefits of homogeneous group membership, it is not advisable to run focus groups comprising both service users or carers
and practitioners.

Simulations have the potential to provide 'a unique and innovative tool that has
not yet been widely applied' in evaluation (Turner and Zimmerman 1994, p.335).
One application typically entails the use of paired role players (man/woman;
white/black; able-bodied/with a disability). The pairs present themselves sepa-
rately to a given service, as similar in terms of eligibility and need. 'To date, paired
role playing has been used principally to test for racial and ethnic discrimination
in housing and employment' (Turner and Zimmerman 1994, p.332); but the
method will work equally well in evaluating the allocation of scarce resources in
social work, where the element of judgement and discretion is present. For
example, a variant of the method using just one researcher has been planned
whereby a professionally qualified social work student with a sight disability will
apply for advertised social work posts, and systematically vary whether the disability is disclosed; this provides a test of the operation of non-discriminatory
employment policies.

A second application is more recent, and represents a development of the use
of vignettes in policy research. Those who evaluate the process of professional
practice come face to face with the invisibility of practice. How may we learn the
ways in which social workers practise? How would different practitioners deal
with the same case? The methods I have discussed hitherto do not directly
address this problem. Wasoff and Dobash have, however, used a promising inno-
vatory method in their study of how a specific piece of law reform was incorporated into the practice of solicitors (Wasoff and Dobash 1992, 1996). The use of
simulated clients in 'natural' settings allowed them to identify practice variations
that could be ascribed with some confidence to differences between lawyers
rather than to differences between cases.

Suppose, for example, that one wishes to carry out a qualitative evaluation of
decisions made by housing managers, medical staff and social workers regarding
the allocation of community care packages. Evaluators using simulated clients
would prepare a small number of detailed case histories designed to test the
practice decisions under consideration. A researcher, practitioner or service-user
representative would take on the scripted role of the client in the case history. The
housing manager, relevant medical staff, and social workers would each interview
the 'client' within the 'natural' setting of their work.

The use of simulated clients has several things going for it. First, social workers
are familiar with the 'family' of methods from which it is drawn. Second, other
methods are not always feasible for practical or ethical reasons. Simulated clients
overcome the ethical problems of seeking the co-operation of genuine clients.
Above all, the method makes practice visible. It will be clear from the brief
description that this method could not be a tool for evaluating particular cases,

but would focus on specific *kinds* of practice. There are limitations to the application of simulation methods. They require resources, time and skills, and they should avoid ethical problems of covert evaluation and entrapment.

Evaluating for social justice

Social workers will need a clear head and free time if they are to delve into the literature on theories of social justice. John Rawls's ideas of justice as fairness mingle with theories of justice based on participatory democracy, and more relativist views of justice operate in tension with neo-Marxist and feminist critical theories. Yet social workers do not need to resolve such intractable debates in order to recognise the daily demands for just practice and inquiry. Janet Finch's research on playgroups illustrates the point (Finch 1985).

Finch's particular interest was in what self-help playgroup provision would mean for working class women living in economically deprived areas. Over a three-year period, through observation and semi-structured interviewing, she was able to document the character of self-help playgroups in such areas.

> I uncovered situations where practice diverged wildly from bourgeois standards of child care and education which most policy makers and academics would take as the norm, and at times were downright dangerous. (Finch 1985, p.117)

She was worried that the publication of her work would further reinforce 'those assumptions deeply embedded in our culture and political life that working class women (especially the urban poor) are inadequate mothers' (p.117). Those who had welcomed her for three years would thus be betrayed. She had to work through these problems. Had she been guilty of taking a middle-class norm and imposing it on these groups? Yet that norm *was* the one to which the women who ran the groups aspired. It was the participants' model and not simply hers. She eventually developed reasoning which avoided the 'deficit' model of explanation, and argued that to view working-class mothers as incompetent is improper and naïve. Finch acknowledges that she is not certain she has fully resolved the issues, and accepts that:

> To argue like this is to take a frankly moral stance, far removed from the model of the objective social scientist... It seems to me that qualitative research on social policy issues will lead inevitably to explicit moral stances of that sort, and that it can never simply provide the 'facts'. (Finch 1985, pp.119–120)

Social work practice and inquiry that promotes empowerment, mutuality and respect will be enriched by a more explicit adherence to standards of justice. Ernest House, the American evaluation theorist, develops the example of negotiating a fair and demanding evaluation agreement (House 1980, chapter 8), in which *all* participants should meet the conditions that they:

- should not be coerced
- are able to argue their position
- accept the terms under which the agreement is reached
- negotiate. This is not simply 'a coincidence among individual choices' (1980, p.165)
- do not pay excessive attention to one's own interests
- adopt an agreement that effects all equally
- select a policy for evaluation that is in the interests of the group to which it applies
- have equal and full information on relevant facts
- avoid undue risk to themselves arising from incompetent and arbitrary evaluations.

House adheres to a reformist view of social justice, which will not secure the agreement of everyone, yet his demanding standards regarding evaluation agreements go well beyond those which typically operate within the field of social work inquiry.

Questions – and Answers?

I have suggested that social workers face a wide-ranging challenge from forms of inquiry that are viewed as ends in themselves. These include participatory reflective inquiry and practice, participatory inquiry for empowerment, evaluating as direct practice, feminist research, and justice-based commitments within research. The examples sketched in the main part of this chapter pose as many questions as they answer. For example, there are *ethical* problems about threats to confidentiality, informed consent, covert inquiry, and the delusion of alliance that qualitative methods sometimes foster (Shaw 1999). The risks of imposition, which have been carefully documented by feminist writers and by some reflective practitioners, will not go away.

There is also a cluster of puzzling problems about who carries out these kinds of inquiry and just what claims are being made about its character. The relationship between participatory forms of inquiry and more traditional forms of research is a vexed issue, and attracts easy generalisations which often fail to do justice to the question.

Work also needs to be undertaken on how such forms of reflective, empowering and methodological practice can be developed. This work will include:

1. Empirical work on how practitioners make evaluative sense of their day-to-day work. Professionals' existing evaluating practices do not provide a blueprint for how such practice should be evaluated. They do, however, provide a starting point from which professionals can begin the development of an evaluating in practice that avoids a decontextualized imposition of ideal models (Shaw and Shaw 1997, 1999).

2. Collaborative practice of the kinds of work discussed in this chapter.

3. The development of opportunities for doctoral work in these fields.

4. Inter-professional learning. The tendency to regard professional competences as exclusive to a given profession is unhelpful.

5. Greater attention by mainstream ethnographers to the evaluative uses of ethnography (e.g. Bloor 1997).

My own sympathies are for a reformist evaluation, which would have the evaluator seek out the data most likely to support programmes that benefit the dispossessed. I recognise the acute sense of dissonance that can arise from arguing for a rigorous evaluative methodology in one breath, and a reformist, partisan advocacy based on the evidence, in the next. But I stay with it for the present.

References

Acker, J., Barry, K. and Esseveld, J. (1983) 'Objectivity and Truth: Problems in Doing Feminist Research.' *Women's Studies International Forum 6,* 4, 423–435.

Barnes, M. and Wistow, G. (1992) (eds) *Researching User Involvement.* Leeds: Nuffield Institute for Health Services Studies, University of Leeds.

Barnes, M. and Wistow, G. (1994) 'Involving Carers in Planning and Review.' In A. Connor and S. Black (eds) *Performance, Review and Quality in Social Care.* London: Jessica Kingsley Publishers.

Bloor, M. (1997) 'Addressing Social Problems through Qualitative Research.' In D. Silverman (ed) *Qualitative Research: Theory, Method and Practice.* London: Sage.

Davis, A. (1992) 'Who Needs User Research? Service Users as Research Subjects or Participants.' In M. Barnes and G. Wistow (eds) *Researching User Involvement.* Leeds: Nuffield Institute for Health Services Studies, University of Leeds.

Dullea, K. and Mullender, A. (1999) 'Evaluation and Empowerment.' In I. Shaw and J. Lishman (eds) *Evaluation and Social Work Practice.* London: Sage.

Edwards, M. (1989) 'The Irrelevance of Development Studies.' *Third World Quarterly 11,* 1, 116–135.

England, H. (1986) *Social Work as Art.* London: Allen and Unwin.

Erikson, E. (1959) 'The Nature of Clinical Inference.' In D. Lerner (ed) *Evidence and Inference.* Illinois, IL: Free Press.

Evans, C. and Fisher, M. (1999) 'Collaborative Evaluation with Service Users.' In I. Shaw and J. Lishman (eds) *Evaluation and Social Work Practice.* London: Sage.

Everitt, A. and Hardiker, P. (1996) *Evaluating for Good Practice.* London: Macmillan.

Finch, J. (1985) 'Social Policy and Education: Problems and Possibilities of Using Qualitative Research.' In R. Burgess (ed) *Issues in Educational Research: Qualitative Methods.* London: Falmer Press.

Fisher, M. (1992) 'Users' Experiences of Agreements in Social Care.' In M. Barnes and G. Wistow (eds) *Researching User Involvement.* Leeds: Nuffield Institute for Health Services Studies, University of Leeds.

Fook, J. (ed) (1996) *The Reflective Researcher: Social Workers' Theories of Practice Research.* St Leonards, NSW: Allen and Unwin.

Fook, J., Munford, R. and Sanders, J. (1999) 'Interviewing and Evaluating.' in I. Shaw and J. Lishman (eds) *Evaluation and Social Work Practice.* London: Sage.

Gibbs, A. (1997) *Focus Groups.* Social Research Update, no. 19, Department of Sociology, University of Surrey.

Gould, N. and Taylor, I. (eds) (1996) *Reflective Learning for Social Work.* Aldershot: Ashgate.

Holman, B. (1987) 'Research from the Underside.' *British Journal of Social Work 17*, 6, 669–683.

House, E. (1980) *Evaluating with Validity.* Beverly Hills, CA: Sage.

House, E. (1991) 'Evaluation and Social Justice: Where are We Now?' In M. McLaughlin and D. Phillips (eds) *Evaluation and Education: At Quarter Century.* Chicago: Chicago University Press.

Humphries, B. (1999) 'Feminist Evaluation.' In I. Shaw and J. Lishman (eds) *Evaluation and Social Work Practice.* London: Sage.

Jarrett, R. (1993) 'Focus Group Interviewing with Low Income Minority Populations.' in D. Morgan (ed) *Successful Focus Groups: Advancing the State of the Art.* Newbury Park, CA: Sage.

Kitzinger, J. (1994) 'Focus Groups: Method or Madness?' In M. Boulton (ed) *Challenge and Innovation: Methodological Advances in Social Research on HIV/AIDS.* London: Taylor and Francis.

Lather, P. (1986) 'Issues of Validity in Openly Ideological Research.' *Interchange 17*, 4, 63–84.

Lather, P. (1991) *Getting Smart: Feminist Research and Pedagogy with/in the Postmodern.* New York: Routledge.

Lincoln, Y. and Guba, E. (1986) 'Research, Evaluation and Policy Analysis: Heuristics and Disciplined Inquiry.' *Policy Studies Review 5*, 3, 546–565.

Miller, J. (1990) *Creating Spaces and Finding Voices: Teachers Collaborating for Empowerment.* New York: State University of New York Press.

Miller, J. and Martens, M. (1990) 'Hierarchy and Imposition in Collaborative Inquiry: Teacher-Researchers' Reflections on Recurrent Dilemmas.' *Educational Foundations 4*, 4, 41–59.

Schon, D. (1983) *The Reflective Practitioner: How Professionals Think in Action.* New York: Basic Books.

Shaw, I. (1996) *Evaluating in Practice.* Aldershot: Ashgate.

Shaw, I. (1997) *Be Your Own Evaluator.* Wrexham: Prospects Publishing.

Shaw, I. (1999) *Qualitative Evaluation* London: Sage Publications.

Shaw, I. and Lishman, J. (eds) (1999) *Evaluation and Social Work Practice.* London: Sage Publications.

Shaw, I. and Shaw, A. (1997) 'Keeping Social Work Honest: Evaluating as Profession and Practice.' *British Journal of Social Work 27*, 6, 847–869.

Shaw, I. and Shaw, A. (1999) 'Game Plans, Buzzes and Sheer Luck: Doing Well in Social Work.' In S. Kirk (ed) *Research Methods: Current Social Work Applications.* Washington, DC: NASW Press.

Stake, R. (1997) 'Advocacy in Evaluation: A Necessary Evil?' In E. Chelimsky and W. Shadish (eds) *Evaluation for the 21st Century.* Thousand Oaks, CA: Sage.

Tanner, K. and Le Riche, P. (1999) 'Work in Progress: The Contribution of Observation to the Development of Good Practice and Evaluation.' In I. Shaw and J. Lishman (eds) *Evaluation and Social Work Practice.* London: Sage.

Truman, C., Humphries, B. and Mertens, D. (1999) *Research in an Unequal World.* Aldershot: Avebury.

Turner, M. and Zimmerman, W. (1994) 'Acting for the Sake of Research.' In J. Wholey, H. Hatry and K. Newcomer (eds) *Handbook of Practical Program Evaluation.* San Francisco, CA: Jossey-Bass.

Wasoff, F. and Dobash, R. (1992) 'Simulated Clients in "Natural" Settings: Constructing a Client to Study Professional Practice.' *Sociology 26,* 2, 333–349.

Wasoff, F. and Dobash, R. (1996) *The Simulated Client: A Method for Studying Professionals Working with Clients.* Aldershot: Avebury.

Weiss, C. (1987) 'Where Politics and Evaluation Met.' In D. Palumbo (ed) *The Politics of Program Evaluation.* Newbury Park, CA: Sage.

Whitmore, E. (1994) 'To Tell the Truth: Working with Oppressed Groups in Participatory Approaches to Issnquiry.' In P. Reason (ed) *Participation in Human Inquiry.* London: Sage.

CHAPTER 3

Totem Not Token

Groupwork as a Vehicle for User Participation

Dave Ward

Introduction

Groups, a major feature of all our lives, are of enormous significance, and until recent times, groupwork commensurately held a key place in the make-up of social work as a discipline. However, the significance of groupwork has shrunk markedly in recent years as the ethos of social work has moved from being about working with people to bring about change, to being about the monitoring and policing of individuals who present problems (Linday and Scally 1997; Ward 1998). At the same time, participation and user involvement have risen in significance to become essential terms in the social policy lexicon (Thompson 1999, p.14), and empowerment has become 'the new touchstone of welfare' (Pithouse and Williamson 1997, p.x). In this chapter we will see how trends can be detected within the rise of participation and user involvement which are similar to those accompanying the demise of groupwork. However, I will argue that if the *quality* of participation and involvement is addressed, and the levels of control and empowerment gained by service users in their dealings with officialdom are taken into account, a reassessment and reassertion of groupwork becomes essential.

The terms participation, user involvement and empowerment are used almost interchangeably, although critical commentators point out that in use each can reveal widely differing underlying ideological positions and values. (Adams 1996; Croft and Beresford 1989, 1992; Humphries 1996; Mullender and Ward 1991; Popple 1995). At one end of the spectrum lie consumerism and linkages with the New Right, and at the other, citizen action and control. Descriptively, these terms can indicate a state of affairs – the extent of people's involvement in the decision-making process, their degree of control over services, activities or projects; or a process – the means for achieving such goals. The theme which will be developed in this paper concerns the question of *collective* or *individual*: the presence or absence of groups and groupwork as a key element of the quality of the 'process' and any 'state of affairs' that may emerge.

User Involvement

User involvement as a leading principle has tended to become somewhat discredited (Shaw 1997). The reorganisation of public services in the 1980s and 1990s around market principles, and around the concept of the user of those services as a quasi-purchaser (DoH 1989), has led to a strong association between user involvement and the consumerism and the conservatism that have become enshrined in the operational discourse of the services. As people have been framed as consumers, needs have been commodified and converted into objects or functions to be met through the operation of the market. The market, so the argument goes, will respond by the creation and distribution of goods and services geared in quantity and quality to the requirements of consumers. This model fails, however, to face up to the underlying contradiction that those public services which are being returned to the market, to be galvanised by its disciplines, only arose in the first instance because of the failure of that very market to provide viable welfare and health provision. It is a discourse which 'starts with the idea of buying the goods and services we want rather than making collective provision for them' (Croft and Beresford 1992, p.32). It is essentially individualistic.

User involvement has come to be the term of choice for those whose interests are to minimise threats to such developments. Influence can be minimised when comment and feedback are organised through single-case complaints systems and mass produced and anonymous questionnaires, devised and controlled by the service provider. These are concurrently the tools of new managerialism and contribute to another side of market discipline, the need to adhere to the tenets of the three 'Es' – effectiveness, economy and efficiency – in order to maximise profit or, in public service parlance, to ensure 'value for money'. According to one former senior civil servant, the consequence has been that, while time and resources are efficiently and economically managed, purpose is lost from sight (Faulkner 1995, p.69). For public employees, he argues, this can lead to a 'filofax' mentality, driving out initiative, distorting priorities, and leading to conformism and a reluctance to question received ideas. Thus mechanisms that offer an illusory promise of providing influence for users are also part of a scheme which in parallel routinises and reduces the activities of the service-providing workforce.

By being sucked into this discourse, user involvement has come to rest unfavourably in the shadow of the other term under review: participation. For example, a project funded by the Joseph Rowntree Foundation in Scotland, The Community Development and Community Care Action Research Project, aims to 'give particular attention to the extension from user involvement to full citizen participation' (Scottish Community Development Centre 1997). In its proposal document, the project sets out in diagram format a framework in which individual user involvement is superseded by collective user involvement and finally community development. It is my contention that user involvement has, by association with the individualistic welfare policies of the New Right, become tainted by the stain of tokenism.

Participation and Partnership

Participation has stronger conceptual foundations than user involvement (Hallet 1987; Richardon 1983). Beresford and Croft (1992) reviewed the term from a historical perspective with rather pessimistic conclusions. What they identified was a pattern of 'cyclical development which rarely seems to build on, or go much further than what has gone before... Typically, participatory schemes have mirrored rather than challenged broader oppressions and discriminations' (p.33).

Beresford and Croft's incisive and critical analysis is particularly pertinent to the theme of this chapter. Reviewing earlier studies on participation and Arnstein's much-quoted and used 'ladder' model (Arnstein 1969),[1] Beresford and Croft comment that the substantive objectives served by participatory arrangements are often not about people's effective involvement and giving them an increased say. They are a means for control rather than a process enabling people to take control (pp.34–35). Participatory arrangements underplay structural issues and focus attention on the dynamics of and interactions within service-user groups and communities. In this way they have 'mirrored rather than challenged broader oppressions and discriminations'(p.33), with the result that pressure for real change has come largely from outside formal participatory mechanisms, from campaigns by groups and organisations of stigmatised and oppressed people. Beresford and Croft cite mental health survivors and disability activists as well as gay and lesbian, feminist and black organisations.

The problem with participation is that the agenda is almost invariably someone else's. People are invited or coerced to be involved. The idea or project is derived from outside their own experiences. Usually it is the more powerful inviting the less powerful to participate and get involved. Fitzpatrick and colleagues, who investigated young people's participation in urban regeneration initiatives, observed that:

> Many adults who accepted the validity of youth involvement had yet to translate this into any change in their own behaviour... They expected young people not to participate on their own terms but to adapt to existing structures, processes and language. (Fitzpatrick, Hastings and Kintrea 1999, p.12)

The evidence is that many of the people with whom social welfare workers work, for example those in poverty, the unemployed, black people, disabled people, homeless young people, feel, and are in reality, excluded in the most basic terms from society's mainstream, both materially and psychologically (Cox and Pritchard 1995). They see themselves as marginalised and blamed for problems which are not of their own making. Such participation by invitation is not their first priority. It may even engender a reaction against professionals who impose agendas, whether in a participative way or not. It can add to a sense of alienation, pushing people further towards rejecting a society which they experience as having failed and rejected them. It is no use professional workers and policy makers continuing to set the agenda, however participatively it is dressed up. If they do so, they will fail to offer people anything with which to engage and may force them further outside. As Campbell (1993) vividly describes, the consequences of such alienation can be devastating.

In sum, participation, while seductive as a descriptive term, has as a form of practice also become co-opted to purposes predominantly geared to the maintenance of the *status quo*, and has had its progressive potential largely squeezed from it. This is not a one-off aberration but a recurring phenomenon. Throughout the last 30 years, following the wide-ranging and varying challenges to traditional forms of authority in the 1960s, a number of participatory themes have come and gone: normalisation, enfranchisement, active citizenship and, currently, stakeholding. Each has held the field for a time but, in due course, has faded from view. They have foundered on the rocks of the inherent contradictions of the notion of participation.

A counter to this rather pessimistic scenario can be found in the work of Waterhouse and McGee (1998) in relation to partnership working in child care. The term partnership is not so ambiguous as involvement and participation, as it clearly incorporates a two-way exchange element. However, it is important not to imply that, simply through a transposition of terms, the issues raised so far can be massaged away. Indeed, partnership has been institutionalised through incorporation into legislation and, for example, partnership is a central tenet of the 1989 Children Act. Nonetheless, in the view of Waterhouse and McGee (1998, p.285), a consideration of the guidance issued by the Department of Health (1991) and subsequent research (DoH 1995) indicates that partnership in day-to-day child care practice can be a meaningful reality. They argue that it entails bringing parents and children into decisions, offering real choices to families, and sharing information and responsibility. Providing that there is openness and clarity about workers' powers and duties, Waterhouse and McGee believe that partnership can be squared with the imbalance of power inherent in the statutory role that social workers carry. Interestingly, child care is one area of social welfare where market relations have not been significantly introduced.

The difficulties for partnership in child care have been well documented and debated (e.g. Parton 1985, 1991 and 1997). In particular, can the supportive and investigative roles involved in prevention and child protection be rendered compatible? There is always the possibility that such partnerships may slip into becoming as disingenuous as the approaches so far considered, disguising particular substantive and political commitments 'as a universal position that gives epistemological and moral privilege' (Hammersley 1995, p.43). However, the terms for partnerships set by Waterhouse and McGee may provide clues to take us forward from the limited visions we have come to attach to user involvement and participation. In these the process is opened up by way of an exchange between user and provider. Young (1999, p.85) summarises the necessary conditions:

- that the intention as well as the process is made explicit

- that people engage in deliberation and discussion which helps them to their understanding and gain a real sense of what is involved

- that people give their conscious and informed consent to engage.

However, what is missing is any specific attention to group and collective interests and action. The process is still essentially individualistic.

Empowerment

Empowerment is *the* social work term of the 1990s. Adams (1996) believes it represents a fundamental 'paradigm shift' (p.33), taking the practice of social work away decisively from the individualistic medical/pathological model. Drawing from the *Dictionary of Social Work* (Thomas and Pierson 1995) for a basic definition, Adams argues that empowerment is concerned with how people gain a *collective control* over their lives to achieve their interests, and is the method by which social workers seek to enhance the power of people who lack it. It represents a change of focus from social work *on people* to social work *with people*. For service users this means the opportunity to break out of the debilitating sense of self-blame created by the ideological repackaging of public ills as private troubles (Wright Mills 1970).

In identifying key themes in empowerment as: 'participation of people in their own empowerment', 'the importance of recognising existing competencies' and 'building on individual and collective strengths', Staples (1990, p.30) also directs attention towards group issues. Indeed this collective focus is embedded in the range of features that are said to be characteristic of empowerment practice.

If empowerment is a process by which power is developed and gained by the powerless themselves (Braye and Preston-Shoot 1995), empowerment practice encourages and enables people to try out and experience new ways of influencing their life chances. This involves not only winning power but *transforming* it (Mullender and Ward 1991, p.6). As Lorde (1984) explains:

> The true focus of revolutionary change is never merely the oppressive situations which we seek to escape, but that piece of the oppressor which is planted deep within each of us, and which knows only the oppressors' tactics, the oppressors relationships. (Lorde 1984, p.123)

In the context of social work practice, Breton (1994) argues that this means an empowering partnership which looks to share power between workers and service users and to challenge both to use it non-oppressively:

> In the face of more and more severe problems, the normal and understandable reaction of caring and dedicated professionals is to become more and more expert, and develop better and better technologies…if empowerment is the goal that reaction is exactly the one professionals should not have. What social workers need to adopt in empowerment work are 'bottom-up' strategies whereby they learn from the oppressed, from those who, more or less effectively, deal first hand with the problems of racism, poverty, sexism, ageism etc; then bringing the best of social work knowledge and expertise, collaborate with the oppressed to build more just societies. (Breton 1994, p.35)

While Adams sees in empowerment something more than just another of the fads which have passed our way, such as 'participation' and 'user involvement', it is fair to say that others are more sceptical. Critics see in the term, as in those others, the potential for it to be a 'conceptual deodorant', used to justify propositions rooted in conflicting ideological positions (Ward 1998); to act as 'a gilded vehicle of social control' (Davis 1986, p.97); and to promote professional self-interest (Baistow 1994; Page 1992).

The slippery and ambiguous nature of empowerment is highlighted in the work of Foucault (1980). Foucault argues against the notion of power as a fixed entity, which some people have and others lack (the way in which the term is used in everyday and, indeed, in professional conversation). Instead, according to Foucault, people simultaneously express power and are affected by it. These exchanges are bounded by what people think is appropriate and normal, and language has a key role in specifying what people take for granted. To engage with the essence of power, Foucault argues, people have to participate in, influence and begin to engage with defining the facts, priorities and responsibilities which we take as given – in fact to challenge the discourses in which we are all enmeshed (Rees 1991). In similar vein Lukes (1974) develops a view of power which focuses not only on the behaviour of specific decision-makers but also on the way that people's interests may be defined by a whole system that works against their interests. For Lukes, power is not only the capacity to impose (if necessary in the face of opposition) but, as echoed in Foucault, also the capacity to set the terms of debate. A good recent example is the previously mentioned repackaging of public issues as private problems by successive governments, so that social explanations of offending have given way to personal culpability. According to Rees (1991) this 'three dimensional view' of power involves more than just a reductionist analysis of competing interests. Implicitly:

> It also raises questions as to what might be in [peoples] interests under different socio-political constraints and this implies the creative exercise of power to produce possibilities which might never have been anticipated... This three dimensional conception of power embodies the spirit and objectives of empowerment. (Rees 1991, p.40)

Consideration of Lukes and Foucault enables us to move beyond 'zero sum' conceptions of power and empowerment – empowerment as something given and received from person to person, so that one person's empowerment must be another person's oppression. Such 'zero sum' perceptions lie behind the pessimistic view that empowerment is just another 'con', serving establishment and professional interests (Baistow 1994; Barry 1996; Page 1992). As Braye and Preston-Shoot put it: 'Power must not be obscured but viewed as a positive concept and used proactively by each party to promote his or her own and respond to the other's interests in the encounter' (1995, p.118). In this way empowerment can give progressive substance to the exchange implicit in partnership.

I have argued elsewhere (Mullender and Ward 1991) that empowerment alone cannot provide an adequate foundation for practice. It must be allied to a commitment to challenging injustice and in particular oppression. I stress the term oppression because it is not ambiguous as to the exploitative nature of economic and social relationships (Kidd and Kumar 1981). This link can draw empowerment away from usages which otherwise devalue the term. Empowerment and oppression are flip sides of the same coin. Both can be understood as a 'state of affairs' within which life chances are constructed, *and* as a 'process' revealing inequalities of power and opportunity. In the case of oppression, the process is one in which the state of affairs is maintained; empowerment is a process of change through achieving power and transforming it. Just as oppression is experienced through personal, everyday events, so empowering practice offers people the chance to experience new ways of being involved in those events.

Running through empowerment is an emphasis on the collective both in action and outcome. In groups, personal troubles can be translated into common concerns. The experience of being with other people in the same position can engender strength and new hope where there was apathy beforehand: a sense of personal responsibility internalised as self-blame can find new productive outlets. Alternative explanations and new options for change and improvement can be opened up. The demoralising isolation of private misfortune, reinforced by public disinterest, or even worse, by condemnation and surveillance, can be replaced in the course of collective enterprise with a new sense of self-confidence and potency, as well as tangible gains, which individuals on their own could not contemplate (Mullender and Ward 1991, p.12).

Moreover, besides achieving material changes and raising the confidence of their members, groups have *transformative* capacity. Tara Mistry's (1989) description of a group for black and white women is a classic example of how empowerment, where affiliated to groupwork, can be tremendously powerful in moving people towards more humane and emancipatory relationships. She describes a mixed-race women's group run by herself, a black woman, and a white woman co-worker. She explains how the group was able to move beyond developing an awareness that, as black and white working-class women, members shared similar problems which had social bases outside their immediate control and were not the result of personal inadequacy. They also confronted and worked on the stereotypes of black people held by their white friends.

Groupwork

In contemporary social work, there is a good deal of evidence of a continuing interest in groups. Indeed there is a considerable amount of work taking place *in* groups. However, much of it is not recognisable as *real* groupwork. It does not pay substantial attention either to the knowledge-base of group dynamics or to the practice-base in groupwork method and skills. Nor does it incorporate the democratic and collective values that are at the core of real groupwork.

What has happened?		
groupwork	has shifted to	work *in* groups
the group as the *instrument* of change	⇨	the group as the *context* for intervention
concern with the dynamics of the group *encounter*	⇨	a pedagogic *instructional* orientation
democratic and *collective* values	⇨	*authoritarian* and *individualistic* values

These characteristics are particularly visible in the group-based cognitive behavioural programmes now in wide use, reflecting what Konopka described as one-to-one treatment with the rest of the members acting as bystanders (cited by Kurland and Salmon 1993, p.8). Writing about work with male sex abusers, Cowburn and Modi (1995) see in such approaches oppressive Eurocentric and heterosexist assumptions, grounded in conformity and obedience, but in fact potentially dangerous in reinforcing abusers' minimalist views of their own responsibility and the harm their actions have caused.

These changes can be contextualised within wider socio-economic changes that have impacted on social work in the 1980s and 1990s. A new ideological climate in which it is possible for a prime minister to claim that 'there is no such thing as society', the introduction of market practices to the delivery of social services, new managerialism, a drive towards client/user specialisms, the emergence of the law as the key defining factor, new 'competency-led' approaches to social work education and training, have made it unfashionable and difficult to own many of the values and purposes of groupwork. These stress that:

- The core process of groupwork is the interaction between a group of people based on mutuality, as the means of achieving group purpose

- Groupwork is anti-oppressive in its context, purpose, method, group relationships and behaviour. (Brown 1996, p.83)

For Douglas (1993, p.31) this means a close connection for real groupwork with concepts of equality and democracy.

Real groupwork may have become unfashionable precisely because it acknowledges that groups develop a life of their own, over which the worker cannot have complete control; that the agenda can be holistic and the process democratic. Group members will raise what is important to them, no matter what 'ground rules' and boundaries have been set. Such free-flowing characteristics are out of kilter with the current climate, emphasising as it does discipline and individual responsibility and, at an organisational level, pre-set objectives and audited outcomes. The result is that for many projects and workers the ideas of real groupwork are unfamiliar or, even worse, are regarded with suspicion.

However, it may be that the time is coming for a radical change of direction. A briefing issued by the National Institute for Social Work (1996) highlights that a major cornerstone for social policy, and a challenge for social work, in the new enlarging Europe is the fight against social exclusion, a theme now adopted for the UK by the post-1997 Labour government. The briefing argues that the challenge of reducing social exclusion demands new approaches to individuals and groups currently denied access to employment or services.

In this context we need to return to the historical connection between groupwork and equality and democracy. The challenge of social exclusion demands that we take account of what we have come to know about the systematic oppression of excluded groups, about anti-oppressive practice and about empowerment. In this context the fundamentals of groups and groupwork, outlined earlier, reassert their significance.

Social Action

Social action emerged in the late 1970s in the field of work with youth offenders. It is now recognised as a distinctive model of empowerment (Williamson 1995), having been first conceptualised in detail as self-directed groupwork (Mullender and Ward 1991), which Payne (1997, p.280) describes as offering 'a clear view of empowerment theory focussed on groupwork settings and processes'. The approach has been recognised as applicable in a wide range of human-service settings and is seen to have wide international currency (Breton 1994; Brown 1996; Jakobsson 1995; Lee 1994; Treu *et al.* 1993).

Social action has been developed by practitioners, academics and service users, reflexively and in partnership, in the course of developing and carrying out field projects and training programmes, and in research and evaluation. Under the aegis of the Centre for Social Action (http: //www.dmu.ac.uk/~dmucsa), social action aims to take an approach to people and communities which focuses on their aspirations and capacities rather than on deficits and negative stereotypes.

There are three main points that distinguish social action:

- A recognition that *all* people have the capacity to create social change and should be given the opportunity

- Professionals work with people in partnership

- The agenda for action is handed over to the people themselves. (Fleming *et al.* 1998)

These have been developed into a set of six key principles which provide a value framework for practice:

- *Valuing others' skills*: everyone has skills and understanding they can draw upon to tackle the problems they face; professionals should not attach negative labels to people with whom they work

- *Rights of participation*: all people have the right to be heard, to define issues facing them and to take action on their own behalf

- *Collaboration*: people acting together can be powerful; those who lack power and influence can gain it through working together; practice should reflect this understanding

- *Understanding context and constraints*: people in difficulty are often confronted by complex issues rooted in social policy, the environment and the economy; practice should reflect this understanding

- *Partnership*: methods of working must reflect non-elitist principles; workers do not 'lead' but facilitate decision making and controlling outcomes; though special skills and knowledge are employed, these do not accord privilege and are not solely the province of the workers

- *Equality of opportunity*: workers strive to challenge inequality and discrimination in relation to race, gender, sexual orientation, age, class, disability
  or any other form of social differentiation.

The shift in perceptions which these principles involve has been powerfully
summarised by the director of an American youth advocacy programme (James
1997):

Problems	⇨	*Solutions*
Deficits	⇨	*Assets*
Clients	⇨	*Citizen decision makers*
Objects	⇨	*Subjects*
Problems in individuals	⇨	*Problems rooted in systems*

Theoretical and practical inspiration comes from the work of Paulo Freire (1972)
and the challenge to apply his ideas in working in the UK. There is much in
common with the theory and practice of community development, where the
challenge is to transfer collective action on structural issues from the
predominantly locality-based context of community work and working with
'ordinary', albeit predominantly poor, people to the fragmented and specialist
concerns of social work. In this the struggles of the black, feminist, and disability
movements (Ahmed 1990; Cress-Welsing 1991; Evans 1994; Gilroy 1987;
Oliver 1992) afford a sense of direction. They indicate the complex way in which
the various dimensions of disadvantage and exclusion are distinctive but still
interlink. Each overarches the others at different times and in particular
conditions, requiring independent action but within a coherent worldview.
Methods developed in social education and social-skills training are adapted for
the exploration of issues and the preparation and implementation of action. (See
Mullender and Ward 1991, for a fully set-out practice methodology.)

Groups are central to the approach developed by Paulo Freire (1972) that lies
at the core of social action and is worth, therefore, explaining in detail. There are
three key elements to Freire's approach: *dialogue*; *'problematisation'*; and
'conscientisation'.

Dialogue is a process which breaks down the traditional relationship between
teacher and taught, worker and service user, replacing it with a partnership where
roles interchange and the participants are co-investigators in creating knowledge
through 'critical reasoning'. It takes place in groups known in Freire's work as
'cultural circles'.

Second, *'problematisation'* is a process of drawing attention to situations that
require action or change, by posing questions. It is a process of challenging

commonly accepted ideas by posing more and more questions, to dig beneath conventional or common-sense explanations of reality (Kidd and Kumar 1981). Problematisation is what gives Freire's work and, I believe, social action, a distinctive critical edge. In simple terms it can be represented by asking the question 'why?'

In professional practice, as in life, we too readily jump from 'what?' questions (what is wrong? what is the problem?) to 'how?' questions (what can we do about it? how should we proceed?). In doing this we unwittingly steer explanations, responsibilities and the scope of solutions to the private world around people and within their existing knowledge and experience. The knowledge and experience have been fashioned by people's positions in society and the processes which keep them there. In asking 'why?' people are encouraged to pursue an issue until the root causes have been identified and exposed. Asking 'why?' gives people the opportunity to 'examine the internal bridles and perceived powerlessness which underpin their sense of self and guide their actions in the world'(Young 1999, p.88). It enables people to break out of the demoralising and self-perpetuating narrowness of vision, introspection and self-blame created by poverty, lack of opportunity and exclusion. With expanded horizons of what is possible, people conceive of new explanations in the wider social, political and economic context and consider how they can identify and engage with these. Asking 'why?' directs the spotlight away from people as problems towards the problems they encounter, and enables them to see opportunities to develop a much wider range of options for action and change. Asking the question 'why?' is the key that unlocks the process.

The third component is '*conscientisation*'. This Freire describes as a permanent critical approach to reality in order to discover it and to unpack and expose the myths that deceive us and help to maintain oppressing, dehumanising structures. Conscientisation goes beyond raising awareness to the development of strategies for bringing about change. Encompassing both action and reflection, it is simultaneously the product and process of ongoing dialogue.

Social action in these terms comes close to matching Adams's (1996) attempt to define empowerment:

> a combination of the traditions of mutual aid, self-help and, more recently, movements of liberation, rights and social activism, strengthened by anti-racism, feminism, critiques of inequalities and oppressions arising from social class, age, disability, sexuality and other differences. It relates closely to movements for users' rights. (p.2)

If empowerment is concerned with how people gain control over their lives to achieve their interests, social action is an approach by which workers, as practitioners and/or researchers, seek to enhance through partnership the capacities and influence of people who are oppressed and excluded. In these terms social action meets the basic credentials of real groupwork.

As social action practice evolved and was articulated, two further factors became apparent. First, embedded in the approach is a process of qualitative inquiry, knowledge-building and evaluation in which practice is closely aligned with research (Gould 1999). Second, the critique of mainstream social work practice, upon which social action practice is grounded, could equally apply to conventional research and evaluation (Humphries and Trueman 1994). The upshot has been the evolution of a parallel approach to research and evaluation (Ward and Fleming, 1999). It highlights the relationship of research and practice as instruments of social change and takes forward the concept of the 're-search-minded practitioner' (Everitt *et al.* 1992) working in partnership with service users (Taylor 1999, p.371).

> First, it is the responsibility of researchers to set in motion a process of participation whereby people identify and define the direction and methods of the research. Second, this means that, although special skills and knowledge are employed, these do not accord privilege and are not solely the province of specialist researchers. In effect, research methods should reflect non-elitist principles and enable service users to empower themselves to make decisions and control outcomes. (Fleming and Ward 1999, p.375)

Social action research engages closely with contemporary debates about the positions and procedures of social research (Beresford and Evans 1999; Dullea and Mullender 1999; Trueman and Humphries 1994). Beresford and Evans (1999) pull together these discussions and identify the emergence of competing paradigms. They highlight a reactionary and dominant paradigm. This stresses research which addresses the effectiveness, efficiency and economy of policy, and is preoccupied with measuring managerially and professionally defined 'outcomes'. The emergence of so-called 'evidence based' practice and policy is one expression. Such research relies heavily on 'scientific' research methods such as random control trials and numerical analysis and thus creates a narrow definition of what counts as 'evidence'. A competing paradigm stresses, they say, changing the role and relations of research. It has emerged from the movements of disabled people, 'survivors', service users, community and citizens' organisations *and* supportive researchers. It represents a shift away from traditional state paternalism and does not share the consumerist ideology of the dominant paradigm. 'It values people's first hand direct experience as a basis for knowledge.' (Beresford and Evans 1999, p.673) Beresford and Evans (p.674) do not demand that 'only research which offers service users the fullest amount of control is adequate or acceptable' but do detect, nevertheless, 'a relationship between the extent of service users' involvement in research and its capacity to serve an empowering function'.

The following example of social action research illustrates some of these themes and the potential gains of research within the second paradigm. The Centre for Social Action had long-standing contact with members of the Somali community in East London through previous work with a homelessness agency. Community leaders approached the Centre to assist with a piece of research about the health and social care needs of Somalis which the local Race Equality Council agreed to fund. A social action researcher acted as research consultant and team facilitator, training members of the community in data-gathering methods and supervising their work (Dyson and Harrison 1996/97). Much of this activity – training, supervision and data collection – took place in groups, as did much of the subsequent work to analyse and present the findings and disseminate them to service providers. The Somali participants were able to control the direction and process of the research with the support of a skilled and clear-minded social action researcher/practitioner. Subsequently, the East London Somali group, in a continuing partnership with the Centre for support and evaluation, has been awarded large-scale European Union funding for a national pilot project for community members who wish to explore the possibilities of returning to Somaliland.

While the potential, for practice and research, of groupwork framed within the social action perspective is being advocated, it is important to acknowledge that social action and its roots in Freire's pedagogy has critics (Barry 1996; Barry, Davies and Williamson 1998/99). It is pointed out that social action and, implicitly, most practice that aspires to be empowering, raises unrealistic expectations about changing the world. It reifies process and leaves real problems of 'managing to survive day to day, finding a job and/or constructive activities and support networks…rarely…defined' (Barry et al. 1998/99, p.68). In so doing it promotes action that inadvertently gives more legitimacy to, rather than questions, the existing social order (Barry 1996, p.7). Further, it is asserted that social action represents an imposed professionally led agenda, no less than any other method, attracting a 'more upwardly-mobile, eloquent section of the population who are not currently deemed rejected or "disempowered"', whilst there remains 'inherent scepticism amongst those currently without power, skills and resources that change could ever be effected from the grassroot' (1996, p.7).

These are serious charges. I reject them on two grounds (Fleming, Harrison and Ward 1998). First, the examples which Barry presents to back up the charges are drawn from her own practice, not anyone else's. As presented, they are not based on the approach laid out here. Indeed, there are examples of social action work which has engaged people in the process of working in partnership on an open and transparent agenda, to achieve tangible material gains countering exclusion and alienation (Fleming et al. 1998; Centre for Social Action 1999).

As an illustration from practice, from perhaps one of the most challenging areas of social work, Butler (1994) writes about a group for women whose children are judged by social services as at risk of significant harm from their parents. She explores how the groupwork engendered an atmosphere of equality, enabling the women 'to explore the humour, sadness and strains of family life and no longer remain silent about these' (p.178). There emerged structural dilemmas facing members which were central to the group agenda: women's sexuality and relationships with male partners that were entangled with the processes of racism and the difficulties of bringing up children of mixed parentage. Faced with relentless hardships, the women easily identified the politics of poverty. Unpacking structural and individual issues was critical to these women's empowerment and the creation of their own solutions to the threats and dilemmas they faced (Butler 1994, p.163).

I would argue, therefore, that while social action is not a panacea and does not overcome the problems of power or the transfer of power, it does maintain a clear position with regard to the rights of service users. In so doing, it promotes a practice that is consistent with progressive social change and a framework within which power can be transferred when the appropriate conditions prevail (Taylor 1999, p.376). Nevertheless, the criticism of Freire leads into a debate of a different order and raises some fundamental questions of which those noted above are surface manifestations. The significant point is made that Freire's work comes from another time and another place:

> [it is a] treatise on educating revolutionaries in oppressed countries about the need to similarly educate, politicise and revolutionise the people... In societies which are highly polarised, such as Brazil, a wholly radical agenda may well be the preferred route. (Barry *et al.* 1998/99, pp.67, 69)

First it must be noted that Freire wrote his seminal work *Pedagogy of the Oppressed* (1972) in the USA, as visiting professor at Harvard. On coming to the United States Freire 'found that repression and exclusion of the poor from power were not limited to developing countries and changed his definition of "third world" to a political, rather than geographical concept' (Branford 1997, p.19). Second, such arguments reflect a 'dualistic' view of the social world (Layder 1994). They pitch the 'third world' against the developed world, as if what is appropriate for one cannot be for the other; process against product; big problems against little ones; changing society against joining it; professional against client; micro against macro; structural/political against the private and personal. Dualistic thinking means that you start with one or the other; it is not possible to do both. In contrast social action adopts a non-dualist position framed within a commitment to emancipation and social justice. I see this as aligned with what Trueman and Humphries (1994, p.14) define as 'anti-discriminatory': 'an active involvement in challenging assumptions based on unequal social relations, through reflexive, explicitly committed participation in the process of social change'. Basically, non-dualist thinking means that it does not matter where you start as long as you have a vision (described by the feminist researchers, Jayaratne and Stewart (1995), as 'partiality') that allows for the complexities and interconnectedness of the social world. It requires a politically committed 'sociological imagination'(Wright Mills 1970).

Following Giddens (1974), social action takes the view that people are shaped by the world around them, but they are also creative beings (Ward 1982). They have their own biographies through which the social world is both reproduced and, at the same, time can be transformed. Framed and constrained by their inheritance and contemporary structures, people do have choices and some control over what happens to them. All people, even the subordinated, are not completely powerless in situations; they have some means in their control to influence and change things.

Aspects of such thinking are also at the heart of current government thinking and policy, the search for regeneration through 'the Third Way' (Giddens 1998). This approach recognises that tackling structural problems is a key feature of tackling poverty and exclusion, and of enabling people to mobilise their creative potential. Undoubtedly it is crucial that the right volume and quality of concrete resources are put in and are targeted to the right places. But this is not enough. Following Giddens's perspective, it is clear that this will not automatically liberate people's capacities to find new and better solutions.

This is where social action and *real* groupwork come in. Without attention to *process* the danger is that people who have been stifled and silenced will not engage. Who will then carry the responsibility for the 'failure' of the policies and be the butt of accusations of wasted resources? It is my fear that it will be the intended recipients, again pathologised and blamed as incapable, unwilling, unmotivated and unworthy. An opportunity exists; the consequences of failure are horrendous, perhaps leading to the creation of what Murray (1999) calls 'custodial democracy', in which 'the mainstream subsidises but also walls off the underclass. In effect, custodial democracy takes as its premise that a substantial portion of the population cannot be expected to function as citizens' (p.7).

To conclude, social action presents an approach to practice which has the capacity to capture the mood of these positive initiatives and to assist the development of forms of participation and involvement which do not deceive, exclude, or unwittingly contain and control. At the heart of social action is attention to group dynamics and groupwork processes, but self-consciously grounded in values and principles through which all aspects of practice should be filtered. Such groupwork is essentially democratic and empowering: it has a place at the centre of democracy if involvement, participation and empowerment are to be totems rather than tokens.

Notes

1. The ladder model has achieved the status of received wisdom and comes up consistently in guides and handbooks for practitioners. Two recent examples are a British Youth Council leaflet (1998) on youth participation, and a Community Development Foundation newsletter (1998/99) featuring a guide to facilitating community regeneration.

References

Adams, R. (1996) *Social Work and Empowerment.* London: Macmillan.

Ahmed, B. (1990) *Black Perspectives in Social Work.* Birmingham: Venture Press.

Arnstein, S. (1969) 'A Ladder of Citizen Participation.' *Journal of the American Institute of Planners* *35*, 4, 216–224.

Baistow, K. (1994) 'Liberation or Regulation? Some Paradoxes of Empowerment.' *Critical Social Policy 42*, 34–46.

Barry, M. (1996) 'The Empowering Process: Leading from Behind?' *Youth and Policy 54*, 1–12.

Barry, M., Davies, A. and Williamson, H. (1998/99) 'An Open Response to the Concerns of the Centre for Social Action in Issue No.60.' *Youth and Policy 62*, 67–70.

Beresford, P. and Evans, C. (1999) 'Research and Empowerment.' *British Journal of Social Work* *29*, 5, 671–677.

Branford, S. (1997) 'Word Power to the Poor', *Guardian*, 10 May.

Braye, S. and Preston-Shoot, M. (1995) *Empowering Practice in Social Care.* Buckingham: Open University Press.

Breton, M. (1994) 'On the Meaning of Empowerment and Empowerment-Oriented Social Work Practice.' *Social Work with Groups 17*, 3, 23–37.

British Youth Council (1998) *Youth Agenda: Participation.* London: British Youth Council.

Brown, A. (1996) 'Groupwork into the Future: Some Personal Reflections.' *Groupwork 9*, 1, 80–96.

Butler, S. (1994) '"All I've got in my purse is mothballs." The Social Action Women's Group', *Groupwork 7*, 2, 163–179.

Campbell, B. (1993) *Goliath: Britain's Dangerous Places.* London: Methuen.

Centre for Social Action (1999) *Bibliography of Social Action.* Leicester: Centre for Social Action, De Montfort University.

Community Development Foundation (1998/99) 'Communities at the Forefront.' *CDF News* *42*, 1–2.

Cowburn, M. and Modi, P. (1995) 'Justice in an Unjust Context: Implications for Working with Adult Male Sex Offenders.' in D. Ward and M. Lacey (eds) *Probation: Working for Justice.* London: Whiting and Birch.

Cox, M. and Pritchard, C. (1995) 'Troubles Come Not Singly but in Battalions: The Pursuit of Social Justice and Probation Practice.' In D. Ward and M. Lacey (eds) *Probation: Working for Justice.* London: Whiting and Birch.

Cress-Welsing, F. (1991) *ISIS Papers.* Chicago: Third World Press.

Croft, S. and Beresford, P. (1989) 'User Involvement, Citizenship and Social Policy.' *Critical Social Policy 26*, 5–18.

Croft, S. and Beresford, P. (1992) 'The Politics of Participation.' *Critical Social Policy 35*, 20–44.

Davis, K. (1986) 'Disabling Definitions: A Comment on Mullender and Ward.' *British Journal of Social Work 16*, 1, 97.

Department of Health (1989) *Caring for People: Community Care in the Next Decade and Beyond.* London: HMSO.

Department of Health. (1991) *Working Together under the Children Act 1989.* London: HMSO.

Department of Health (1995) *Child Protection: Messages from Research.* London: HMSO.

Douglas, T. (1993) *A Theory of Groupwork Practice.* London: Macmillan.

Dullea, K. and Mullender, A. (1999) 'Evaluation and Empowerment.' In I. Shaw and J. Lishman (eds) *Evaluation and Social Work Practice.* London: Sage.

Dyson, S. and Harrison, M. (1996/97) 'Black Community Members as Researchers: Working with Community Groups in the Research Process.' *Groupwork 9,* 2, 203–220.

Evans, M. (ed) (1994) *The Woman Question.* London: Sage.

Everitt, A., Hardiker, P., Littlewood, J. and Mullender, A. (1992) *Applied Research for Better Practice.* London: Macmillan.

Faulkner, D. (1995) 'The Criminal Justice Act 1991: Policy, Legislation and Practice.' In D. Ward and M. Lacey (eds) *Probation: Working for Justice.* London: Whiting and Birch.

Fitzpatrick, S., Hastings, A. and Kintrea, K. (1999) 'Young People's Participation in Urban Regeneration.' *Child Right 154,* 11–12.

Fleming, J., Harrison, M. and Ward, D. (1998) 'Social Action Can be an Empowering Process.' *Youth and Policy 60,* 46–62.

Fleming, J. and Ward, D. (1999) 'Research as Empowerment: The Social Action Approach.' In W. Shera and L. Wells (eds) *Empowerment Practice in Social Work: Developing Richer Conceptual Foundations.* Toronto: Canadian Scholars Press.

Foucault, M. (1980) *Power, Knowledge: Selected Interviews and Other Writings.* New York: Pantheon.

Freire, P. (1972) *Pedagogy of the Oppressed.* Harmondsworth: Penguin.

Giddens, A. (1984) *The Constitution of Society.* Cambridge: Polity Press.

Giddens, A. (1998) *The Third Way.* Cambridge: Polity Press.

Gilroy, P. (1987) *There Ain't No Black in the Union Jack.* London: Hutchinson.

Gould, N. (1999) 'Qualitative Practice Evaluation.' In I. Shaw and J. Lishman (eds) *Evaluation and Social Work Practice.* London: Sage.

Hallet, C. (1987) *Critical Issues in Participation.* London: Association of Community Workers.

Hammersley, M. (1995) *The Politics of Social Research.* London: Sage.

Humphries, B. (1996) *Critical Perspectives on Empowerment.* Birmingham: Venture Press.

Humphries, B. and Trueman, C. (eds) (1994) *Rethinking Social Research.* Aldershot: Avebury.

Jakobsson, G. (ed) (1995) *Social Work in an International Perspective.* Helsinki: Helsinki University Press.

James, T. (1997) 'Empowerment through Social Change.' *Bridges,* Summer, 6–7.

Jayaratne, T. and Stewart, A. (1995) 'Quantitative and Qualitative Methods in the Social Sciences: Feminist Issues and Practical Strategies.' In J. Holland and M. Blair with S. Sheldon (eds) *Debates and Issues in Feminist Pedagogy.* Buckingham: Open University Press.

Kidd, R. and Kumar, K. (1981) 'Coopting Freire: A Critical Analysis of Pseudo-Freirian Adult Education.' Reprinted in *Social Action 2,* 2, 11–18 (1994).

Kurland, R. and Salmon, R. (1993) 'Groupwork versus Casework in a Group.' *Groupwork 6,* 1, 5–16.

Layder, D. (1994) *Understanding Social Theory.* London: Sage.

Lee, J. (1994) *The Empowerment Approach to Social Work Practice.* New York: Columbia University Press.

Lindsay, T. and Scally, M. (1997) 'Teaching and Assessing Groupwork in Social Work.' Paper presented at the Seventh European Groupwork Symposium, Cork, July.

Lorde, A. (1984) *Sister Outsider.* Freedom, CA: Crossing Press.

Lukes, S. (1974) *Power: A Radical View.* London: Macmillan.

Mistry, T. (1989) 'Establishing a Model of Feminist Groupwork in the Probation Service.' *Groupwork 2,* 2, 145–158.

Mullender, A. and Ward, D. (1991) *Self-Directed Groupwork: Users Take Action for Empowerment.* London: Whiting and Birch.

Murray, C. (1999) 'All Locked up in the American Dream.' *The Sunday Times,* 7 February.

National Institute for Social Work (1996) 'Social Exclusion, Civil Society and Social Work.' *Policy Briefings No. 18.* London: NISW.

Oliver, M. (1992) 'Changing the Social Relations of Research Production.' *Disability, Handicap and Society 7,* 2, 101–114.

Page, R. (1992) 'Empowerment, Oppression and Beyond: A Coherent Strategy? A Reply to Mullender and Ward (CSP Issue 32).' *Critical Social Policy 35,* 89–92.

Parton, N. (1985) *The Politics of Child Abuse.* London: Macmillan.

Parton, N. (1991) *Governing the Family: Child Care, Child Protection and the State.* London: Macmillan.

Parton, N. (ed) (1997) *Child Protection and Family Support: Tensions, Contradictions and Possibilities.* London: Routledge.

Payne, M. (1997) *Modern Social Work Theory* (second edition). London: Macmillan.

Pithouse, A., and Williamson, H. (1997) 'Introduction, Apology and Polemic.' In A.Pithouse and H. Williamson (eds) *Engaging Users in Welfare Services.* Birmingham: Venture Press.

Popple, K. (1995) *Analysing Community Work: Its Theory and Practice.* Buckingham: Open University Press.

Rees, S. (1991) *Achieving Power.* Sydney: Allen and Unwin.

Richardson, A. (1983) *Participation.* London: Routledge and Kegan Paul.

Scottish Community Development Centre (1997) 'Proposal to Joseph Rowntree Foundation.' Glasgow: SCDC (unpublished).

Shaw, I. (1997) 'Engaging the User: Participation, Empowerment and the Rhetoric of Quality.' In A. Pithouse and H. Williamson (eds) *Engaging Users in Welfare Services.* Birmingham: Venture Press.

Staples, L. (1990) 'Powerful Ideas about Empowerment.' *Administration in Social Work 14,* 2, 29–41.

Taylor, G. (1999) 'Empowerment, Identity and Participatory Research.' *Disability and Society 14,* 3, 369–384.

Thomas, M. and Pierson, J. (1995) *Dictionary of Social Work.* London: Collins.

Thompson, A. (1999) 'User Friendly.' *Community Care* 8–14 April, 14–15.

Treu, H-E., Salustowicz, P., Oldenburg, E., Offe, H. and Neuser, H. (eds) (1993) *Theorie und Praxis der Bekampfung der Langzeitarbeitslosigkeit in der EG.* Weinheim, Germany: Deutscher Studien Verlag.

Trueman, C. and Humphries, B. (1994) 'Rethinking Social Research: Research in an Unequal World.' In B. Humphries and C. Trueman *Rethinking Social Research.* Aldershot: Avebury.

Ward, D. (ed) (1982) *Give em a Break: Social Action by Young People at Risk and in Trouble.* Leicester: National Youth Bureau.

Ward, D. (1998) 'Groupwork,' In R. Adams, L. Dominelli and M. Payne (eds), *Social Work: Themes, Issues and Critical Debates.* London: Macmillan.

Waterhouse, L. and McGee, J. (1998) 'Social Work with Children and Families.' In R. Adams, L. Dominelli and M. Payne (eds) *Social Work: Themes, Issues and Critical Debates*. London: Macmillan.

Williamson, H. (ed) (1995) *Social Action for Young People*. Lyme Regis: Russell House.

Wright Mills, C. (1970) *The Sociological Imagination*. Harmondsworth: Penguin.

Young, K. (1999) 'The Youth Worker as Guide, Philosopher and Friend.' In S. Banks (ed) *Ethical Issues in Youth Work*. London: Routledge.

CHAPTER 4

Action Research for the Development of Children's Services in Ukraine

Jennie Fleming

Introduction

The author has written this chapter on behalf, and with the agreement of, all those involved in Ukraine and Britain with the project for the development of children's services in Ukraine. The Centre for Social Action, De Montfort University, England has been working in partnership with the Ukrainian Institute of Social Research, Kyiv for many years. This collaboration is one in which the Ukrainian partners are in the 'driving seat' and the Centre sees its role as facilitating a process of critical reflection which should culminate in considered action enabling people to move services for children from where they are now, closer to where they want them to be. It is an approach that emphasises both empowerment for all involved and the rights of the child. *The Dictionary of Social Work* (Thomas and Pierson 1995) gives a basic definition of empowerment as being concerned with how people gain a collective control over their lives to achieve their interests, and the method by which social workers seek to enhance the power of people who lack it. It represents a change of focus from social work on people to social work with people.

This chapter will outline the development of a multi-agency project to develop child-centred child care provision in Ukraine in line with the United Nations Convention on the Rights of the Child. The project is a four-way partnership between the Ukrainian Institute for Social Research (ISR), the Centre for Social Action, Unicef Ukraine and the All Ukrainian Committee of Children's Rights, a non-governmental organisation. It is a negotiated relationship based on the sharing of knowledge, skills and experience both between and amongst Ukrainian and British colleagues.

All the organisations in the project share a commitment to working in partnership both with each other and also with the organisations providing child care in Ukraine at present. All are committed to the implementation in Ukraine of the UN

Convention on the Rights of the Child and to a programme of innovative solutions to the growing problems of children in public care.

The Situation in Ukraine

> Ukraine is going through a transition period, the goal of which is the creation of a democratic society and a market economy. However the processes of state-building and transition to a new economic model, different in principle, have caused many problems which are impossible to solve at once. (Valeriy Smoliy, Deputy Prime Minister of Ukraine, in Steshenko 1998)

The deep economic crisis in Ukraine today is a result of the dismantling of the former Soviet unified economy; also, the previous state economy was heavily reliant on the military industrial complex and the production of capital goods. Productivity since 1993 has fallen by more than a half. Data on per capita income shows that in 1996 63 per cent of the population of Ukraine lived below the poverty line. Income stratification is also increasing. In 1996 the wealthiest 10 per cent of the population received a third of all personal income (Unicef 1997, pp.10–11). The situation has got worse since these figures were produced.

Poverty, unemployment and general social upheaval were created by the rapid political change that has taken place over recent years. The gulf between economic progress and social deprivation is vast and Unicef (1997, p.vii) states that it can be clearly demonstrated through the 'worsening position of a group of children whose voice to the outside world is rarely heard: children in public care'. The problem of children in public care did not become fully apparent until after the events of 1989, and the invisibility of these children prior to then was due to a 'tendency to repress rather than acknowledge social difficulties' according to Cemlyn and Vdovenko (1995, p.17).

In 1993 there were over 83,000 children in public care in Ukraine (Unicef 1997, p.67). Rates of receiving children into public care have increased dramatically since 1989. Of all the countries monitored for the 1998 Unicef report, Ukraine had the highest deterioration (88%) in the 95 welfare indicators, which included poverty, nutrition, health, mortality, education, social cohesion and child and family protection (for further discussion of these issues see Steshenko 1998). These children are mostly living in large institutions.

As the political, social and economical systems of society have changed, so has the situation of the institutions. For example, all residential children's institutions are affected by the huge budget shortages, because the state does not earmark sufficient resources for their needs. Nowadays nearly all institutions require immediate overhaul and reconstruction and new equipment and resources. Lack of finances affects the provision for children, particularly those who are unwell or requiring specialist support (Ukrainian Institute of Social Research 1998). This is the context in which the work described is being undertaken.

Partnerships between East and West

Those involved in work between two cultures will have vastly different ideas of how research, evaluation and practice development should be conducted. The methodologies will be different, as will the cultural, social and academic traditions. Marsden and Oakley (1990) recognise the tensions here and state that: 'It is important to recognise these differing interests and to work through a methodology which can provide a forum where these might be publicly dealt with and which can produce something which is less hierarchical'(1990, p.9). The role of the consultant in developing countries has been much criticised, not least within the context of Eastern Europe. There is much potential to create tension and harm when the consultancy is based purely upon the knowledge and experience of a foreigner who attempts to transfer practices and methods from one cultural situation to another without regard for either specific national or local differences (Aubrey 1998a).

From the very beginning of the consultancy process it would appear that there are unequal relationships. The inference is often that the Western consultant has the cure for a particular situation and that the recipients in Eastern Europe must simply listen and learn. To continue with the medical metaphor, the consultant can heal what is wrong, because the recipient can not. Gilbert (1998) pursues the metaphor thus: 'Called in to investigate a case of an ailing business or organisation, they carry out a diagnosis, prescribe a course of action...they present a large bill and then move on to the next patient' (p.340).

A TACIS (Technical Aid for the Commonwelath of Independent States) report (1997) criticised management development programmes for their unnecessary bureaucracy and their lack of sensitivity towards beneficiaries. There are many factors that have contributed towards the irritation of Eastern Europeans. Gilbert (1998) provides several examples which include:

> Resentment at the rates of remuneration that Western consultants attract, irritation with consultants who after six or seven visits still do not understand more than a smattering of the language and dismay that few consultants seem prepared to live in the country for more than a few days at a time. (p.341)

Because of this lack of knowledge of language Westerners inevitably also have a very limited understanding of the complex social situation in which the language has been shaped and developed.

Mikkelsen (1995) maintains that all those involved in the development field are potentially guilty of using development situations to enhance either their own professional reputation or that of their institution or agency. She reinforces the fact that participatory development should be owned by those that understand the situation of their community, and uses Arnfred and Bentzon (1990) to illustrate her point: 'To get things moving in the right direction, development planners, practitioners and researchers alike, have to give up one of the fundamental self-established rights – the right to define what is the problem, whose problem it is, how to solve it and why'(p.36).

In this project there are many stakeholders – the Ukrainian researchers and trainers, the managers of the children's homes, the potential foster carers, the children, to name but a few. All these people have differing perceptions of the project and differing expectations, before one brings into the relationship the British participants. It is against this background and history of East–West relationships that the partnership is operating. Being aware of the difficulties and pitfalls is the easy part; trying to develop practice and relationships on a basis of equality and empowerment is the challenge with which we all struggle. Freire places emphasis on the need for dialogue in any development work: 'It is not our role to speak to the people about our view of the world, nor to attempt to impose that view on them, but rather to dialogue with the people about their views and ours' (1970, p.77).

The De-institutionalisation of Child Care Project

The project is multi-funded, the UK costs being met by De Montfort University and the Know How Fund. Unicef pays all the costs in Ukraine as part of its programme 'Transforming State Institutional Care of Children in Ukraine'. The project was divided up in to four parts, although there were close links between all of them:

- Work with residential children's homes to encourage the development of models of work that best meet the child's interests and foster their abilities to live independently once they are adult

- Work to develop the foundation stones of a system of foster care in Ukraine

- Developing models of support for families in crisis appropriate to Ukraine; this stage was research-based

- Developing community-based social support for disabled children and their families.

The project had a *research element* in order to develop a firm information base on the situation of children living apart from their families in Ukraine. It also established how the law relating to the removal of parental rights works in practice, making comparisons with other countries and finding out about models of family support in other countries. The results were explored with Ukrainian professionals, parents and children so that appropriate models of family support for Ukraine could begin to be developed.

There was a *training and practice development element* involving four separate training/practice development seminars, each with three parts. These addressed work with disabled children, the development of foster care, creating less institutional environments within children's homes, and evaluation.

The distinction between research, training and practice development is not clear, as there is overlap between all three. The parts of the project were developed through discussion with the main partners. A detailed framework for each component was developed by the British and Ukrainian partners. All the work and research activity was undertaken by Ukrainians, the role of the British professionals being to run training seminars, offer support and advice and provide the Ukrainians with information about child care in other countries.

The Ukrainian participants were a multi-disciplinary team. The programme was headed by an experienced researcher from the ISR and the key players in the project were the staff of the Institute, who all had considerable experience of traditional research. Those who attended the seminars and developed the practice were a wider group who included the staff of the ISR and also psychologists, heads of children's institutions and people running foster family homes.

The British participants were also a multi-disciplinary team including youth and social workers with a wide range of experiences: fostering, residential work, undertaking social action work, being in care themselves, being foster parents. In addition to those who facilitated the seminars, the Centre for Social Action employed a British man living in Kyiv (and an ex-foster carer himself) who supported the Ukrainians and aided communication. The whole programme is also being evaluated by a Ph.D. student at De Montfort University as the core of her thesis on the transfer of knowledge between East and West.

Methodology

The aim of the social action methodology is to enable people to develop their own solutions to their own problems. The input and exercises in the seminars aim to provide people with the necessary tools of analysis that are relevant to their circumstances. It is important in a country like Ukraine where the social and economic situation is rapidly changing that proposals are not inflexible – tools of analysis are needed in order to develop appropriate solutions that take into account the changing situation.

The CSA has run a series of seminars on this project for managers and practitioners who work directly with children in Kyiv and Odessa. The focus on *practice* is intentional, as it is here that the real change for children will come. Whilst good and appropriate legislation is important, it is through changing practice that real improvements in children's lives are achieved.

The seminars are participative. We start from the assumption that we all have things to learn from each other and that we are all both teachers and learners (Freire 1970, p.53). Our aim is to build on the capacities that exist already in the group to enable people to share and use all the skills, knowledge and experience of participants. The process we go through is one of problem posing and problem exploration. For example, the group might consider their own childhood and think about adults they liked and those they did not like, and then go on to explore why this was, and which characteristics they responded to in adults. This could be done through discussion, mime, drawing or writing. The seminars also provide people with a model of working that they can adapt to enable children and young people to use their skills, knowledge and experiences to identify their own issues and concerns and take an active part in developing their own solutions to them.

The work of the Centre for Social Action is based on clear and explicit values that underpin and inform its undertakings. Values are the standards and ideals through which we judge the actions of ourselves and others (Badham and Eadie forthcoming). The central value that runs through all the work is a commitment to empowerment. Staples (1990) identifies key themes in empowerment as: 'participation of people in their own empowerment', 'the importance of recognising existing competencies' and 'building on individual and collective strengths' (p.30). Empowerment is the process by which power is developed or taken by the powerless themselves.

Empowering practice offers people the chance to try out and experience new ways of influencing their life chances. It looks to share power between parties and to challenge them all to use it non-oppressively. It is this model that we are endeavouring to put into practice in our work in Ukraine, to facilitate a process by which our Ukrainian colleagues empower themselves and in turn work with the children and potential foster families in a way that also results in their empowerment.

Empowerment Research

In the United Kingdom empowerment issues have begun to be played out in the arena of research, with the insistence of service users that they have a right to participate, and to control, the definition and assessment of need and the formulation of services (Davis and Mullender 1994); there are also new legal requirements on service providers to consult widely in their planning and review processes. The consequent active involvement of service users in the research process, rather than as passive objects, presents new challenges for established research practice and methods. This way of looking at research was new to our Ukrainian research colleagues but they quickly and easily saw the relevance of it, and particularly its appropriateness to a rapidly changing society such as Ukraine. They readily adopted and adapted it, and explored its application for themselves.

Most positivist researchers aim 'not to disturb the world they are studying: their aim, instead, is to trawl their data collecting net quietly through the social world' (Graham and Jones 1992, p.239). Social scientists who take this approach use tools such as surveys or questionnaires to capture and understand the subject matter under scrutiny. In contrast to the 'positive tradition is the interpretative tradition in which an understanding of the social world and the subject matter studied is generated from the people'. This second theme is more concerned with understanding social phenomena, and interprets them from the viewpoint of the people themselves (Silverman 1993). The argument is that human beings are active participants who live in a changing environment.

Feuerstein (1986) offers a complete set of steps for what she terms 'participatory evaluation' and recommends that all parties who are involved with the project or programme under evaluation are involved at all stages of the process. This will include selecting objectives and indicators, deciding upon evaluation methods, collecting the data and analysing and using the results (p.x). The process continues in this participatory way, with decisions being made collaboratively throughout. This is very similar to the approach developed by the Centre for Social Action (see Fleming 1997; Fleming and Wattley 1998). As far as is feasible, we work together with all the parties involved at all levels and at all stages of a research project. They participate in the refinement of the objectives, in the formulation of the questions to be addressed and the methods of information collection and in due course, in the interpretation of the findings. This forms the basis of a collaborative research approach which draws out qualitative and quantitative data, using a range of data-collection methods.

In research, training and practice development we consider that asking people the question 'why?' is the key that unlocks the process and leads to forms of social change activity that challenge a *status quo*. In social action we ask 'Why does the problem exist, what are its causes?', 'Why are there so many children in institutions in Ukraine?' We encourage people to pursue the question 'why?' until the root causes of a problem have been identified. This stage is one of the distinctive characteristics of the social action approach (Mullender and Ward 1990). Leaving out this stage confines explanations and responsibilities and the scope of the solution to the private world around people and within their existing knowledge and experience. It is a development from individual concerns to an analysis of the structures within which they exist. This is the process we facilitated in the first seminars in Kyiv – it was adapted to the particularities of the Ukrainian situation, through discussion and dialogue.

The value of the whole method lies particularly in the depths of richness of the qualitative data gathered; it can provide vivid descriptions and clear insights into problems and opportunities. By using a collaborative format and a combination of methods, a range of perspectives is brought to bear on data and meanings are attributed to them, to achieve both sensitivity to participants and, through triangulation, research validity (Patton 1990).

The benefits of this approach for the situation in Ukraine came about because all those concerned with the problems and issues of state child care were involved, thus securing widespread ownership of findings and achieving support for the implementation of solutions. We have found that the process also engenders knowledge, skills and structures which can be sustained after research involvement is over: for example, the group of committed parents, professionals and academics who are determined to develop a system of Ukrainian foster care. What takes place is a seamless interaction, and progression, of research and development work, as is clearly illustrated in the work in Kyiv and Odessa.

Setting The Research Agenda

Social action research works on the basis that research should not be detached from practical activities. Projects should learn from the information produced by the research, as it emerges, and should incorporate it into the process. This means that people at all levels must have close links with the research and a commitment to take on the process and its results in their own activities. Thus, all parties are involved in discussions about what information should be collected, why and from whom, how it should be collected, and how it should be presented and used. What is important at this stage is not to specify a number of predetermined questions based on researchers' perspectives, but to ensure that the research methods deployed are sufficiently flexible and open for issues to be introduced by participants and to be added from emerging data.

For example, in the children's home project the researchers spoke to graduates of children's homes to establish what areas and issues needed exploration in the next stages. They were also involved in discussions about what were the best ways to involve residents of the children's home in the project and how to get the most accurate information. The young people involved had much to contribute in deciding the best ways of collecting information.

A variety of information collection methods are available to achieve this. In Ukraine these included:

- review of secondary sources, policy documents, correspondence, international materials and practice examples

- direct observation

- guided conversations with key individuals and groups

- critical incident analysis to look at how certain problems areas are dealt with

- case studies of organisations or individuals
- focus groups
- SWOT analyses (looking at the strengths, weaknesses, opportunities and threats in particular situations)
- questionnaires
- statistical data. (See also Mikkelsen 1995, Ch.3)

Data was analysed throughout the project by a variety of means. Thematic coding of the qualitative information was undertaken. Emergent themes were discussed with the participants – children, potential foster carers, workers in institutions. By having a range of people and methods of looking at the same situation, triangulation is achieved.

Outcomes

The project has been even more successful than perhaps had been originally anticipated. Its significant areas of achievement compared to the original objectives are set out below:

- The effect of the legal system on child care decisions has been examined and the findings are ready for publication
- The Ukrainian practice of bringing up of children has been studied
- Research has been conducted in boarding schools in Kyiv and Odessa to find out what happens within them
- Focus groups with graduates of boarding schools have been conducted
- Causes for conflict situations in families that result in children being placed into institutions or the removal of parental rights have been thoroughly studied. The report *Troubled Families* was published
- Practical help was given to heads of some boarding schools in Kyiv and Odessa who were keen to improve their organisations
- Training has been provided for the heads of boarding schools; the trainers have visited three times
- Practical recommendations in terms of improving conditions for the keeping and upbringing of children have been carefully worked out and published
- Social workers who will prepare professionals for foster family support have been selected and trained

- Experience of the introduction, selection, training and support systems of fostering in other countries has been studied

- Via publications in the local press, TV and radio programmes (including phone-in programmes) in Kyiv and Odessa, Ukrainian people have been told about the idea and objectives of fostering for Ukraine

- Potential foster families in Kyiv and Odessa have been identified and selected and have received training

- Thirty-four Ukrainians attended the European Foster Care Conference in Hungary and gave a presentation of their work, as well as making many useful contacts and attending workshops

- The Cabinet of Ministers' principles for foster care have been analysed and improvements suggested

- Disability training for district officials, staff working with disabled children and the parents of disabled children has been enthusiastically received

- The whole project has made a major impact in raising the profile of family-based alternatives to children's institutions in Ukraine, and has encouraged debate and discussions about how children are cared for

- Four books about the project and its findings have been published (Komaroua *et al.* 1998; Volynets *et al.* 1998a, 1998b; Yakoba 1998).

Evaluation from the Viewpoint of Ukrainian Partners

All the seminars were formally evaluated at the time. The notes of the Ph.D. student's interviews with participants throughout the project have been available (Aubrey 1998b) and some information was collected by the author specifically to include in this chapter.

Some participants of the seminars have told us that they have gone straight to work and tried some of the exercises with the young people with whom they work, and have been impressed with how well the young people have articulated their views. At one seminar about working with disabled children, one participant said that the children had, 'become intensely aware of the issues and recognised my responsibility to do something about it' (Wilson and Keenan 1998, p.8). People have said what a revelation it has been to realise that small things can make big differences – for example, listening to what children and young people have to say. From the evaluations of the seminars we have been told that people have found it helpful to look at problems differently and to be creative and innovative in thinking of how to change things. 'We realise that asking the question "why?" is really important. There are problems but we are able to look at them in a totally different way. We realise that we must find Ukrainian answers to Ukrainian problems.'

Participants often say that they feel the courses start very slowly; however, by the time the seminar is over, they say they understand why this is so: 'I see now that it is important to start slowly, it is important to consider things from every point of view and to think about all aspects and how it is constructed. It is a good way to work.' Importantly, it is also fun – people work hard but enjoy themselves too; this has surprised them but has also encouraged them to use the methods with children and young people.

Perceptions of involvement and participation

People commented on the research methodology and how appropriate they felt it was to their situation:

> We learnt another way of research, no not another way, but a different approach. The methods we learned were more practical and I like this way, especially for social work. We need to combine theory and practice... In my mind it is a practical project, we learned to do small but practical things step by step.

> The research went into directions we did not expect. The work with the children's homes gave us information we would never have known to ask for. By not going in with fixed ideas, but open questions we ended up with information we did not expect and in directions we had not foreseen.

They also commented about how other participants had been involved and the impact of this involvement on them all:

> People, like the parents in Odessa, they see their ideas recognised and included in everything we did. It was new to them and a surprise – they were pleased. We worked with them, like you do with us – we do not teach.

> We realise now the importance of talking to the children. Children told us of being beaten – no director did.

The responsibility of what they are doing

Very quickly people realised the enormous significance of this project. They knew it could have profound influence on children's lives. In the children's home part of the project the researchers were particularly affected emotionally by what they found out about the lives of the children living there. The reality of the children's lives was reflected in the results of collecting information in different ways.

> The children are very dependent on the staff in the homes. We used questionnaires, focus groups in the homes and individual conversations outside the home. I did this last one without the directors of the homes knowing. I told them an NGO had invited the children to a party. With the questionnaires we got little information, later we discovered sometimes the staff had told the children what to answer. In the focus groups we got formal, official information, 'I don't like my mother, but my father is nice'. But when the children were alone with the researcher it was different – sometimes they talked for three or four hours. Some of the things they told us were terrible. Pure sociological evaluation would not reflect what we have done in this project.

> I am scared for the children if it is known they have told us these things.

The value of international partnerships

Many people acknowledged the benefits of the transfer and exchange of knowledge between partners, and recognised the values we were trying to demonstrate.

> It was very pleasant to see foreign partners who were real partners, not teachers, so many people come to teach us what we already know. Here we developed methodics that joined together your experience and ours – I believe there was mutual learning. You recognised we were already clever and came to have conversations with us – not tell us. We can feel the respect you come with.

Blocks and Difficulties

Language

The issue of language is one we are very conscious of, particularly since none of the workers from the Centre for Social Action speak more Russian than to be polite with greetings or adequately manage to shop for dinner in the market. Increasingly it is Ukrainian not Russian that is the language of choice, particularly in politics and academia, if not yet with the person in the street in Kyiv or Odessa. We have excellent interpreters for most of our work, but language is more than just the meaning of the words. Not all language difficulties can be simply overcome by using an interpreter. There are deeper differences and complex sets of meanings that may not be understood even with fluency in Russian or Ukrainian.

> Sometimes it is very difficult to interpret one word – English words like empowerment or capacity building, for example, even youth participation in my language. It is not enough to say youth participation, you should add youth participation in the decision-making process... you can't just say

capacity building and expect every one to understand – it is something new for Ukraine.

There is no word for fostering in the Russian or Ukrainian languages; at present they have chosen to use the English word:

> To offer people fostering, first you have to name it and the word should contain some positive meaning for the majority of the population… In Russia they use the word 'patronage' for fostering, but that's a medical term, and by the way it is not a Russian or Ukrainian word and we don't like it. If we used the English word 'fostering' we would make the process much more complicated. It is a small thing, but very important – it hampers progress.

Lack of cultural awareness

As has already been discussed, the British participants lack knowledge about Ukrainian life, culture, legal system, child care practice; in this situation they also lack knowledge of the language. Some people felt this was a serious limitation.

> It is important that people from the West understand the situation in Ukraine. It is very different here and unless people know about the country in context, it is difficult to provide training for a small aspect of social work. People are very, very poor. I have a sister and brother-in-law and they are both disabled and have one child. They receive 80 Hrivna a month and 60 of that goes on rent. Trainers cannot understand the situation unless they have been through it themselves. How can they come and work unless they know about what it is like for people? They have only their Western expectations and they base their training on their Western experience. The wider picture in terms of fostering and adoption is very complicated. Even ten foster children is difficult, when people do not have money to feed themselves, they do not want an extra child. People come for two weeks and have no idea about anything, the politics, the situation of people and the nature of the social problems – I think they need this.

The situation in Ukraine

There are many ministries responsible for children in Ukraine, and this makes co-ordination and liaison very difficult. The ISR has good links with the Ministry of Family and Youth, but recognises the need for wider links. It has been very difficult to get some of the information required from different ministries, such as information on the finances of children's homes. 'When we were trying to analyse material from ministries, we could not get access from the Ministry. We did not expect them to be so reluctant – they simply would not release information.'

The Ukranian legal system requires a law to be passed to allow any new development or procedure, and at present there is no law that allows fostering. A considerable amount of work has been done on developing draft law, and there has been much debate in the project about how far fostering can be developed without this new law.

The project is working in an environment of very little public knowledge or understanding of foster care. Although much work has been done – for example radio phone-ins and newspaper articles – there is still much more to be done to change public opinion and create an awareness of the situation of children in state care.

> It is still the same old understanding of the problem, people still think that there is some institution that should be responsible, but it does not exist any more – people are not concerned because they still think that there is an institution in charge.

> One year ago we were surprised about the idea of fostering – placing a child in another family. Now we are deep in the topic, but we cannot expect others to have the same understanding. For a huge proportion of the population fostering is strange and not easy to understand.

There is also a lack of awareness of the issues from policy makers: 'There is a lack of understanding from most of the government officials about the problem and they do not believe that the system could be effective in this country... I think it is lack of information that causes this lack of understanding.'

Different approaches

There are dilemmas with the empowerment action research approach, not least the concern that the method can be forced upon people by funders or organisations (Mikkelsen 1995). The approach defines itself as a bottom-up model, and yet if these communities accept the approach without the conviction that it is the most appropriate model, it could be suggested that it is simply one more oppressive development technique that is essentially hierarchical and top-down.

There are many differences in the approaches of Britain and Ukraine. We have found much more emphasis on psychological testing, and reliance on psychologists, in Ukraine than in the UK. The language and the concepts behind language are different; for example, Ukrainian colleagues talk of 'problem families' rather than families who face problems, and they use terms such as nervous breakdown, traumatic stress syndrome and anti-social behaviour in very different ways. This different approach has been the subject of much debate.

The Future – Continuing to Develop Empowerment

All the partners realise that this one-year project has been just the beginning of a much longer programme and all are keen to continue to develop practice and policy to de-institutionalise child care in Ukraine.

As well as developing the project further along the lines already begun, some specific areas to pursue have been identified. For example:

- working to increase the voice of the children in this project, and towards their greater active participation

- looking at how it could be possible to develop ways for children to move straight from the street into foster care

- undertaking more intensive work with the staff team of one children's home/boarding school to facilitate the development of child-centred policy and practice and using this as an example for others of what can be done.

- developing an NGO, e.g. Ukrainian Foster Care Association, to work in co-operation with the state.

The ISR, Unicef and CSA are all committed to the idea of Ukrainian people taking this collaboration forward: 'We do not want to stop, there is much more to find out. We have a big responsibility to the children'; 'We need to talk very loudly about what we have found – we have no choice. We cannot go back to not knowing now.'

Conclusions: Learning Together

Our Ukrainian colleagues have made mammoth strides in the ten months since this particular programme has begun – incredible progress has been made towards establishing a system of foster care, and in thinking about how children's homes are organised and how to develop Ukrainian family support systems. All the people from Britain who have been involved in this programme have been inspired and stimulated by their work in Ukraine. We have learnt so much; it has challenged us and enabled us to improve our practice in the UK. We have been humbled by the commitment of our Ukrainian colleagues. Never once have we heard them say, 'It is too difficult' or, 'The problem is too large'. What they say is, 'We will find a way.'

All the British workers are totally committed to the vision they share and want to see the project through – but in keeping with the guiding principles; it is up to the Ukrainian partners to make decisions on what their future role is.

Genuinely empowering research and practice entails a demanding agenda. In this chapter, I have tried to outline how the values and processes of a UK-based organisation can be made meaningful and useful to people in another country. I am not saying that social action can be a panacea for all problems. Indeed, we must be cautious and not over-estimate the impact of the approach. There are many things still to be learnt both about working for empowerment and about working in partnership with people from another country. However, our experience shows that the philosophy and methods described are effective in ensuring participation. It is through wide participation that people become empowered to ensure that services which are appropriate to their culture, and which meet their needs, will develop.

Acknowledgements

This whole project has depended on the work and commitment of many people. It is important to take the opportunity to name a few of them: Alexander Yaramenko, Ludmyla Volynets, Nadiya Komarova, Natalie Salabaj, Iyrna Ivanova, Iryna Pesha, Yuliya Yakabova, Alexandra Antonova-Turchenko, Anna Svyatnenko, Natalia Petrova, Jo Aubrey, Ian Boulton, Cathy Burdge, Chris Gardiner, Mark Harrison, Chris Hollis, Marie Seeley, David Ward, Unicef, Sergai Naboka, Nadya Valentyuk and the other translators; of course, the participants of the seminars; and most particularly, the children who took part in this project and for whom we all hope for a brighter future.

References

Arnfred, S. and Bentzon, A. (1990) *The Language of Development Studies.* New Social Science Monographs. Roskilde: Roskilde University Centre.

Aubrey, J. (1998a) 'A History and Critique of Development Literature and its Application to Eastern Europe.' Unpublished paper.

Aubrey, J. (1998b) 'Transcripts of Interviews with Ukrainian Participants.' Unpublished.

Badham, B. and Eadie, T. (forthcoming) 'Social Work in the Voluntary Sector: Holding on and Moving Forward.' In S. Bulter and M. Lymbrey (eds) *Social Work Ideals and Practice Realities.* London: Jessica Kingsley Publishers.

Cemlyn, S. and Vdovenko, T. (1995) 'Social Work in Russia and UK – What are We Exchanging?' *Social Work Education 14*, 1.

Davis, K. and Mullender, A. (1994) *Key Issues in Disability: Rights or Charity. The Future of Welfare.* Special edition of *Social Action Journal 2*, 1. London: Whiting and Birch.

Feuerstein, M. (1986) *Partners in Evaluation – Evaluating Development and Community Programmes with Participants.* Basingstoke: Macmillan.

Fleming, J. (1997) 'Research in the Context of Human Services in Crisis.' In R. Adams (ed) *Crisis in the Human Services: National and International Issues.* Kingston upon Hull: University of Lincolnshire and Humberside.

Fleming, J. and Wattley, R. (1998) 'One Who Teaches from Experience: Social Action and the Development of Anti-Racist Research and Practice.' In M. Lavalette (ed) *Anti-Racism and Social Welfare.* Aldershot: Ashgate.

Freire, P. (1970) *Pedagogy of the Oppressed.* Harmondsworth: Penguin.

Gilbert, K. (1998) '"Consultancy Fatigue": Epidemiology, Symptoms and Prevention.' *Leadership and Organisation Development Journal 19*,6, 340–346.

Graham, H. and Jones, J. (1992) 'Community Development and Research.' *Community Development Journal 24*, 3, 235–241.

Komarova, N., Volynets, L., Salabaj, N. and Pesha, I. (1998) *Scientific Methodological Recommendations for Social Workers on the Preparation of Foster Parents*. Kyiv, Ukraine: Institute of Social Research.

Marsden, D. and Oakley, P. (1990) *Evaluating Social Development*. Oxford: Oxfam.

Mikkelsen, B. (1995) *Methods for Development Work and Research: A Guide for Practitioners*. London: Sage.

Mullender, A. and Ward, D. (1991) *Self-directed Groupwork: Users Take Action for Empowerment*. London: Whiting and Birch.

Patton, M. (1990) *Qualitative Research Methods*. London: Sage.

Silverman, D. (1993) *Interpreting Qualitative Data: Methods for Analysing Talk, Text and Interaction*. London: Sage.

Staples, L. (1990) 'Powerful Ideas about Empowerment.' *Administration in Social Work 14*, 2, 29–41.

Steshenko, V. (ed) (1998) *The Health of Women and Children in Ukraine*. Kyiv, Ukraine: Unicef.

TACIS (1997) *Interim Evaluation*. Brussels: European Community.

Thomas, M. and Pierson, J. (1995) *The Dictionary of Social Work*. London: Collins.

Ukrainian Institute of Social Research (1998) 'System of State Institutional Care in Ukraine: Reality, Problems and Ways of Improvement.' Paper prepared for the International Foster Care Conference in Hungary, August 1998.

Unicef (1997) *Children at Risk in Central and Eastern Europe: Perils and Promises*. Florence, Italy: Unicef.

Unicef/UNDP (1996) *Children and Motherhood in Ukraine*. Kyiv, Ukraine: Unicef.

Volynets, L., Komarova, N., Antonova-Turchenko, I., Ivanova, I. and Pesha, I. (1998a) *Social Orphans in Ukraine: An Expert Analysis of the Current Ukrainian System of Child Care and Education*. Kyiv, Ukraine: Institute of Social Research.

Volynets, L., Komarova, N., Ivanova, I. and Antonova-Turshenko, I. (1998b) *Methodical Recommendations about the Protection of Children and Education in Children's Homes on the Principles based on the UN Convention on Children's Rights*. Kyiv, Ukraine: Institute of Social Research.

Wilson, C. and Keenan, E. 'Report on the Disability Issues Training Conducted by the Centre for Social Action, De Montfort University, Leicester, UK on behalf of UNICEF'. Kyiv, Ukraine. Unpublished.

Yakoba, Y. (1998) *Problems of Family, Children and Parents*. Kyiv, Ukraine: Institute of Social Research.

CHAPTER 5

Family Involvement in Child Protection
The Use of Family Group Conferences
Kate Morris and Carmel Shepherd

Introduction

Family involvement in planning for children at risk of significant harm has gener-ated considerable professional debate and academic research (DoH 1995; Thoburn 1992). Professionals and family members have struggled to find effec-tive mechanisms for meaningful participation, and to reflect the expectations in law and guidance that working partnerships be established between service users and professionals (DoH 1988). 'Whilst I understand why it [the child protection investigation] had to happen, what I don't understand is why it had to be so damaging to me, to my children, to my family' (Morris, Smith and Potts (video) 1996).

In 1992 Haringey Social Services and Area Child Protection Committee took the decision to pilot the use of family group conferences (FGCs) in their child protection services. This innovative project was researched and monitored by the internal project manager and the University of Sheffield. Since the initial trial period the FGC model is now fully incorporated into the local child protection services and is promoted within the authority's Children's Service Plans. This chapter details this pilot scheme and the accompanying research. The findings are summarised and their implications discussed. In conclusion some broader issues are explored and ways forward are identified.

Family Group Conferences

An overview

FGCs are increasingly part of child care services in the UK (Morris, Marsh and Wiffen 1998). Originating in New Zealand, the FGC model enables the family to form the primary planning group when there is the need for a plan to assist their child/children. The model is applicable to all areas of child care practice – including youth justice (Jackson 1998). The model has some key features that should be present if the planning process is to be accurately described as an FGC:

- 'Family' is widely interpreted and should include all those within the child's network – for example relatives, friends, significant others

- The co-ordinator must be 'independent', that is they should neither manage nor provide services to the child and their family

- The process should always include time for private family planning – without any professionals present

- The principles of the family plan should be agreed unless the plan places the child at risk of significant harm. (Resources are negotiated following this initial agreement.)

The process is relatively simple, and can be summarised as in Figure 5.1.

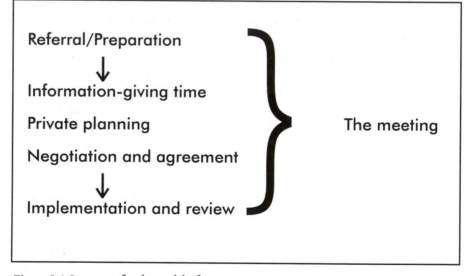

Figure 5.1 Summary for the model of FGCs

The model focuses on facilitating effective family planning for children and young people. Once a referral is made the co-ordinator identifies the child's network and convenes a meeting. The meeting has three stages – information giving, private planning time, and negotiation and agreement of the family plan.

The role of the co-ordinator is crucial. He or she is charged with the responsibility of managing the process, of involving and preparing participants and of chairing the information-giving stage. As many of the family needs as possible are accommodated – venues, timing, particular traditions. The co-ordinator will also ensure that the relevant professionals attend and are able to share their knowledge, duties and resources. The model intends that the co-ordinator should reflect the language and culture of the family. The process will be held in the family's chosen language and professionals who do not share the language should be accompanied by interpreters/translators. The model is an inclusive approach, the child is a full participant and arrangements should reflect this – for example in the use of advocates/supporters and child-friendly venues. The co-ordinator has the right to exclude family members. This will usually only occur where there are issues of physical risk or intimidation, inhibiting drugs/alcohol use or mental health difficulties that clearly identify a risk of harm to the individual if participation occurs.

Nationally, the use of the model has gained momentum and there have been various accompanying research reports (Crow and Marsh 1997a; Jackson 1998; Lupton, Barnard and Swall-Yarrington 1995; Morris and Tunnard 1996). The model is effective, with some 94 per cent of families producing safe and effective plans for their children (Crow and Marsh 1997b). Little evidence exists to indicate that the model should only be used with particular needs or difficulties, and the research would suggest that it is potentially helpful in all areas of practice. Certainly families perceive this to be a positive way forward and are, if effectively prepared, able to participate and plan for their children (Wiffen and Morris 1998).

Family group conferences in child protection

The use of FGCs in situations where a child is at risk of significant harm is contentious. The model is perceived to have a role where there is a need for informal, negotiated services – other settings generate more concern (DoH 1998). Although there is no evidence that FGCs in child protection increase risk, professional anxieties can distort their use, as experience in authorities piloting the model indicates (Family Rights Group 1994–96). There are therefore some practical baselines to adopt when using FGCs in child protection:

- The initial investigation should be complete – no one can plan effectively if the child's situation is only partially identified. FGCs are not an investigative model

- There should be some shared acknowledgement between professionals and families that risk is an issue – there must be sufficient family concern to make planning viable

- The family should be told all relevant information – safe plans cannot be generated if key protective information cannot be shared

- The focus, as ever, is the child and their needs – any plan produced must reflect this expectation and directly address the needs of the child

• Professionals must be explicit about their roles, duties and any risk assessments – the model does not remove from them professional duties towards children at risk of significant harm.

Ultimately this model provides for effective family participation in helping to make children safe. Given that the majority of children whose names are placed on the Child Protection Register live within their families, FGCs can offer a means of actively involving the family network in producing protective plans (Marsh and Crow; Morris and Tunnard 1996).

The Haringey project

The impetus for an FGC project in Haringey originated from individual team managers in the children and families teams and from a training officer who wished to consider more effective ways of involving children and families in decision-making processes. While the usefulness of FGCs in the UK had been demonstrated elsewhere, limited work had been developed in the area of child protection. Services to children at risk of significant harm and to looked-after children form the main focus in the children and families teams in Haringey. The particular interest of the Family Rights Group (FRG) in introducing FGCs into these areas of work provided the opportunity for forming a partnership between FRG, the University of Sheffield and Haringey under the auspices of the Department of Health (Shepherd 1997).

The Haringey Project aimed to evaluate the use of the FGC model for families whose children's names were placed on the Child Protection Register, and for children within the care system. The criteria for referrals were clearly defined, and the time-scales for making referrals were set out. These were outlined for front-line social workers as shown in Figure 5.2.

Haringey had particular reasons for introducing compulsory criteria for making referrals for an FGC within set timescales. In existing pilot schemes elsewhere in the country professionals were able to opt into the FGC project, thereby potentially impacting the research outcomes because of a pre-existing commitment to partnership and service-user involvement. The Haringey project was keen to introduce a more objective element to the process of referral without predetermining factors for 'promoting' success. There were also concerns amongst the team managers in Haringey that front-line staff might be reluctant to make referrals because of a tendency to underestimate the abilities of families to form plans that could protect their children. Additional concerns that staff might be anxious about referring because of 'exposing' their own practice to the scrutiny of research convinced the team managers responsible for agreeing criteria for referrals that the 'power' for participation should not lie with individual front-line staff. The agreed timescales were also introduced in an attempt to ensure an organisational authority for the project, allowing the independent co-ordinators to determine the willingness and commitment of families to partic-ipate in the process. In this way, whilst some families chose not to proceed with an FGC, at least every family who met the project criteria could be offered the same consistent service.

Ten independent co-ordinators were appointed after a national recruitment campaign. They were paid on a sessional basis and their varied professional back-grounds included information officer, mediator, social worker, teacher and solici-tor. Between them the co-ordinators spoke some seven different languages and their ethnic backgrounds comprised black Caribbean, African, Greek, Irish and white European. The co-ordinators were unable to reflect all the languages spoken or needed for the families referred to the project. In particular, none of the co-ordinators spoke Turkish. A number of interpreters received training about FGCs and they were appointed to work together with the co-ordinators when necessary.

Client group	Referrals *must* take place when the following conditions apply
Child protection work **Timing of referrals:** Within two weeks of the child protection conference	1. When child/ren are placed on the Child Protection Register following an initial case conference AND When the category for registration is *not* sexual abuse and/or where HIV and AIDS are an issue. 2. When children have been placed on the Child Protection Register for two or more years AND When the registration is *not* under the category of sexual abuse and/or where parents are excluded from attending the child protection conference.
Looked-after children **Timing of referrals:** Within two weeks of initial planning meeting accommodating the child/ren and before the child's initial looked-after children review.	1. All requests for children to be looked after, including when court proceedings are applied for. 2. All children for two years or more who are not in a secure placement. *Note:* These referrals should be made within two weeks of a recommendation from the Looked-after children review.

Figure 5.2. Criteria for referrals to FGC.

Preparation for the project began in 1994 and it ran from 1995 to 1997. The project was managed by a project manager whose tasks included:

- the co-ordination of the monthly meetings of the multi-agency steering group (education, health, police child protection team and social services)

- liaison with Family Rights Group, the University of Sheffield and the Department of Health

- the appointment, allocation and supervision of co-ordinators

- promoting and maintaining a high profile for the project within the authority (holding briefing meetings with front-line staff and senior managers and producing quarterly newsletters).

Of the 47 families referred to the project, 29 completed the whole FGC process. The following details two case examples:

Both parents of two young children were drug addicts and as a consequence were considered by social services to be unable to provide adequate care for their children. Care proceedings were initiated and the children were placed with foster carers. A referral for an FGC was made. An FGC was held with family members able to attend and agree a plan. The family plans secured the children's future within the extended family. It outlined supportive services for the identified carers and the children as well as contact arrangements between the children and their parents. Care proceedings were withdrawn, offsetting at the very least the costs of the FGC. The family plan was able to reflect naturally the particular needs and wishes of the children in the context of their existing family network.

A black African child with disabilities was initially referred to social services by his school, following concern about injuries believed to have been caused by his mother. This single parent was horrified by the actions of the social services, and deeply distressed by the decision to place her son's name on the Child Protection Register. The carer refused to meet social workers or work with them in any way. Care proceedings were planned, but before these were initiated a referral was made for an FGC. In this case two co-ordinators were appointed to work together as race, culture and gender issues were thought to have contributed to the difficulties in establishing a working relationship between the carer and social services. Unlike the social workers, the co-ordinators were able to work with the child and the mother to identify the extended family. An FGC was held which identified appropriate resources for the child and his mother, including previously rejected comprehensive educational support within the special education system.

The Research

The research explored both the view of the professionals and the experiences of the families. The University of Sheffield undertook a broad-based piece of research with the participating professionals and the co-ordinators. This built on work being undertaken nationally by the University and aimed to place any findings in this context. Initial data was collected via questionnaires completed by the co-ordinators after the conference. Professionals attending the FGCs were also asked to complete and return a short questionnaire. Follow-up telephone interviews were undertaken between three months and fifteen months after the FGC, giving information about outcomes for almost three-quarters of the families involved (Crow and Marsh 1997a). Alongside this Sheffield University research, the Haringey project team sought the experiences and views of family members through a series of interviews.

Professionals' views

The research with professionals (including the co-ordinators) wanted to consider a number of aspects of the pilot scheme: core data about the type, purpose and process of the FGCs, the professional perceptions of the outcomes, the cost implications of using the model, and particular issues to do with ethnicity and culture. The response rate for the questionnaires was high, suggesting that professionals were keen to inform the development of the project. A 'feedback loop' was also established to allow professionals regular updates of the findings via newsletters and open meetings. This ensured that professionals were able to see the outcome of their involvement in the research, and encouraged further participation.

Professional perceptions of the processes were positive overall, with only 5 per cent seeing the FGC as 'poor'. Over 50 per cent of the respondents were positively surprised at how the meeting went, particularly at the family's commitment, friendliness and ability. This indicates a tendency for professionals to underestimate the ability of the families to manage the FGC process. No professional reported feeling dissatisfied with the family plan; social workers were more likely to say they were 'partially satisfied' with the plan while other professionals were more often 'very satisfied'.

Professionals reported that they felt the involvement of the extended family was reassuring, as was the family 'ownership' of the plan. The private planning time was seen as empowering and a positive experience for the family. Three main areas of concern were identified: that the timing of the FGC must be appropriate to avoid setting the family up to fail, that the model might raise too high expectations of the agencies, and that at times extended family attendance was poor.

The cost implications of the model appear, from this research, to be neutral. When compared with existing planning processes, no significant cost differences were identified. However, the model was perceived to have been helpful in preventing family breakdown or use of state care for one-third of the children and as such can be seen as cost-effective.

Outcome research for this model is hampered by the limited comparable data for other decision-making models. Indeed, there is an issue about the intensity of research for a user-driven model, compared to the historically relatively light focus on outcomes for professional models. In Haringey the vast majority of family plans were agreed and implemented, and at follow-up 70 per cent of these plans continued to be maintained. The research indicated that family plans were seen as at least as protective as professional plans. The rate of removal of the child's name from the Child Protection Register was relatively high; a further indication that the use of FGCs may reduce concerns about risk.

Over two-thirds of the FGCs considered involved black or ethnic minority families. Issues raised by the families are explored later. However, the research does suggest that for some groups, such as Caribbean families, this model is more acceptable than for others, such as Irish travellers.

> The findings from this study broadly support other studies in this area, all the indications are that the Conferences do increase family involvement, and can be carried out in a wide area of practice. There are gains, varying from slight to substantial, for the welfare of the children concerned. (Crow and Marsh 1997a, p.16)

Family experiences

It was felt important that the process of researching the family's experiences should reflect the principles of the FGC model. In practice this meant using independent interviewers and where possible ensuring that the language of the family was shared by the interviewer. Some 11 families agreed to meet with the interviewers and all these families had experienced an FGC at least two months prior to the interview.

The areas that the project wished to explore further with families were:

- family views about the co-ordinator

- family views about the length of time it took before an FGC was held. The average time from the appointment of the co-ordinator to setting up an FGC was eight to ten weeks, a concern for the agencies. Was this process too slow, too fast or just right for the families?

- family perceptions of the usefulness of the FGC model.

Overall the families said the gender, race, ethnicity or religion of the co-ordinator was not an issue, but that it was important to them that the co-ordinator spoke their chosen language. Interestingly, eight of the families said that the social workers did not ask them about their preferences in the appointment of the co-ordinator, although preferences were stated on their referral forms. It appears that social workers made the assumption that families would prefer the co-ordinator to reflect the family's own race, culture or gender. The family research suggests this is not the case; it depends whether the family believes that some of their difficulties are influenced by such factors. One carer did say that it was important for the co-ordinator to reflect the gender and ethnicity of her son, as these were important issues for him. The majority of families did not have a preference about the co-ordinator's gender or ethnicity; however, there were some other, individual circumstances where these factors were important.

For 8 of the 11 respondents, the independence of the co-ordinator was very important. Two said independence was 'quite important'. None considered the independence of the co-ordinator to be neutral, not very important or irrelevant. All explained that independence meant to them that the co-ordinator was an outsider who 'had nothing to do with social services' and someone who had 'no vested interests'. Clearly independence is an important factor and is perceived as such by the families. Although families knew that the local authority paid the co-ordinator, it was important to them that the co-ordinator had no role to play other than facilitating the FGC process.

For families, any delay in holding the FGC was presented as less important than allowing sufficient time for all relevant family members to be contacted and helped to attend. It appears that speed is not an essential factor for families and that it is more important to ensure that all relevant members of the family are well prepared for the FGC meeting. Admittedly, families have other commitments as well and it is essential for the co-ordinator to be flexible and sensitive to the pacing required by the family. This information has significance beyond FGCs and begins to tell us something about the impact of professional timing and timescales.

The families who formulated a care plan in the sample reported satisfaction with the plan and almost all those interviewed said that their family carried out their part of the plan 'fully'. One family said that their son only 'partly' kept to their part of the plan. Most worryingly, only one family said that social services carried out their part of the plan 'fully'. All the remainder said that the social services only 'partly' carried out their part of the plan.

> My son came back to live at home after the FGC. But as soon as he came back, Social Services washed their hands of him and closed the file, without notice. The least they could have done was to call me to ask how things are going. It took me two months to get a new social worker.

> The Social Services were supposed to have a meeting with us two weeks after the date of the FGC, but it never took place; we were supposed to have another meeting in six months' time which has not happened. They dragged their feet.

Overall, all the families said that they believed the FGC to be a helpful and useful way of helping families. This included the families who were unable to formulate a care plan. It was important to them to try to solve their own problems. Families made it clear that they wanted social workers to be involved in giving them the services they identified and which had been agreed. Families felt there was little point to an FGC unless the professionals were committed to making the plans work and helping the families to achieve their aims. The implications of these experiences are that FGCs can only benefit the children and their families if social workers and their managers are committed to the process, the outcomes and the plans designed with and by families.

Issues and Dilemmas

Any research that explores the use of FGCs can, by virtue of the private nature of the planning time, only consider outcomes. The closed nature of the decision-making process means it is impossible to consider the processes involved in reaching the plans. Anyone who is part of the private planning time should be significant to the child. Neutral observers will inevitably impact the processes – how many of us would feel uncomfortable and alter our behaviour if our family life was being watched? Hence the research can answer only some questions – professional anxieties about power dynamics, the role of particular family members and how a certain plan was reached can only be considered in terms of outcomes. If the plan is safe, the family processes by which the plan was reached are out of the professional domain. If the plan is unsafe, then professionals must deal with this accordingly, and intervene in the family processes to ensure the child's safety.

The focus on outcomes for Haringey was to a large extent professionally driven. The research considered outcomes as defined by the service providers – the rates of registration, the numbers of cases involving proceedings. The financial costs of tracking large groups of family members over a period of time to hear continually their experiences and views was not within the project budget. Whilst the project was able to evaluate outcomes via professional processes, evaluation of direct family perceptions was not possible on an ongoing basis. Research elsewhere helps us to begin to understand the longer-term impact of FGCs for families; a two-year study of 100 children for whom FGCs have been held is currently being undertaken by Marsh and Crow, but for Haringey only a short-term evaluation was possible.

The decision to build in a feedback 'loop' for participants in the project was important. It reflected the partnership intentions of the work and aimed to maintain a level of engagement between the research and development team and the staff implementing the model. The resource constraints prevented such a process of reporting back being possible for families. Whilst co-ordinators could provide families with information that placed individual experiences in a context, further development is needed to devise strategies for families to hear about the research and inform its future development.

The project demonstrated a level of social-worker resistance towards the use of FGCs in child protection. A number of staff continued not to refer to the project despite clear guidelines indicating that they should do so. There are a number of possible explanations for this reluctance to participate. These include attitude and values to do with family involvement, difficulties in adopting new practices, and front-line professional resistance to compulsory referral criteria. The research would suggest that preconceived attitudes and beliefs about the families they worked with contributed to a large extent to professionals' resistance. This was demonstrated by the social workers' feedback to the researchers about their surprise at the families' commitment and capacities to meet and make plans for their children.

Whatever the explanation for Haringey, projects elsewhere indicate that this experience is not unique. The evaluation of training and feedback to the project steering group suggests that for Haringey staff, the sharing of power with families was particularly problematic. The area of child protection causes particular professional anxieties about risk and accountability. The FGC model has to occur within a setting that addresses these concerns and allows workers to participate effectively. Whilst attempts were made in Haringey to create such an environment, for example the endorsement of the Area Child Protection Committee (ACPC), the front-line staff and their immediate managers continued to feel anxious, believing that the model would generate accountability without responsibility. User involvement can only be effective in these circumstances if significant preparation occurs, with very clear messages about rights and responsibilities. Families are being enabled to share with professionals planning for their children. This brings with it responsibility for the families as well as rights. The Haringey experience would suggest that broad-based training for professionals and service users in effective participation and partnership would be a positive way forward. Experience in other areas such as youth justice also indicates that these dilemmas are not unique (Jackson and Morris 1999).

The organisational context for partnership projects, as indicated by the Haringey experience, needs careful consideration. For staff to embrace a model of active service-user involvement they must themselves feel empowered within their agencies. Staff who feel powerless and demoralised find it difficult to appreciate the crucial role they have in enabling families to become partners in the planning process (Morris and Shepherd 1999). As interviews with the families indicated, families do anticipate a helpful and positive role for social workers, but in a manner that is respectful, inclusive and builds on the strengths of families rather than their weakness. Research elsewhere indicates that such an inclusive approach to families is a prerequisite to effective planning and services (Bullock, Little and Millham 1993).

Haringey was unique in specifically exploring issues in relation to race and gender in the FGC process and in particular in 'matching' co-ordinators with families. The research findings and the project experience raised questions about the assumptions being made by professionals about families' choices. The model embodies each family's traditions and practices in planning for their children. The Haringey experience demonstrated that families will have their particular priorities about the right person to facilitate this process. Generalised professional assumptions about ethnicity have been shown to be unhelpful. For families, co-ordinators sharing the same language and being clearly independent from the local authority were the key priorities. Professionals tended to assume that families' priority would be a 'match' of ethnicity, race and religion. However, this was not the case. Ultimately, this experience reinforces the need for professionals to ask families rather than work on assumptions that may not reflect family needs.

Language was a significant issue for the Haringey project. Effective services cannot be provided effectively without the co-ordinator speaking the chosen language of the family. Haringey did not have sufficient co-ordinators who spoke the full range of the community languages spoken by the families referred to the project. Interpreters were specifically trained about the model when working with co-ordinators, a knowledge-base that became crucial in contributing effectively to the FGC process for families. In one case both a British Sign Language and a Turkish speaking interpreter were required for the family to be able to communicate with each other, the co-ordinator and the professionals. This was the first time the family were able to express themselves, and the meeting went on for six hours. For these children and their family, their need was actually about being able to communicate and in doing so, the presenting problems were solved. Prior to the FGC, the communication difficulties had prevented services being taken up, which was perceived by the professionals as a resistance to change. In fact, the family was simply unable to use the services being offered. The FGC, by virtue of its use of the family languages, solved the problems that were misunderstood by the professionals. Such a complex scenario is not unique, but for families it can lead to inappropriate and severe social work intervention.

Ways Forward

The research from Haringey indicates that this is a model of planning that families feel they can participate in and endorse. The families' comments through the research tell us a great deal about the FGC model, but also about their experiences of the broader child welfare services. The Haringey research was limited, and somewhat professionally driven. The next steps would seem to be the development of ongoing systems for user comments and feedback which directly inform the use of FGCs in the UK. Such an approach could involve the creation of user panels to comment on and promote further projects and research, the involvement of users in training and the opportunity for users to disseminate their experiences more widely. Furthermore, existing FGC research has limited direct representation of children's experiences. In Haringey the high attendance levels by children suggest they are interested in the meetings, and keen to be participants. Future research needs to grasp the challenges of listening to children in a way that informs practice and does not burden the child with unfair responsibilities.

The significant role of the co-ordinator in making the FGC successful for children and families cannot be underestimated. Research from Haringey and elsewhere demonstrates the vital role played by the co-ordinator. Family messages about the role of the co-ordinator begin to tell us something about the key attributes and skills of good co-ordinators. Their independence and their chosen language are just two examples. Further service-user research would enable us to understand in more detail the most appropriate skills for co-ordinators.

The use of service-user models such as FGCs has significant implications for existing professional systems. The Haringey research indicates that families will find the model useful at different times. This demands flexible professional systems which can accommodate different families' planning needs. Existing child protection procedures are rigid, and set particular timescales. These do not reflect the needs of families and struggle to respond positively to families' model of planning. The Haringey experience suggests that if families are to have a meaningful role in planning to protect their children, professional systems must allow negotiation and discretion at a local level.

The Haringey FGC project demonstrates that families can and do make safe plans for their children where there are child protection concerns. This approach is nor merely about family participation in professional planning, but locates the decision-making process within the family. The pilot project in Haringey does contribute to our broad understanding that FGCs are useful in all areas of child care provision. Recent central government consultative guidance suggests strongly that FGCs belong in the area of family support (DoH 1998). The evidence from Haringey suggests otherwise and it would be to the detriment of good planning for children if the use of FGCs were curtailed by professional anxieties rather than evidence-based practice.

Conclusion

The work in Haringey demonstrates that FGCs in child protection work are a safe and useful model for effective service-user participation. The model enables families to produce plans, which appear to be at least as safe as those produced by professionals. The project also allowed an exploration of professional attitudes and values that inform the approaches taken when providing services to children and their families.

The model is only one method of achieving active partnership and participation. FGCs cannot and do not provide the way forward for all families. Haringey and the extensive FGC work elsewhere demonstrates the effectiveness of FGCs; the challenge lies in the model becoming part of a broader development of service-user involvement in protective services for children.

Acknowledgements

The authors wish to acknowledge fully the work of Professor Peter Marsh and Gill Crow, Research Fellow, University of Sheffield, who have kindly given their permission for their research findings to be extensively reported in this chapter.

References

Bullock, R., Little, M. and Millham, S. (1993) *Going Home: The Return of Children Separated from their Families.* Aldershot: Dartmouth.

Crow, G. and Marsh, P. (1997a) 'Haringey FGC Project: Report to the Department Health' (unpublished).

Crow, G. and Marsh, P. (1997b) *Family Group Conferences, Partnership and Child Welfare: A Research Report on Four Pilot Projects in England and Wales.* Sheffield: University of Sheffield.

Department of Health (1995) *Child Protection: Messages from Research.* London: HMSO.

Department of Health (1998) *Consultation Document: Revised Guidance for Inter-Agency Co-operation for the Protection of Children.* London: Department of Health.

Department of Health and Social Security (1988) *Working Together: A Guide to Arrangements for Inter-Agency Co-operation for the Protection of Children from Abuse.* London: HMSO.

Family Rights Group (1994–96) *Family Group Conferences: A Newsletter.* London: Family Rights Group.

Jackson, S. (1998) 'Family Group Conferences in Youth Justice: The Issues for Implementation in England and Wales.' *The Howard Journal of Criminal Justice 37,* 1, 34–50.

Jackson, S. and Morris, K. (1999) 'Family Group Conferences: User Empowerment or Self Reliance? A Development on Lupton.' Forthcoming, *British Journal of Social Work 29,* 621–630.

Lupton, C., Barnard, S. and Swall-Yarrington, M. (1995) *Family Planning? An Evaluation of the Family Group Conference Model.* Portsmouth: University of Portsmouth/SSRIU.

Marsh, P. and Crow, G. (1998) *Family Group Conferences in Child Welfare.* Oxford: Blackwells.

Morris, K. Marsh, P. and Wiffen, J. (1998) *Family Group Conferences: A Training Pack.* London: Family Rights Group.

Morris, K. and Shepherd, C. (1999) 'Quality Social Work with Children and Families.' Forthcoming, *Child and Family Social Work.*

Morris, K. and Tunnard, J. (1996) *Family Group Conferences: Messages from UK Research and Practice.* London: Family Rights Group.

Morris, K., Smith, K. and Potts, M. (1996) *Child Protection Enquiries: Mothers Talk about Their Experiences: A Training Video and Guide.* London: FRG/NCH Action for Children/Department of Health.

Shepherd, C. (1997) 'Haringey FGC Project: Report to the Department of Health' (unpublished).

Thoburn, J. (ed) (1992) *Participation in Practice – Involving Families in Child Protection: A Reader.* Norwich: UEA/Department of Health.

Wiffen, J. and Morris, K. (1998) *Family Group Conferences: A Guide for Families.* London: Family Rights Group.

CHAPTER 6

Politics into Practice

The Production of a Disabled Person's Guide to Accessing Community Care Assessments

Kathryn Ellis and Kirstein Rummery

Introduction

This chapter explores the authors' experiences of working with disabled people and their organisations to produce a guide to accessing community care assessments. The project formed part of a wider investigation, carried out between 1995 and 1996, into the accessibility of care management and assessment systems to disabled people and carers two years after full implementation of the 1990 National Health Service and Community Care Act (NHSCCA). The findings were based on observations of assessment practice in six social work teams, spread over two local authorities, and interviews conducted with 50 disabled people and 23 carers who had experienced an assessment by the teams involved (Davis, Ellis and Rummery 1997). By incorporating into the dissemination strategy a 'disabled person's guide to accessing assessment' based on the findings, the proposers of the main study hoped to ensure that the investigation would be of direct benefit to people with physical and sensory impairments.

The guide project can be linked to Rapoport's (1970) definition of action research as 'a general mode of inquiry that seeks to contribute to the practical concerns of people in a problematic situation and to the goals of social science in a mutually acceptable ethical framework' (p.95). In terms of addressing disabled people's practical concerns, lack of information about agency policies and services is frequently identified as a barrier to accessing community care. Yet an earlier study, similarly based on observations of assessment practice, suggested that the most significant barrier to meaningful participation in needs assessment by disabled people and carers was the mediation of formal procedures and available information by front-line practitioners (Ellis 1993). However tightly prescribed arrangements for assessment and care management appeared to be in government guidance accompanying the NHSCCA, the proposers of the later study felt that these informal practices were likely to remain significant at point of entry to new systems. In the guide we hoped to introduce disabled people to some of the 'tricks of the trade' deployed by front-line assessors and to suggest strategies for countering them.

'The goals of social science' are addressed in this chapter by linking our experiences as social researchers to the broader concepts and issues involved in user participation and action research. Any discussion of user involvement in social research rests on a critical examination of underlying power dynamics, whilst the 'ethical framework' of our action research consisted in working democratically with disabled people and their organisations to produce the guide. We therefore first consider the extent to which our wider study conformed to the policy- and practice-related research methodologies developed by the disability movement, before moving on to explore the links between these approaches and 'empowering' action research. This analysis forms the basis for the critical evaluation in subsequent sections of the chapter of our own methodology in producing the guide, and of the extent to which our democratic aspirations were realised in practice.

The Politics of Disability Research

Drawing on the work of theorists within the disability movement (Morris 1991; Oliver 1990), the research team took as its starting point the view that disabled people constitute an oppressed social group. From this standpoint, inequalities of power and other resources ultimately stem from dominant assumptions about disabled individuals as the tragic victims of impaired bodies and minds. Disability theorists have reconceptualised 'disability' as a social creation located in the structural and attitudinal barriers of able-bodied society.

The disability movement has also developed its own methodologies to counter the institutionalisation of oppressive social relations in the medical labels and categories that underpin both welfare policy and practice and policy research. The emancipatory research paradigm, outlined by Oliver (1992), is generally viewed as the 'gold standard' of policy research and development involving disabled people. Reconstructed as a political rather than a technical activity, emancipatory research is geared towards 'the systematic demystification of the structures and processes which create disability' (Barnes 1992, p.22). Relations between researcher and researched are renegotiated in ways which enable disabled people – traditionally the objects of research – to articulate, become conscious of and develop understandings of their own experiences (Everitt 1998).

Where disability-related research is sponsored by traditional research institutions, however, participatory methodology is the pragmatic solution to the constraints imposed by funders' priorities (Zarb 1992). Researchers engaged in emancipatory research both commit to its goals and accede control over the research agenda to disabled people and their organisations. By contrast, participatory research involves sharing power with disabled people and their organisations rather than working under their direction and control.

The wider research study of which the production of the guide forms part should be seen as an example of participatory rather than emancipatory research. The proposal was developed in consultation with disabled people and their organisations, and there was an explicit commitment to working within the social model of disability on the part of both the sponsors and the research team. This, in turn, informed the recruitment of the researcher, the composition of the project advisory group, the methodology and dissemination strategy. Yet the sponsors' priorities were still partly rooted in a rational, social-administration tradition of policy research. That is, the underlying assumption governing the funding of research was that change interventions are properly based on a rational analysis of social problems and on the 'facts' derived from empirical investigation. Operating within the social model would suggest a political challenge to the very basis on which existing policy and practice in social care are constructed and an acknowledgement of the need for alternative approaches. However, our proposal had to satisfy funding criteria based on policy relevance, and the report of the findings was judged, in part, in terms of its potential for effecting progressive change within the parameters of current policy and practice. Any recommendations based on the radical transformation of social care in line with the demands of the disability movement were therefore beyond the scope of the funding specification.

Nevertheless, as Zarb (1992) argues, participatory research still offers the means of challenging disablist policies and practices. Our research findings were designed to be of direct assistance to disabled people and their organisations by supporting them either to challenge the discriminatory impact of new arrangements or to co-operate with service providers in developing more relevant and participatory procedures. In particular, as the next section seeks to demonstrate, the guide project was designed as a tool of empowerment both in terms of process and outcome.

Empowering Action Research

In their text on action research in health and social care, Hart and Bond (1995) provide a useful typology of four 'ideal types' ranged along a continuum from experimental research on the left through organisational and professionalising research to empowering research on the right (pp.40–43). The shift from left to right signifies a move away from a consensus towards a conflict model of society. On this distinction turn further key differences in the ways in which the 'problem' to be solved is defined, the nature of the desired change and the method for bringing this about, and the relationship between researcher and researched. As

Hart and Bond (1995) suggest, their typology reveals the primacy of context in selecting an appropriate strategy, including power relations.

Our commitment to conceptualising disability within a social model brought our own project closest to the 'empowering' type of action research and a conflict view of social relations. The 'problem' was not individual disabled people but the disabling procedures and practices which served to impede their access to assessment and community care services. Moreover, the primary aim of the guide project was to provide practical assistance to disabled people in negotiating barriers to the support they required. As Hart and Bond (1995) argue, the outcomes of empowering research are more likely to be action-focused than research-focused. Hammersley (1995) makes a similar point when he suggests that the objective of this type of action research is less the production of knowledge than the success of a particular practical or political project.

Yet, as indicated earlier, the production of the guide was seen as a process as well as a task to be accomplished. Where problems are framed within a consensus model of society, Hart and Bond (1995) point out that the method of change selected will tend to be social education or social work treatment. Within a conflict model, however, the favoured method is more likely to be changes in political consciousness and organisation. Through the production of the guide we aimed to promote collaborative working between social researchers and disabled people's organisations in the dissemination of research findings to user audiences. The guide itself, moreover, was designed to encourage individual disabled people to act strategically within their own assessment encounters and gain access to the services on which many are obliged to depend.

The level of commitment to democratic relations between participants also differs according to the type of action research. In the empowering model, where the relationship between the researcher and 'subjects' is described by Hart and Bond (1995) as 'co-researcher/co-change agent', it is other participants who determine the level and type of involvement of the action researcher. Empowering action research is less a technique used on or on behalf of other people to produce particular outcomes than a process of empowerment in which researcher and researched work collaboratively.

Although we attempted to take our lead from disabled people, however, the guide had been commissioned by the sponsors of the main research project rather than by organisations of disabled people. Consequently, as subsequent discussion seeks to demonstrate, our democratic aspirations were compromised in practice by our primary accountability to the funding body and by the definition of our project as participatory rather than emancipatory.

Producing the Guide

Setting up the guide panel

The empowering model suggests that the participants in action research should be largely self-selected (Hart and Bond 1995). As a result of an approach to a local disability resource centre for advice, two representatives of this organisation and the representative of another local organisation were invited to join the panel. At the first meeting of the guide panel, ways of widening representation were discussed. This eventually led to a representative of a local deaf forum joining the panel. At the suggestion of the project director, a member of the local community health council with a particular interest in access issues was invited to join the panel. This caused the researcher some discomfort at the first meeting, when it was decided that organisations rather than individuals should be represented on the panel. Moreover, when the decision was made to exclude informal carers from the panel, an exception had to be made for her partner/carer who accompanied her to the meeting.

In selecting the panel, the issue of distinguishing between organisations of and for disabled people was not made by other participants in the manner anticipated. The local organisation suggested by our initial contact turned out to be an organisation for disabled people, that is, one controlled by an able-bodied majority. We were even more taken aback by the proposal at the initial meeting that two members of staff from the local social services department be invited to join. Moreover, as one worked in a team for people with learning difficulties, panel members thought it was unnecessary to seek direct representation from that particular constituency. Although these recommendations ran counter to our own views about disabled people representing themselves, we gave primacy to the principle of taking our lead from guide panel members.

Establishing the purposes of the guide

In action research of the empowering type, the 'problem' properly emerges from the everyday practices and experiences of group members (Hart and Bond 1995); and, indeed, there was some renegotiation of the outcomes of our own project over the course of early panel meetings.

From the outset, the panel members were keen to ensure that the guide was based on information that disabled people themselves had identified as useful. Accordingly, a survey was conducted through local and national newsletters to establish the type of information that individual disabled people and their organisations would like to see included in a guide about community care assessments. National and local organisations of and for disabled people were also contacted by circular to find out what sort of guidance already existed. What this survey revealed was not only that no similar publication existed, but that there was considerable interest in such a guide amongst disabled people and their organisations.

Two representatives of an organisation of disabled people from another region requested further involvement and were invited by members to join the panel.

The original proposers of the project had envisaged a national audience for the guide on the basis that, local variations notwithstanding, it would serve to highlight common issues surrounding access to assessment. Participants, however, brought a local knowledge and understanding of assessment and care management systems to bear on panel discussions. The researcher felt uncomfortable at having to continually remind participants that the scope of the guide was national and that local procedures and practices were not necessarily replicated elsewhere.

Early meetings also progressed slowly because local representatives used the occasion to catch up on news. Whilst panel members who were not part of this local network initially felt excluded by 'cliqueyness', their involvement eased the tension concerning the scope of the guide as other members came to value their differing experiences. Nevertheless the concern with local agendas was a recurrent theme at guide meetings. Before the second site for the fieldwork on the main project had been finalised, some panel members representing local organisations lobbied for inclusion of 'their' authority so that the researchers could address particular issues. The researcher had to make it clear that the choice of site was beyond her power to make.

Whilst some of the decisions taken by the panel were surprising when measured against the principles of emancipatory research, there was a shared understanding of the hierarchical relations between service providers and disabled people and the way that power was exercised. During a discussion about a glossary of terminology used in assessment, for example, the panel rejected the suggestion that a local authority employee could act as an 'advocate'. Nor, given practitioners' tendency to use information strategically and protectively when assessing need, did the majority of members subscribe to the view expressed by one participant that the guide could serve as a vehicle for improving professional practice. As Hart and Bond (1995) point out, there is a clear distinction between the educative base of the empowering and professionalising types of action research. The former is directed towards enhancing user control, whereas the latter is focused on enhancing professional control and the ability of the individual practitioner to control the work situation.

The guide panel believed that the way to counter front-line discretion was to provide disabled people with comprehensive information about their entitlements under relevant legislation, rulings and official guidance as well as to point users towards any locally available information, such as community care plans, charters and eligibility criteria, that might assist them in making their case. In the words of one panel member, the guide should be a 'bill of rights with instructions'. The findings of the main research study, combined with panel members' own experiences, would also be used to offer insights into the way in which policy and procedures were renegotiated in everyday practice. These unofficial versions of assessment would be useful in highlighting the most effective referral routes, the type of question users should ask and the way answers should be interpreted.

The desired approach to be achieved by the guide was 'puzzle-solving'. By being taken through assessment step-by-step, users could be assisted to anticipate the differing stages of, and routes through systems, to take appropriate action, and to know what to do if they were unsuccessful at any stage. Meeting the wider objective of enabling disabled people to participate fully in the assessment process further depended on information being presented in accessible ways. This meant publishing the guide in a range of formats and languages, and using diagrams and pictures in addition to text in order to enhance its accessibility to Deaf people and people with learning difficulties. In line with a philosophy of empowerment, the idea also emerged of an interactive guide that would promote users' participation in assessment. Detachable forms would enable people to assert their right to an assessment or make a self-assessment of their needs. Personal action plans would allow users to make individualised records of their assessment and any other relevant information or actions.

Translating principles into practice

The cost of producing the guide in its elaborated format exceeded the allotted budget. Moreover, neither the research team nor other panel members had the time or other resources to undertake the additional work. Encouraged by the sponsors, a successful bid for further money was made to fund a consultant/researcher to collect the additional information, produce a working draft and desktop publish the final version. Although the post was advertised twice, in the event the successful bid for the contract was made by the organisation for disabled people represented on the panel, whose representative then stood down.

Once the contract had been entered into, panel meetings became both more formal and more focused. The panel assumed responsibility for overseeing the quality of the work produced, and future meetings were timetabled around a series of deadlines designed to ensure that the guide was produced to schedule.

The first draft was heavily criticised by the panel for falling short of the aims and objectives thrashed out at earlier meetings. The guide not only failed to provide relevant, accurate and comprehensive information on the legislative and organisational frameworks of assessment, but also failed to meet the criterion of user-friendliness and accessibility to be achieved by varying the presentation of information through diagrams, bullet points, inset boxes, illustrations and so on. The first draft also omitted the interactive features envisaged by the panel.

The politics of disability underlying the production of the guide became more explicit in some of the concerns articulated by panel members. In particular:

- The structure and language used in the draft were criticised as provider-driven rather than disabled person-centred. If terms such as 'disabled person', 'carer', 'advocate', 'community care assessment', 'screening', 'allocation', 'to live in the community', '24 hour clock' were used, then they required clarification in the glossary.

- The draft was further criticised for not taking the autonomy of the disabled person as the starting point or making it clear that people could exercise choice about who should attend the assessment, where it should take place, the most appropriate type and level of assessment or, indeed, whether to be assessed at all.

- At the same time, disabled people's experience of internalised oppression should be acknowledged. Simple injunctions to complain in writing were unhelpful unless individuals were reminded they could enlist the support of an advocate or friend.

- Where conflict between a disabled person and carer arose, the needs of the former should be treated as paramount. It should be pointed out that disabled people could also be carers, but otherwise carers should be directed to seek a separate assessment.

The first draft was also criticised for reproducing policy rhetoric rather than drawing on the findings of the main study and panel members' own experiences in order to present the reality of assessment from the disabled person's perspective. The intention to offer 'insider knowledge', so that guide-users could act strategically within assessment encounters, had not been translated into practice. People needed to know, for example, that:

- Referrals could be made, or information sought from family members or other carers, without the knowledge of the disabled person

- Details given over the telephone could form part of an initial screening, so that an assessment could be conducted over the telephone without the person concerned even being aware an assessment had taken place

- People might be told they would not receive a service because it was too expensive, or might be given a list of housework/care agencies to organise their own

- Assessments could take different forms – from a five-minute discussion at a hospital bedside to an hour-long meeting with a number of different professionals

- Any information people provided would probably be stored on a database

- It was unlikely people would receive very full information from social services departments about their assessment

- Even if an assessor acknowledged people's needs, they would not necessarily be met

- A service review could signal a move on the part of the agency to try to withdraw a service.

Although the second draft was much improved, considerable work remained if the guide was to meet the specification developed by the panel. As the contracted organisation felt unable to complete the work satisfactorily, members of the research team redrafted the guide. It was then desktop published with the addition of clipart illustrations produced by a computer consultant. The local disability resource centre took over the final production and sale of the guide.

Action Research as Empowerment: An Evaluation

In this section we attempt to assess the extent to which we achieved our objective of working democratically with disabled people's organisations to produce a guide of practical value to individual users. As we have already argued, such an evaluation rests on an appreciation of power relations both between providers and recipients of welfare and between researchers and researched.

For the disability movement, the prevailing relations of welfare production serve to reinforce the identity of disabled people as passive, dependent and needy and to segregate them from the mainstream. In the area of social care, counter-strategies have included the development of alternative forms of support through organisations of disabled people and the promotion of inclusive citizenship in the place of segregation in 'special' services. Emancipatory research, which is grounded in similar epistemological and political traditions, has been promoted as a means of challenging the disablist relations of research production.

As our research proposal had been developed before the guide panel was convened, and the means of research production and distribution remained largely under the control of the researchers, we were clearly not engaged in emancipatory research. Indeed Oliver (1996) makes a clear distinction between emancipatory research on the one hand and participatory, applied and action research on the other. The latter methodologies may allow the excluded to be included in the game, but emancipatory strategies are based on the conceptualisation and creation of a different game where no one is excluded in the first place. Yet we have presented empowering action research as a process and not just as a means of accomplishing a discrete task. We would argue that the *process* of including the excluded changes the rules of the game both for those traditionally excluded and for those who have been implicated in their exclusion. Empowering action research not only enabled us to confront hierarchical research relations, but ensured that disabled people were active participants in the project who reshaped the scope and form of the guide in line with a shared commitment to tackling disablism in service provision, and to self-empowerment.

Reason (1988) suggests that the task of the group in collaborative research is to find a degree of fit between the more or less formally agreed purposes and processes of the official inquiry and the purposes, questions and approaches which participants bring with them. Within the empowering model of action research, Hart and Bond (1995) similarly argue that shared objectives between the key stakeholders are only partially possible and require constant renegotiation over the course of the action. In our own project, we found that the immediate concerns of participant organisations lay with local service provision. The perceived need to maintain effective working relations with other local organisations, including statutory agencies, clearly influenced the recruitment of the initial panel, and local concerns threatened to dominate the proceedings of early meetings.

During this early stage, we could perhaps have maintained a closer focus on the production of the guide during the meetings proper if time had been built in before or after panel meetings for members to meet informally to exchange local news. Gradually, though, the panel began to renegotiate the nature and scope of the guide. Although the 'market research' suggested by the panel yielded only a low response, the survey was important in fostering a sense of ownership of the guide amongst participants. The resulting uncertainty was less comfortable for the researcher, however, who struggled to manage a twin commitment to open discussion and decision making by the panel on the one hand and the production of a coherent guide to deadline on the other. After all, however much we sought to take our lead from disabled people, our ultimate accountability was to the funders.

Brechin (1993) describes a similar tension in her role as researcher in a collaborative project involving people with learning difficulties. When the process of creating an enabling environment for sharing ideas appeared to dominate the purpose of meetings, she was tempted to place limits on that sharing and take control. Yet this period turned out to be an essential aspect of the group taking charge of itself. Only then could the researcher adopt a more facilitative, less controlling role. As Hedges (1985) argues, social interactions may be particularly important in action research where the research is designed to change as well as study a situation. The very process of group discussion can identify common views and lead to a sense that collective action is an effective way of tackling problems.

In retrospect, although progress was slow during early panel meetings, this was an important period in the development of a shared understanding of the way in which the guide should address the power dynamics underlying community care assessments. A consensus emerged, through discussion, that the aim of the guide was to promote a rights-based approach to assessment amongst users and encourage their active participation in the process. A further aim of the guide was identified as demystifying the process of assessment by providing information about the formal and informal processes involved. Guide users should be alerted not only to prioritisation criteria but to the 'tricks of trade' used by practitioners to deny access or ration demand.

This, in turn, reflected our own understanding of power relations in social care which, as in the case of the relations of research production, we believed to be more fluid and dynamic than sometimes represented by disability theorists. Our analysis of assessment practice as street-level bureaucracy, for example, suggests that some accounts of new arrangements for community care may be over-deterministic (Ellis, Davis and Rummery 1999). Albeit to varying degrees, front-line practitioners within administrative systems of assessment and care management enjoy relative autonomy. This, in turn, provides a space for disabled people with 'insider knowledge' to act strategically in their assessment encounters and gain access to resources. Additionally, under some circumstances, professionals may act as allies. Our findings suggest that discretionary power is used

---

- As a political rather than a technical activity, empowering action research should not be viewed solely as the means of accomplishing a discrete task but also as a *process* of self-empowerment by marginalised groups.

- Empowerment as a process involves key stakeholders in continually negotiating and renegotiating the purposes and outcomes of the action, and keeping the nature and scope of their involvement under constant review.

- In the case of action research involving people with physical and sensory impairments, the politics of disability underlying the action may need to be made explicit, as consensus between participants based on textbook definitions cannot be assumed.

- When seeking to involve local organisations in a national project, account needs to be taken of the extent to which their legitimacy and funding are rooted in local political and organisational networks.

- The budget for meetings should reflect the centrality of the process of forming collaborative working relationships to empowering action research; and in the case of people with physical and sensory impairments, such costs as personal assistance, interpreting and translating support may need to be covered.

Figure 6.1. Pointers to future practice

negatively or positively depending on a number of localised contingencies, including the ways in which professional, consumerist and user-led discourses of empowerment are mobilised by social work teams in their everyday assessment practice (Davis *et al.* 1997). The guide offered the means of disseminating these findings to disabled people and their organisations and improving access to the support on which many individuals are obliged to rely.

The hard-won sense of shared purpose about the guide, thrashed out at early meetings, appeared to be threatened at one stage by under-funding. Panel meetings involved unanticipated expenses, such as the travel and accommodation costs of members from outside the region. Nor, without proper remuneration, were participants able to undertake much work on the guide outside meetings. As this left the researcher with more to do than originally envisaged, additional funding had to be sought to enable the extra work to be contracted out. Fortunately the revised specification for the guide was in line with the sponsors' commitment to empowering research, and the additional resources were readily agreed.

Moreover, the focus of panel meetings sharpened still further once the work was contracted out. The discussion of matters such as the job specification, for example, led to a clear articulation of the guide's aims. The often fierce criticism of successive drafts, however painful, was probably even more important in crystallising a shared understanding about the guide's form and content and about the politics it should express. Consequently, even though the research team undertook the final write-up, they did so on the basis of a clearly defined set of principles and methods developed by the panel.

The decision of the panel to include a local service provider in the group proved costly, however, and should perhaps have been more vigorously challenged by the research team. It later emerged that a member of the organisation contracted to produce the guide also received a service package from the social services department represented on the panel. This contributed to a general hesitancy on the part of the organisation to adopt a critical stance towards local authority service providers and to produce the 'realistic' guide to assessment envisaged by the panel. For a small, fragile organisation which feared jeopardising effective working relationships with a statutory agency, possibly even funding, the stakes were just too high. Relations between the panel and this organisation were made even more complex because, during the course of the project, the staff working on the guide were in conflict with the governing body about the philosophy and future direction of the organisation.

We have summarised in Figure 6.1 the key pointers to future practice which we have drawn from our participation in the project as social researchers. Provided its limitations and pitfalls are understood, we would argue that participatory action research can represent an effective challenge to the hierarchical relations of welfare and research production. Being clear about power relations is a necessary but insufficient condition for empowerment. As Hugman (1998) points out, this has to be grasped and worked through in direct practice. In retrospect, it was asking a great deal of a group of small, under-funded voluntary agencies, operating in a particular locality, to take on work from which they would derive little direct benefit. The work of the panel might usefully have been redirected towards developing the template for a national guide adaptable for local use. On the plus side, a panel of disabled people's organisations took charge of the research project and reshaped the guide into a tool of self-empowerment for individual disabled people.

Conclusion

Central to our analysis of the action research project outlined in this chapter has been an appreciation of the power play between key stakeholders. From its inception, the production of the guide was influenced by power relations between able-bodied and disabled participants, between research sponsors and research team, between researchers and researched. The de-politicised accounts of rational social management, and more recently managerialism, tend to screen powerful interests from view altogether (see Chapter 13 for a fuller discussion). At the same time, our understanding of relations of power in research and welfare production is more differentiated and contingent than accounts by some disability theorists. We would suggest that the principles of empowering action research provide a framework within which more democratic ways of conducting research with disabled people and their organisations can be worked through. Yet the actual practices adopted in any particular project depend on the actors involved and the specific context within which the action is conceived and developed. This in turn requires an approach to practising research similar to that which Hugman (1998) recommends that the 'caring professions' adopt in their practice of social welfare (pp.203–207). That is to say, professional researchers must engage actively and reflexively with the moral dimensions of research work in their everyday practice. At the same time, ethical issues must be situated in their appropriate structural and organisational contexts. Only then can the researcher, as the caring professional, effectively engage in a dialogue with people which is based on shared citizenship.

References

Barnes, C. (1992) 'Qualitative Research: Valuable or Irrelevant?' *Disability, Handicap and Society* 7, 2, 115–124.

Brechin, A. (1993) 'Sharing.' In P. Shakespeare, D. Atkinson and S. French (eds) *Reflecting on Research Practice: Issues in Health and Social Welfare*. Buckingham: Open University Press.

Davis, A., Ellis, K. and Rummery, K. (1997) *Access to Assessment: Perspectives of Practitioners, Disabled People and Carers*. Bristol: Policy Press

Ellis, K. (1993) *Squaring the Circle: User and Carer Participation in Needs Assessment.* York: Joseph Rowntree Foundation/Community Care.

Ellis, K., Davis, A. and Rummery, K. (1999) 'Needs Assessment, "Street-Level Bureaucracy" and the New Community Care.' *Journal of Social Policy and Administration 33*, 3, 262–280.

Everitt, A. (1998) 'Research and Development in Social Work.' In R. Adams, L. Dominelli and M. Payne (eds) *Social Work: Themes. Issues and Critical Debates.* Basingstoke: Macmillan.

Hammersley, M. (1995) *The Politics of Social Research.* London: Sage.

Hart, E. and Bond, M. (1995) *Action Research for Health and Social Care: A Guide to Practice.* Buckingham: Open University Press.

Hedges, A. (1985) 'Group Interviewing.' In R. Walker (ed) *Applied Qualitative Research.* Aldershot: Gower.

Hugman, R. (1998) *Social Welfare and Social Value: The Role of Caring Professions.* Basingstoke: Macmillan.

Morris, J. (1991) *Pride against Prejudice: Transforming Attitudes to Disability.* London: The Women's Press.

Oliver, M. (1990) *The Politics of Disablement: A Sociological Approach.* Basingstoke: Macmillan.

Oliver, M. (1992) 'Changing the Social Relations of Research Production?' *Disability, Handicap and Society 7*, 2, 101–114.

Oliver, M. (1996) 'A Sociology of Disability or a Disablist Sociology?' In L. Barton (ed) *Disability and Society: Emerging Issues and Insights.* Harlow: Longman.

Rapoport, R. (1970) 'Three Dilemmas of Action Research. *Human Relations 23*, 499–513.

Reason, P. (1988) 'Introduction.' In P. Reason (ed) *Human Inquiry in Action. Developments in New Paradigm Research.* London: Sage.

Zarb, G. (1992) 'On the Road to Damascus: First Steps towards Changing the Relations of Disability Research Production.' *Disability, Handicap and Society 7*, 2, 125–138.

CHAPTER 7

Breaking the Ice

Developing Strategies for Collaborative Working with Carers of Older People with Mental Health Problems

Helen Rogers

Introduction

The principle of incorporating carers' views in the development and evaluation of services has become relatively common in the past decade (see e.g. Barnes 1997; Barnes and Wistow 1995; Martin and Gaster 1993). However, translating the rhetoric into reality is more difficult than it seems. Problems arise on a number of fronts – how do you engage with carers who do not see themselves as part of a homogeneous group? How do you overcome the paternalistic enthusiasm that inevitably exists when paid employees from statutory organisations try to work alongside unpaid carers without fully understanding their circumstances? What sort of relationship needs to be established between the parties to facilitate open and regular communication? What information needs to be made available, when and to whom?

During the projects featured in this chapter, these and other questions were raised and, in the main, answered. What resulted, however, was not a 'blueprint' for working with carers but an increased awareness of their issues, concerns and restraints. At the same time, key personnel involved in the projects within the organisation began to consider more carefully their own assumptions about the demands placed on carers. In this regard, they began to develop a better insight into how these demands affected carers not only in terms of their daily lives, but also of their willingness or enthusiasm to engage with statutory bodies in a participatory manner. The impact of this clearer understanding of carers' views and needs, coupled with a re-examination of the intrinsic values of the organisation, meant that the hurdles and barriers which had previously hindered attempts at effective participation and collaboration with carers could be removed.

This chapter is about working with carers of older people with mental health problems (including dementia), on a series of staged projects. It has a dual focus in that it describes the services which were established as a direct response to carers' needs and also (and possibly more importantly) how this was achieved. My intention is to consider three areas. First, I shall consider briefly some of the hurdles and barriers that contextualise the difficulties faced by both statutory bodies and carers of older people with mental health problems in terms of collaborative working. Second, I shall describe the work undertaken, which, like that of other contributors to this book, is set within an action research framework; and finally, I shall highlight some of the lessons learnt during the projects.

Identifying Hurdles and Barriers

Statutory bodies and cultural change

Since 1979, health and social care agencies in the public sector have wrestled with numerous structural and cultural reforms. New management structures, processes and philosophies express a 'new orthodoxy' about how to run services (Stewart and Stoker 1995). Initial changes in practice gathered pace and coherence in the 1980s, acquiring the label of new public management (NPM) by the 1990s (Walsh 1995). The fundamental intent of this new managerial orthodoxy was to challenge the traditional bureaucratic modes of operation based on rule following, specialism, hierarchy and line management. New public management promotes operating principles based on efficiency, quality, flexibility, competition, performance standards and 'customer satisfaction'. Adjustments to this radical shift in emphasis took time to filter through the organisations in both a strategic and an operational sense.

Studies which took place in the early 1990s indicated that although statutory organisations had a genuine desire (as well as a requirement) to improve their relationship with users and carers, they had a long way to go (see e.g. Glendinning and Bewley 1992; Hoyes et al. 1993; Martin and Gaster 1993). Fundamentally, the conclusions reached in these studies were similar. The authors identified a number of key points which, if not addressed during consultation exercises, would unwittingly exclude the individuals with whom they wished to engage. In summary these points include:

1. Access – not only physical access but the cost implications of travelling to a venue, and the availability of a sitting service

2. Clarity and appropriateness of information – individuals cannot be expected to participate if they are unaware or unsure of the scope and purpose of the objective

3. Support and advocacy – necessary because many people are not used to being asked for their views

4. Timing – must be considered because it is essential in giving people time to form opinions

5. Commitment – to the process of listening and responding to views.

These very basic principles still form the ground rules for ongoing or regular consultation exercises but they do not go far enough in highlighting the complexities of working collaboratively with, for example, carers of older people with mental health problems. Unravelling some of the complexities leads to a closer examination of widely held perceptions which may or may not be grounded in false assumptions.

Do carers see themselves as carers?

The short answer is not always. Various factors influence the way carers of people with mental health problems see themselves. First, the contemporary use of the term 'carer' has been developed within social care agencies and it bears the mark of that origin (Twigg, Atkin and Perring 1990). The point is frequently made by carers that they do not see themselves as such; the term is unfamiliar to them and, some would argue, at odds with how they perceive their actions. They regard what they do as an extension of family or personal relations rather than as the work of a carer, a term which has formal, quasi-employment overtones. Second, and following on from this point, there is no simple definition of being a carer. Conceptually, the term centres on the performance of tasks which are both supportive in nature and grounded in pre-existing relationships of kinship or friendship (Thomas 1993). It is, however, often difficult to distinguish such carer relations from the ordinary patterns of care and dependency characteristic of interpersonal, family and gender relations. At what point does a partner, son, daughter or neighbour cease being such in order formally to take on or be assigned the role of carer?

Third, the notion that carers of older people with mental health problems are a homogeneous group of individuals is open to question. They may share a common ground derived from the activity of care-giving, but the impact on their lives in respect of financial and employment sacrifices, the loss of a social life, friends and freedom and adapting to a new role, will be different in each case (see e.g. Archbold 1983; Barnes *et al.* 1981; Dunkle 1985). Finally, there is a degree of fluidity between the role of carer and that of service user. The type and frequency of support which carers of older people with mental health problems need in order to continue as carers is determined by the degree of emotional stress and physical demands placed on them either by themselves, by the state or by 'significant others'.

Stress and strain among carers of older people with mental health problems

While phrases such as 'looking after', 'caring for' and 'tending to ' may be adequate to describe the role of some carers of older people with mental health problems, for others they are extreme understatements and fall short of providing palpable descriptions of their experiences.

Incontinence, night-time disturbance, lapses of personal hygiene, apathy and lack of communication, demands for attention and uncharacteristic anti-social behaviour have all been identified as contributing to the levels of stress experienced by carers (Gilleard 1984; Greene *et al.* 1982; Pearlin *et al.* 1990). A number of studies have highlighted the existence of increased stress levels where carers feel that they have not only lost 'control' over the actions of the person they are caring for, but have also suffered 'lost opportunities' which were anticipated and planned for at an earlier stage in the relationship (Braithwaite 1990; Morris, Morris and Britton 1989; Motenko 1989).

Gender matters. Male carers consistently report higher morale and lower distress – even when the demands are considered to be the same as for females (Gilhooly 1984; Jerrom, Mian and Rukanyake 1993; Levin, Sinclair and Garbach 1983). Zarit, Todd and Zarit (1986) contrasted the position of older men with that of older women providing care to their respective spouses who were experiencing mental health problems. Their findings suggest that men are more willing to 'share' care-giving with formal and informal services, and experience less of a 'threat' in terms of their self-esteem. The authors conclude that socialisation experiences make 'switching off' harder for female than male carers, even when support is available. Eagles *et al.* (1987) undertook a more detailed consideration of the factors which influence the willingness of either male or female spouses to accept formal support, and concluded that it was not necessarily the gender of the carer that was important but the presence of mitigating factors. The factors they identified included:

- the type of level of problem behaviour
- the quality of the relationship between the care giver and receiver
- cognitive styles and coping mechanisms used by the carer
- the availability and appropriateness of formal and informal support
- levels of satisfaction derived from the caring role.

To summarise the first section of this chapter, three points stand out. First, statutory organisations have had to deal with major structural and cultural changes during the past 20 years which have demanded a new emphasis on the way that they develop and provide services. Second, this new emphasis has brought to the forefront the need to work more closely with the people who come into contact with their services. The stumbling block, however, is that while statutory bodies may enthusiastically embrace the notion of working more closely with, in this case, carers of older people with mental health problems, their eagerness may not always be reciprocated because the carers have more immediate demands on their time and energy. Third, if carers of older people with mental health problems are to be active participants in service development and evaluation, then there is an obligation on the part of the statutory bodies to understand their specific limitations, restraints and concerns.

Recognising the importance of these factors influenced the way in which the framework was constructed for the projects described below.

The Project

The organisational context

The projects were located within the Older People's Directorate of Shropshire's Mental Health NHS Trust and focused on working with carers of older people with mental health problems and carers of people affected by dementia irrespective of their age. Since the completion of the projects, the organisation has merged with another to form Shropshire's Community and Mental Health Services NHS Trust. The Directorate however, has remained as an identifiable entity.

Like most other health providers, the Trust supplies in-patient, out-patient and community-based services for children and young people, adults and older people with mental health problems.

Until 1993, virtually all the services provided by the Trust were centralised, being based at Shelton Hospital (the original asylum). Gradually, the social work team, community mental health nurses, the day centre and out-patient facilities were decanted into the community. However, the majority of in-patient facilities for both adults and older people remained on the hospital site.

Corporately, the Trust offers opportunities for members of staff, service users and their carers to comment on the way services have or continue to be developed, through a range of mechanisms, including:

- bi-monthly public meetings
- staff and in-patient suggestion schemes
- the establishment of a patients' council
- regular informal and formal meetings with community-based voluntary and user groups including the Wheelchair User's Group, MIND, and the National Schizophrenia Fellowship
- undertaking consultation exercises focusing on specific developments.

These mechanisms coupled with a compliance with some of the operating principles underpinning new public management (quality assurance, flexibility, and the establishment of performance standards), provided sufficient evidence for the Trust to be awarded the Charter Mark on two successive occasions.

Whilst the Trust as a whole demonstrated a commitment to consultation, the quality assurance manager (the current author) in conjunction with senior members of clinical staff based in the services for the Older People's Directorate, wanted to explore ways in which more collaborative and participatory styles of practice could be achieved during the development of services. Fundamentally, this meant creating an environment that was more conducive to enabling carers of older people with mental health problems to identify shortfalls in existing service provision and to offer solutions which would lead to improvements. Although this approach was not deemed by the Trust as a major departure from the normative standards used during previous consultation and evaluation exercises, it was considered to be rather innovative and slightly radical; encouraging carers to set their own agenda was not something that had been done before. Ensuing from this was the concern that the priorities identified by the carers of older people with mental health problems in terms of service developments would not necessarily be the same as the Trust's. It became apparent to those involved in the projects that the positional shift from 'consulting with' to 'participating with' carers had wider implications than had first been anticipated. In order to justify this new approach, both the process and the outcomes needed to be located within a methodological framework – the most appropriate one being an action research approach.

A fundamental premise of community-based action research according to Stringer (1996), is that it begins with an interest in 'the problems of a group, a community or an organisation' (p.9). Its purpose is to assist people in their understanding of their situation and thus resolve problems that confront them. The principles of collaboration which underpin action research provide a starting point for all the stakeholders involved in a research project to develop a relationship which is based on a shared understanding of both the problem which needs addressing, and the circumstances which led to its identification. According to Stringer (1996), action research follows a routine based on 'looking' (building a picture which describes the situation), 'thinking' (the what, how and why questions associated with identifying problems and solutions) and 'acting' (planning and implementing changes and evaluating their impact). The process, however, is not linear but cyclical, and the actions of looking, thinking and acting occur on an ongoing basis; indeed, this is what happened in the following projects.

Stage one

EVALUATING SERVICES – THE PROCESS

Structured surveys and focus groups had been previously used in the Trust, but they tended to be targeted towards service users rather than carers. They were undertaken annually and their emphasis was primarily on determining levels of user satisfaction with existing services. No evaluative work of any substance had been undertaken with carers of older people with mental health problems. Whilst on the one hand, this was an advantage since any developmental work with carers could begin with a clean sheet, the potential drawback was that carers could highlight a number of service deficiencies which, from an organisational perspective, might be difficult to respond to.

This was one of the issues that prompted the development of a project group which consisted of the quality assurance manager, clinical managers, community mental health nurses and consultant psychiatrists from the Older People's Directorate. The remit of the group was not only to establish a process of evaluation which emphasised a participatory style of working with carers of older people with mental health problems, but also to anticipate some of the likely outcomes in terms of service developments which would need to be addressed. The project team purposely did not want to be too prescriptive with carers concerning the areas they could comment on during the evaluation, but equally, they did not want to be put in a position of being unable to respond to carers' needs. Two areas were identified as being likely sources of concern for carers: first, a delay between being seen by the family doctor and a referral to mental health services, and second, a general lack of information about mental health problems including causal factors, support networks and service availability. Clearly, at the planning stage there was no way of knowing whether these were indeed concerns that carers had, but the significance of discussing potential problems and superficially identifying solutions highlighted the commitment to working with carers in addressing their concerns, rather than just to listening to them.

The project team considered that the most effective method of eliciting the views of carers of older people with mental health problems was through the use of a structured questionnaire (with both open and closed questions), followed by a series of focus groups. Designing the questionnaire was relatively simple in comparison to the difficulties the project group faced in terms of identifying their target population and gaining access to it.

Accessing carers' groups for the purpose of identifying the target population was one option which was considered but discarded as problematic for a number of reasons. As noted above, not all carers see themselves as such; care-giving tends to be viewed as an extension of family and interpersonal relations. For these people, membership of a carers' group would be inappropriate. Conversely, carers who do identify themselves as such may not attend groups because they do not exist in their area, or if they do, transport may be a problem. Some carers have other commitments including a job or further family responsibilities which deter their attendance, whilst others are unable or unwilling to leave the person they care for either alone or with another person. A second option was to lift the names and addresses of the next of kin from the case records of the service user. Apart from the obvious issues associated with this course of action in terms of ethics and breaches of confidentiality, it would be inappropriate to assume that the next of kin was 'the carer'. The final option (and the one pursued) involved the community mental health nurses. Not only were they in a position to identify the number of carers, in the main they had regular contact with the majority of them.

The project group members were keen to avoid any unnecessary intrusion into the carers' lives. Whilst they were enthusiastic about embarking on the first stage of what was hoped would be a continuing dialogue with carers, group members were cautious in not assuming that carers would share the same view. In this respect, the method by which the questionnaire was distributed was important. Regular contact between the community mental health nurses and the carers provided the opportunity for the questionnaire to be delivered by hand during pre-planned visits. This approach offered a number of advantages. First, it avoided unnecessary breaches of confidentiality in terms of naming the carers (which would have occurred if the questionnaire had been posted). Second, it side-stepped the problem of carers receiving possibly unwanted and unexpected communication from the Trust. Third, the nurses could provide a casual and gentle reminder to the carers if they had overlooked the questionnaire. The main drawback associated with this method was the risk that the nurses could get drawn into helping with its completion; this was not the intention.

Two outstanding issues remained. A number of community mental health nurses expressed concern that some of the carers with whom they worked were experiencing considerable social and psychological difficulties of their own. It would therefore be inappropriate and insensitive to encourage them to engage, at this time, in what was essentially a Trust-led initiative. Examples of these difficulties included some carers' reluctance to accept the presence of a mental health problem, not least because of the stigma that this brings but also in terms of changes in the dynamics of the relationship; lost opportunities; and in some instances, witnessing further degeneration. Consequently, the nurses were given a degree of discretion about delivering questionnaires to carers in these or similar circumstances. The second outstanding issues revolved around the provision of information which would accompany the questionnaire. Too much could act as a deterrent, too little would be insufficient to explain the objectives of the exercise. Eventually, a simple information pack was put together. Each pack contained:

1. an explanatory letter concerning the reasons why the Older People's Directorate wanted to work more closely with carers

2. a structured questionnaire containing both open and closed questions focusing on biographic details (age, gender etc.), current service usage and unmet needs

3. an invitation to attend a focus group (including a clarification of what this was) with choices of times and venues, an offer of the reimbursement of travelling expenses and any costs incurred in accessing a 'sitting service'

4. two stamped addressed reply envelopes to be returned to the quality assurance manager, one for the questionnaire and one for accepting or declining the invitation to the focus group.

While the questionnaires were anonymous, it was hoped that by addressing the responses to the quality assurance manager (who was not part of the Older People's Directorate) further fears of identifying the carers could be allayed.

Deliberately, the timescale for the distribution and the return of the questionnaires was quite lengthy (from February to the end of April 1996). This was to ensure that each of the community mental health nurses could visit all the potential respondents as part of their normal routine.

OUTCOMES OF THE EVALUATION

The community mental health nurses initially identified 228 carers, and 179 information packs were distributed. A total of 37 per cent (n = 66) of the questionnaires were returned and 42 people accepted the invitation to take part in the focus groups.

Overall, the responses received relating to the type and level of service provided by the Trust were favourable. However, three common themes emerged from the questionnaire.

1. Carers reported that they had insufficient knowledge and understanding of functional and organic mental health problems (particularly in terms of early onset dementia).

2. They were unclear about what services were available and how they could access them. A number of queries related to services provided by social and health care agencies, for example, their rights to an assessment of their needs (under the Carers (Recognition and Services) Act 1995 (DoH 1996)), and accessing respite and day care facilities. Others concerned a carer's entitlement to welfare benefits and, in some cases, access to legal advice regarding the relevance or otherwise of the power of attorney.

3. Virtually all the carers felt that they had experienced a delay between consulting their general practitioner for advice about the care receiver's mental health problem and being referred to specialist mental health services.

These points formed the basis of the discussions in each of the seven geographically spread focus groups, which were facilitated by the quality assurance manager. Essentially, the purpose of the focus groups was twofold: to give carers an opportunity to discuss their concerns in order to help them to develop solutions to highlighted problems, and to establish an environment in which carers could be encouraged to work more closely with the Older People's Directorate. It was the latter aim which stimulated debates in all the focus groups. Most carers described themselves as having a passive role in relation to the Directorate; if services did not meet their needs, they did not use them. They made no attempt to express their views because they did not know who to talk to or indeed if they did, they were unsure of how their opinions would be received. While the carers from the focus groups valued the opportunity to discuss various aspects of existing service provision, they believed that the Directorate had a considerable amount of work to do before it could convince carers that it genuinely wanted to develop services in response to their views and needs.

Stage two

PSYCHO-EDUCATIONAL SESSIONS WITH CARERS OF PEOPLE AFFECTED BY DEMENTIA

I mentioned earlier in the chapter that caring for older people with mental health problems is stressful. In some respects, the stress is worsened when there is an absence of, or limited access to practical and emotional support and a lack of understanding of the behavioural and general medical aspects of mental health problems (particularly dementia). As a direct result of nurses and social workers engaging with carers and listening to their concerns surrounding these issues, a series of six psycho-educational sessions for carers of people affected by dementia was undertaken over a 12-week period in both the east and the west of the county.

There were three objectives for this project:

- to respond to the needs of carers which were highlighted in both the questionnaire and focus groups, by providing information on the medical aspects of dementia

- to provide information about other services which were available to carers

- to encourage the development of support networks.

In addition to these, the Older People's Directorate wanted to evaluate the effectiveness of the sessions from the carers' point of view, in order to determine whether the approach was beneficial.

The majority of carers who attended the focus groups had said that they were happy about being contacted by the Directorate regarding future initiatives, but this still left a number of carers with whom caution needed to be exercised. In order to overcome this problem, community mental health nurses, social workers and members of in-patient staff were asked to identify carers who following discussions, had expressed an interest in attending the sessions. Letters of invitation were then sent to these carers, offering additional places for other family members and friends if they were required. While the project team members had hoped that participants would attend all the sessions, it was recognised that this might not be possible either because not all the sessions were relevant or because carers had more immediate demands on their time.

Each of the sessions had a different focus and included information and discussions on behavioural and medical aspects of mental health problems; legal advice from a local solicitor; welfare rights advice from the Citizens' Advice Bureau; details on accessing social services, voluntary organisations, and mental health services; and advice on 'managing difficult behaviour'.

At the beginning of the first session in both locations, carers were given a pack containing a modified version of the Alzheimer's Disease Society's 'knowledge test' (used in this instance as a quiz to promote discussion), a 'relative's stress scale' to provide a baseline measurement of a carer's existing stress levels (Greene *et al.* 1982), and some explanatory notes relating to the sessions. The 'test' and the stress scale were repeated at the beginning of the final session. While the results of the 'test' indicated an improvement in the overall knowledge-base of the carers, the results from the stress scale indicated that they were experiencing higher levels of stress. This provoked a number of questions for both the project team and members of staff working with the carers:

1. Were the reported increases in stress levels due to the content of the sessions or to other factors affecting the carers?

2. In responding to carers' need for information relating to dementia, how is a balance achieved between providing general information about possible degeneration without causing alarm?

3. If some carers perceive that they are ill informed, how do they know what questions to ask, to whom and when?

Despite the reported increase in stress levels, what became apparent during the sessions was the emergence of a relaxed, yet structured environment where it was 'acceptable' to discuss a whole range of mental health problems. Apart from being described by the carers as helpful and to an extent fun, the process had contributed to some form of 'equalising' of the participants. This was a positive and yet unintended consequence of the sessions and as such, the reasons for it are subject to conjecture. First, the distinctions between those people who were carers and those who were members of staff were less obvious than in a clinical setting. Second, the sessions took place in a comfortable and welcoming community education centre which had no association with mental health services. Third, the use of the 'test' provided a light-hearted way of identifying knowledge gaps; when the consultant psychiatrist offered the wrong answer to one of the questions, it caused considerable amusement. Finally, the sessions demonstrated that the Older People's Directorate was determined to improve the flexibility and responsiveness of its services by offering such a programme.

Stage three
CLOSING THE GAP

The final phase of the staged projects involved working with GPs and other members of the primary health care team to reduce the delays between the diagnosis of the mental health problem and a referral to the specialist services. This was a concern that had been raised in both the questionnaire and the focus groups by the carers, and the purpose of the project was to consider ways in which professional practice, within primary health care services, could change in order to reduce such delays. Following a number of lengthy discussions between members of the project group and GPs, three shared objectives were identified:

- To improve access to community mental health nurses for the primary health care team

- To improve access to community mental health nurses for carers who wish to meet with them outside of their own home

- To establish early contact between community mental health nurses and individuals affected by functional and organic mental health problems.

There were three parts to this project. First, in order to assess the viability and effectiveness of basing a community mental health nurse at a practice, a pilot study was established. In this instance, one of the primary functions of the community mental health nurse was to raise the profile of mental health problems of older people by providing advice and information to colleagues within primary health care teams, and where appropriate to co-work with them. Second, the outcomes of the pilot (which were generally positive), indicated that the model should be extended to incorporate six other practices (both fundholding and non-fundholding, in rural and urban settings) within the county. The final part of the project was the introduction of a simple screening tool that could be used by all primary health care teams as a means of identifying cognitive impairment. A certain score triggered automatic referral to the community mental health nurse who would follow up their assessment and incorporate the use of the 'mini mental state examination'. Confirmation of cognitive impairment was then referred back to the GP for further physical investigations and possible referral to a consultant psychiatrist; the community mental health nurse would continue to be involved.

At the end of the project the various professional groups were asked, during single-discipline focus groups, to evaluate the project. On the whole, the GPs reported that there had been an overall improvement in the type and level of communication with mental health services which, they believed, had led to an improvement in patient care. None of them, however, had used the screening tool. A number of primary health care team members who at the beginning of the project had made it quite clear that they were reluctant to take part, had not meandered from their initial position. They justified their actions on the grounds that their existing workload was only just manageable without dealing with what they considered to be the responsibilities of another health provider. Furthermore, they described themselves as general nurses not mental health nurses, and were therefore not equipped with the skills to work with people with mental health problems. In contrast to these, 'the reluctant participants', there were a significant number of 'the committed enthusiasts' who had recognised the benefit of working collaboratively and who had capitalised on the opportunity to work with nurses with different skills. Indeed, a number of them had passed the screening tool on to colleagues in different practices who incorporated it into their own clinical practice.

There was mixed reaction from the community mental health nurses. Most of them had witnessed an increase in the amount of referrals over and above the number they would normally expect but they felt that this was probably due to their increased visibility in the practice rather than a commitment to the principles of joint working. Some of them had found it quite difficult to work with colleagues who were from the same profession but who had completely different views about multi-disciplinary practice. For others, the experience had been very positive.

In some respects, the objectives of the project had been met. The practices, which were staffed by 'committed enthusiasts', requested a continuation of the project in some shape or form since they valued any initiative which would improve services to their patients. The 'reluctant participants' did not share this view.

Lessons Learnt from the Projects

In the introduction to this chapter, a number of questions were raised which, with both hindsight and the experience of working with carers of older people with mental health problems, can now be answered. In addition to these however, other considerations materialised during the projects which are worthy of further discussion.

Adapting to organisational change

A new professional discourse has been developing alongside the structural and cultural change within health and social care organisations. This discourse contains a number of terms which have their origins in the ethos of the private sector. Initially, notions of performance management, value for money, efficiency ratios and effectiveness measures were seen as alien, having no association with the traditional modes of bureaucratic operations. However, with regular usage, coupled with a new orientation in service delivery, they have become more meaningful and acceptable. Similarly, the concepts of consultation, participation and service-user involvement have been absorbed into the organisational vocabulary forming an essential part of this professional discourse. There is a risk, however, that familiarity with the terms will lead to the assumption that people who are outside the formal health and social care sector understand both the meanings of the terms and their applications. This is clearly not always the case. Furthermore, it is the assumptions that surround the use of the terminology which are problematic.

The first lesson learnt from the series of staged projects described above was that carers of older people with mental health problems are not a group of homogenous individuals who meet on a regular basis for mutual support and the opportunity to comment on health and social care services. Indeed, as noted from the work of Twigg *et al.* (1990), not all carers see themselves as such and therefore, in some ways, exclude themselves from attending groups which are likely to be targeted during consultation and evaluation exercises. Additionally, following discussions with carers during the projects, it became apparent that the terms consultation, participation and collaboration were as alien to them as the terms which had initially caused problems for practitioners within health and social care agencies during the 1980s and 1990s. Essentially, the words were not part of the carers' discourse and as such their meanings and applications were unfamiliar to them.

Understanding the demands on carers

A second lesson learnt was that the priorities of carers are very different from those of health and social care agencies when it comes to engaging in discussions concerning service developments. The operating principles enshrined in the managerial orthodoxy of new public sector management naturally steer organisations in the direction of such priorities as establishing mechanisms for assessing 'customer satisfaction' and working more closely with users of their services. For most of the carers in this study, their priorities meant ensuring that the person to whom they provided care was not left alone for more than ten minutes because they had a tendency to wander or misuse simple appliances, or ensuring that sufficient bed linen was available because of incontinence, or coping with hours of silence from a person who previously was out-going, sociable and chatty. Any 'free time' is used carefully. The carers who were prepared to use their time in a way that could impact positively on the levels of available support by engaging with the Older People's Directorate had to be convinced that the process would be worth while. This brings us to the third lesson.

The project team was aware that carers' time is precious, and so the objective of engaging with them had to be meaningful. This was the main reason why the approach adopted for the projects was based on participation rather than on the relatively passive notion of consultation, and also why carers were encouraged to set the agenda for future developments. However, the team did not want to be in a position of raising expectations for carers which subsequently it could not meet. This explains the rather lengthy planning process associated with development of the service evaluation exercise: it encompassed debates around the likely areas of concern for carers.

Developing a relationship

Using an action research framework for the projects outlined in this chapter was helpful not only in terms of the evaluation of the work but also because the routine provided by Stringer (1996) of 'looking', 'thinking' and 'acting' could be applied to virtually every stage of the process. Moreover, implicit in such a framework is the notion that the stakeholders involved work collaboratively to build positive working relationships based on a mutual understanding of each others' limitations and restraints in order to produce a more communicative approach. For the project team, the series of staged projects was the first real attempt to work with carers of older people with mental health problems and the members were mindful that carelessness in the planning stage could have a detrimental effect on the development of a relationship based on trust. Simplistically, the quality assurance manager played the role of devil's advocate by asking the 'how would you like it if…' questions. In this respect, the team was able to unpack some of the assumptions which surround such standard practice of statutory organisations as, for example, the distribution of a questionnaire. Additionally, the focus groups and the psycho-educational sessions took place outside the hospital environment because the team recognised that what was a 'normal' and non-threatening environment for them was not necessarily perceived as such by the carers. Any association with mental health services is shrouded in stigma and unease. This more thoughtful approach to working with carers has had its rewards, which were not only demonstrated by the relaxed atmosphere which emerged during the psycho-educational sessions but also in subsequent work with carers of older people with mental health problems. Since the completion of the projects, a number of small-scale developments have occurred as a result of carers feeling comfortable in approaching members of staff with their ideas about how improvements could be made.

Implementing changes

Within the Older People's Directorate, implementing change brought about at the suggestion of carers has not been a major problem. However, the difficulties occur when changes in practice are dependent on another arm of the health service. This was demonstrated during the work with some of the primary health care teams. A reluctance to recognise their shortcomings in mental health knowledge and the benefits of multi-disciplinary working meant an unnecessary delay in referring a person with mental health problems to a more specialised service. A lack of awareness of the complexities and implications experienced by carers in similar circumstances suggests that this is an area for further work.

Conclusion

Introducing a participatory style of working with carers of older people with mental health problems is more difficult than it first appears. Considerable time is spent ensuring not only that the process is workable, but that the outcomes are achievable. Furthermore, a commitment from the organisation and from the carers is needed in order for participation to work. This, however, relies on both parties having an understanding of their own and each others' restrictions and limitations, which in itself takes time to establish. Notwithstanding these points, the benefits far outweigh the drawbacks.

Note

The Primary Health Care Team project received the NHS Executive, West Midlands 1996/97 Award for Innovations in Nursing Practice.

References

Archbold, P.G. (1983) 'Impact of Parent-Caring on Women.' *Family Relations 32*, 39–45.

Barnes, M. (1997) *Care, Communities and Citizens.* London: Longman.

Barnes, M. and Wistow, G. (1995) *User Orientated Community Care: An Overview of Findings from an Evaluation of the Birmingham Community Care Special Action Project.* Leeds: Nuffield Institute for Health, University of Leeds.

Barnes, R.F., Raskind, M.A., Scott, M. and Murphy, C. (1981) 'Problems of Families Caring for Alzheimer Patients: Use of a Support Group.' *Journal of the American Geriatrics Society 29*, 80–85.

Braithwaite, V.A. (1990) *Bound to Care.* Sydney: Allen and Unwin.

Department of Health (1996) *Carers (Recognition and Services) Act, Policy Guidance.* London: HMSO.

Dunkle, R. (1985) 'Comparing the Depression of Elders in Two Types of Caregiving Arrangements.' *Family Relations 34*, 235–240.

Eagles, J.N., Craig, A., Rawlinson, F., Restall, D.B., Beattie, J.A.G. and Besson, J.A.O. (1987) 'The Psychological Well Being of Supporters of the Demented Elderly.' *British Journal of Psychiatry 150*, 293–298.

Gilhooly, M.L.M. (1984) 'The Social Aspect of Dementia.' In I.G. Hanley and J. Hodge (eds) *Psychological Approaches to the Care of the Elderly*. London: Croom-Helm.

Gilleard, C.J. (1984) 'Problems Posed for Supporting Relatives of Geriatric and Psychogeriatric Day Patients.' *Acta Psychiatrica Scandinavica 70*, 198–208.

Glendinning, C. and Bewley, C. (1992) *Involving Disabled People in Community Care Planning: The First Steps*. Manchester: Department of Social Policy and Social Work, University of Manchester.

Greene, J.G., Smith, R., Gardiner, M. and Timbury, G.C. (1982) 'Measuring Behavioural Disturbance of Elderly Demented Patients in the Community and its Effects on Relatives: A Factor Analytical Study.' *Age and Ageing 11*, 121–126.

Hoyes, L., Jeffers, S., Lart, R., Means, R. and Taylor, M. (1993) *User Empowerment and the Reform of Community Care: An Interim Assessment*. Bristol: School for Advanced Urban Studies.

Jerrom, B., Mian, I., Rukanyake, N.G. (1993) 'Stress on Relative Caregivers of Dementia Sufferers and Predictors of the Breakdown of Community Care.' *International Journal of Geriatric Psychiatry 8*, 331–337.

Levin, E., Sinclair, I. and Garbach, P. (1983) *The Supporters of Confused Elderly Persons at Home*. DHSS Commissioned Research Project, vols. 1, 2, and 3. London: National Institute for Social Work Research Unit.

Martin, L. and Gaster, L. (1993) 'Community Care Planning in Wolverhampton.' In R. Smith, L. Gaster, L. Harrison, R. Means and P. Thistlethwaite *Working Together for Better Community Care*. Bristol: School for Advanced Urban Studies.

Morris, R.G., Morris, L.W. and Britton, P.G. (1989) 'Cognitive Style and Perceived Control in Spouse Caregivers of Dementia Sufferers.' *British Journal of Medical Psychology 62*, 173–179.

Motenko, A.K. (1989) 'The Frustrations, Gratification and Well Being of Dementia Caregivers.' *Gerontologist 29*, 166–172.

Pearlin, L., Mullan, J.T., Semple, S.J. and Skaff, M.M. (1990) 'Caregiving and the Stress Process: An Overview of Concepts and their Measures.' *Gerontologist 30*, 583–594.

Stewart, J. and Stoker, G. (1995) 'Fifteen Years of Local Government Restructuring 1979–1994: An Evaluation.' In J. Stewart and G. Stoker (eds) *Local Government in the 1990s*. London: Macmillan.

Stringer, E.T. (1996) *Action Research: A Handbook for Practitioners*. Thousand Oaks, CA: Sage.

Thomas, C. (1993) 'De-Constructing Concepts of Care.' *Sociology 27*, 4, 649–669.

Twigg, J., Atkin, K. and Perring, C. (1990) *Carers and Services: A Review of Research*. London: HMSO.

Walsh, K. (1995) *Public Services and Market Mechanisms*. London: Macmillan.

Zarit, S.H., Todd, P.A. and Zarit, M. (1986) 'Subjective Burden of Husbands and Wives as Caregivers: A Longitudinal Study.' *Gerontologist 26*, 260–266.

CHAPTER 8

Listening to Children

Meeting the Needs of Young Carers

Chris Dearden and Saul Becker

Nobody seems to care what other people have to put up with – what they have to go through – they don't give a thought for the person who stays behind and looks after the sick person. (Miriam, now an adult but caring since age 15, quoted in Aldridge and Becker 1993, p.31)

Introduction

Young carers are children and young people under the age of 18 who provide personal care or support to a relative in the community. That relative is usually a parent but could be a sibling, grandparent or other family member who may have physical health problems or disabilities, mental health problems, learning difficulties, may be misusing alcohol or drugs, or may be frail and elderly. The upper age of 18 is usually used to denote the boundary between young and adult carers, as under-18s have not yet achieved the age of majority; as children, they are seen as vulnerable and are protected by specific children's legislation.

There are no precise figures on the number of young carers nationally. Early studies in the 1980s suggested a figure of between 10,000 and 15,000 (O'Neill 1988), while a later evaluation of support services for young carers suggested the number may be 15,000 to 40,000 (Mahon and Higgins 1995). Secondary analysis of the 1985 General Household Survey data indicates that 17 per cent of adult carers age 16 and over were caring before they became 16, and a third of these were assisting parents (Parker 1992, 1994). Thus a significant number of adult carers began caring as children. More recently the Department of Health has attempted to establish national figures and suggests there may be between 19,000 and 50,000 young carers (Walker 1996). However, the Department of Health takes as its definition those young people who provide, or intend to provide, substantial care on a regular basis. We focus on the *impact* caring has on children's lives, rather than solely on the amount of time spent caring Thus, using an impact definition, the figure is likely to be substantially higher. We do know that, in the UK, almost three million children under the age of 16 (equivalent to 23 per cent of all children) live in households where one family member has a chronic physical or mental health problem (Becker, Aldridge and Dearden 1998). Thus the potential number of young carers is likely to be significantly higher than 50,000.

Whispers in the Dark: A 'Hidden' Problem?

> The scandal of young people in their early teens, or younger, providing physically arduous and emotionally draining care for their parents – including every intimate act of personal hygiene – is uncomfortable and painful for those involved. Those not involved prefer not to think about it. (White 1989, p.23)

The issue of young caring has only recently emerged onto the social policy agenda although Aldridge and Becker (1993) suggest that it is not a new phenomenon but has probably existed for centuries. Before research was conducted, young carers had no voice and we knew very little about them. The feminist literature on caring ignored *children* who care, and the growing interest in, and literature about, children's rights failed to acknowledged their particular needs; young carers were invisible and neglected.

Because the UK has no overt family policy, but rather a series of social policies which implicitly assume familist ideologies, much of what goes on 'behind closed doors' remains hidden from view unless it transgresses acceptable norms and values, or breaks the law and is discovered. While community care policy assumes that family, friends and neighbours will provide most of the care to sick or disabled family members with the state stepping in to fill the gaps (see e.g. DoH 1989; Griffiths Report 1988), children are perceived as vulnerable and are protected by legislation such as the Children Act of 1989 and the 1989 UN Convention on the Rights of the Child, ratified by the UK government in 1991. Thus, while adult carers can be seen to be conforming to society's norms, the notion of children acting as carers transgresses such norms since children are perceived as the dependants of adults, and childhood is viewed as a protected phase.

However, it is not caring *per se* which transgresses such norms. Some degree of caring in childhood is to be valued as part of 'healthy' child development. All young people should grow and develop in line with their physical and emotional ability and maturity, and caring for and about family members is part of this gradual development and maturation. Young carers are children who are involved in *exaggerated* levels or types of caring which often impact negatively on them. For example, they may be providing support and assistance for a great number of hours each day, or they may be providing less care in terms of hours but that care may be of a physically arduous or intimate and embarrassing nature. Caring may have a negative impact on their ability to socialise with peers or perform to their full potential in education which may result in longer-term problems within the labour market or further/higher education. There is, therefore, considerable agreement regarding the characteristics that define the experiences and condition of young carers: these concern their involvement in levels or forms of caring which have a restrictive or negative impact on their childhood (Becker *et al.* 1998).

Some of the earliest research into young caring aimed to highlight the issue and to estimate the number of young carers, either locally or nationally (O'Neill 1988; Page 1988). While these studies failed in their attempts to determine the extent of young caring, they did succeed in raising awareness of the issue and were instrumental in stimulating further research. The first study to contact young carers directly and to ask them about their experiences and needs was conducted in Merseyside (Bilsborrow 1992) and led to the setting-up of the first two desig-nated support services for young carers. Other small-scale research studies and awareness-raising publications have concentrated on the needs and experiences of children supporting family members with specific health needs, such as Par-kinson's disease (Grimshaw 1991), mental health problems (Elliott 1992; Landells and Pritlove 1994), Huntington's disease (Tyler 1990), multiple sclero-sis (Segal and Simkins 1993), AIDS and HIV (Imrie and Coombes 1995).

As further research has been conducted throughout the 1990s we have begun to understand more about the needs and experiences of young carers; about the outcomes of caring unsupported (or with limited support); and about the profes-sional support and services which young people and their families feel they need and which would make their lives easier. The wide dissemination of research findings and the media interest in the issue have resulted in professionals, practi-tioners and the wider public becoming more aware of the issues.

The Young Carers Research Group (YCRG) was established in 1992 and its first piece of research, published one year later (Aldridge and Becker 1993), received wide media coverage and resulted in an early day motion in Parliament. The aims of the Group's ongoing programme of work are to give children and young people a voice; to raise awareness of the issues; and to inform and improve policy and practice. In this chapter we will draw on the Group's work, both small-scale qualitative and larger quantitative studies, to demonstrate how research can improve the participation and involvement in social care delivery of a group of previously 'hidden' and vulnerable children.

Giving Young Carers a Voice: Methodological Issues

> I agreed to take part in this research because it's important everyone knows how we feel and how we've been ignored. Something has got to be done to help young carers. (Alison, age 18, quoted in Aldridge and Becker 1993, p.80)

The methodology adopted by the YCRG has been largely qualitative in nature, using a grounded theory approach (Glaser and Strauss 1967) to analysis, allowing the young carers' words and ideas to form the building blocks of our own understanding. Interviews have been arranged around broad themes with priority given to the meanings young people attach to their own experiences. Later pieces of research (Dearden and Becker 1995a, 1998a) have incorporated a quantitative element, enabling us to generate statistical data about young carers. This quantitative analysis has become possible in recent years as support services for young carers have developed and, as a group, have become much easier to identify and access for research purposes.

One of the particular problems of early research was the identification of potential respondents. As there were no specific support services available for young carers, they were especially difficult to identify. The Group's first piece of research (Aldridge and Becker 1993) relied on the formation of a multi-disciplinary steering group of interested professionals from a range of statutory and voluntary welfare agencies. These professionals used their own personal and professional contacts and raised awareness within their own agencies and organisations to assist in the identification of potential young carers. Although time-consuming, this approach worked well and has usually been the model adopted by subsequent young carer support services. These specialist services have tended to begin with a group of interested individuals who have formed an interest or steering group, raised awareness locally, and often made funding applications to continue their work once local young carers have been identified. In many cases the original group has become the project steering or management group.

A second, and potentially more damaging, problem is that of identifying problems or issues which we, as researchers, are unable to solve. Giving young people a voice and asking them to identify problems is ethically difficult if there are no available services which can offer support. The decision made by the Group has been to offer information, where available, or to try to obtain information or identify a relevant organisation that can offer the advice or support required by families. Permission has been obtained to do so and no confidential information has been shared with other agencies without the express consent of individual respondents. In our later research, respondents were identified via support services and any issues raised could be referred back to project staff, again with the express consent of respondents. Thus, we have avoided the pitfall of raising false hopes or expectations and have tried to clarify and answer any specific queries raised by respondents.

The early work of the Group was exploratory, and semi-structured interviews were felt to be the best methodology to adopt in order to explore a hitherto unknown area. Although the interviews with young carers were arranged around themes, the loose structure offered the interviewer the opportunity to follow avenues opened up by the young people themselves. This type of interviewing, 'conversations with a purpose' (Lindlof 1995), has worked very well with young people and has resulted in a wealth of rich data. The words of the young people are very powerful and have been used to good effect in research publications and in awareness-raising presentations to social welfare professionals. This form of social research has been empowering to young people, giving them a voice and enabling them to tell their stories. Our subsequent research has also adopted this methodology but has been informed by quantitative data collected from young carers' designated support services (Dearden and Becker 1995a, 1998a). This dual approach has enabled us to generate statistical data about young carers' age, gender, ethnicity, caring tasks, educational experiences etc., while the words of the young people remain paramount.

Engaging young people in interviews has been relatively problem-free. Although some interview respondents have been naturally shy and reticent, the majority have been very willing to talk about their experiences – possibly because they have had few opportunities to do so in the past and value the opportunity to share their knowledge and experiences with someone who believes them and is non-judgemental.

The issue of informed consent is critical to research with children and young people. Interviews have usually been conducted either at the respondent's own home or at a young carers' project, where young people feel safe. Parental permission (in addition to permission from young people themselves) has been obtained for interviews with young people under the age of 16, while those over 16 have usually been in a position to make an informed decision themselves. There are exceptions to this rule, notably with young people with learning difficulties, where parental permission has been sought regardless of the age of the young carer. In one case a decision was taken not to continue with an arranged interview with a young woman with learning difficulties as we were uncertain whether the respondent was fully aware of the consequences of being interviewed. Care has been taken to interview children and young people alone, to allow them the opportunity to discuss issues freely without parental presence. Equally, parents have been reassured that the aim is not to discuss personal family matters 'behind their backs' but to allow the children the opportunity to talk freely. In some cases a project worker has been present during interviews, usually where the respondent is particularly shy or nervous, and has been able to act as an 'independent observer' while providing reassurance to the respondent.

All respondents are assured that they are under no obligation to answer any questions posed by the researcher, that they can terminate the interview at any time and that the information shared will not be divulged to other family members or to professionals involved with the families. They are also assured that real names will not be included in research reports and that care will be taken to protect their anonymity. The YCRG has never released details of any respondents to the media – despite frequent requests, pleas and threats!

Younger respondents are often interested in the recording equipment used and have been shown how to switch equipment on and off so that they can exercise greater control over the interview process, pausing or terminating this process themselves. Younger respondents are also offered the opportunity to listen to themselves on tape – often the source of much amusement, but again a way of increasing involvement in the interview process.

There are several advantages to the methodology adopted. Because young carers have been a 'hidden' welfare group, whose experiences have only recently been acknowledged, loosely structured interviews have the advantage of avoiding imposing our own interpretations and structures on their experiences. The interviews can go in any direction to take account of themes raised by the young people but not previously considered by the interviewer. Furthermore, alternative methods such as questionnaire surveys would fail to give the depth of data, knowledge and understanding that the chosen methodology has yielded. However, the research and the methodology have received criticism from other academics, whose agendas are, perhaps, different from our own.

Writing from a disability rights perspective, authors such as Keith and Morris (1995) have questioned the whole notion of 'young carers', suggesting that to label the children of disabled parents as carers undermines those parents and suggests that they are in some way 'inadequate', when the crux of the problem is their lack of adequate and appropriate professional support and services. They suggest that if disabled people received the services that they require and to which they have a right under disability legislation, their children would not be drawn into caring roles. Others (Olsen 1996; Parker and Olsen 1995) have questioned whether the findings of small-scale qualitative studies can be generalised to a larger population. The debate generated by these critiques and the replies from the YCRG (Aldridge and Becker 1996), has informed the development of policy and practice in the latter part of the 1990s, and most writers, whether from a disability rights or a children's rights perspective, now advocate family-based support which takes into account the expressed needs of all members of a family, rather than parent or child in isolation. The methodological criticisms have also been addressed, since the findings from larger-scale studies (Dearden and Becker 1995a, 1998a) have been remarkably similar to those of earlier smaller-scale work.

There is now a broad consensus on the needs and experiences of young carers, particularly those whose families receive little or no support from welfare service providers and who are coping with family illness or disability in relative isolation. There remain differences between the disability rights perspective and the children and family rights paradigm regarding the appropriate response to the issue of young caring. From a children and family rights perspective, we would argue that although a more family-based approach to meeting needs is essential, there are some children who may require specific designated services to support them as *children* who are also carers (i.e. they are children first). There are also some cases where support is essential because of conflicts of interest between parents and children, and other instances where parents may, for whatever reason, refuse external support for themselves. From a disability rights perspective, support and services to disabled parents are paramount, and specialist support services for young carers are viewed as deflecting scarce resources from such support. There is also a fear that, once young carers' support services are established, the 'problem' will be viewed as solved and nothing more will be done to support disabled parents. In our view, however, these anxieties do not justify ignoring the voices of children who are carers.

Listening to Children

> I didn't used to talk about it. I didn't want anybody knowing our business. I still don't but I've grown up a lot, I've had to. You've got to. (Claire, age 16, quoted in Aldridge and Becker 1993, p.46)

The first two pieces of research conducted by the YCRG focused on identifying the needs and experiences of a small number of young carers (Aldridge and Becker 1993) and their parents (Aldridge and Becker 1994). The young people who took part in this research had never before been consulted by professionals and had not had the opportunity to recount their experiences or been included in any decision-making processes by welfare service providers. Their parents confirmed that the needs and wishes of their children had been overlooked and ignored by service providers:

> They don't ever talk to the girls about caring. The nurse comes round occasionally and the health visitor and they all know my daughters care, but they've not said anything about it though. (Mrs Winterbottom, quoted in Aldridge and Becker 1994, p.5)

For many of the young people involved in this research, the interview process was cathartic, offering them their first opportunity to discuss their feelings regarding caring and to say what support would make, or would have made, their lives easier. It is perhaps not surprising that the young people found it difficult to articulate fully the types of *services* which would help them, but they had no difficulty in expressing their needs. These needs may be broadly categorised under three headings: the need for information, the need for someone to talk to, and the need for practical support (Aldridge and Becker 1993). Parents found it even harder to suggest ways in which their children might be supported and few could identify any specific needs their children had as *carers* (Aldridge and Becker 1994).

This early work led Aldridge and Becker (1993) to hypothesise that, within families, it is often one child who is 'elected' into the caring role by other family members. Once caring becomes established, the child is then socialised into the role, perceiving it as natural and unable to envisage alternatives. They found that the lives of the young people were often very restricted as they had little free time for 'normal' childhood activities. These restrictions could also extend to school and educational experiences, resulting in absenteeism, persistent lateness and difficulties in completing homework and joining extracurricular activities. Children were seen to be performing a range of tasks from basic domestic duties, such as cleaning, cooking, etc. to very personal, intimate care such as bathing and toileting. While the children demonstrated a commitment to performing these tasks as a means of supporting family members, none were comfortable with providing intimate care.

Parents too felt their children were often constrained by their caring roles (Aldridge and Becker 1994) and they experienced guilt at having to rely on their children's support despite the fact that it was usually the absence of practical, appropriate professional support services which led to this. The findings from the research with parents suggested that they had mixed feelings about their children adopting caring roles. There was evidence of some preferring their own children to 'outsiders', while others found the situation unacceptable but had few, if any, alternatives. Parents were also uncomfortable with their children having to provide personal care.

Later larger-scale surveys of young carers' projects around the UK have confirmed many of the findings of these early, exploratory studies. Our first national survey (Dearden and Becker 1995a) collected data on 641 young carers. Sixty per cent of the young people were living in lone-parent families and most were providing support to mothers with ill health or disabilities. While early studies had suggested this may be the case, this larger data-set provided confirmation. It appeared that in two-parent families children helped to support a range of relatives with health problems, while in lone-parent families they tended to provide support for lone mothers in the absence of other adults. Our most recent survey (Dearden and Becker 1998a), which collected data about 2303 young carers, confirms this and indicates that most care recipients (57%) were experiencing physical health problems or disabilities, although a quarter had mental ill health. As in Aldridge and Becker's (1993) study, the young people were involved in a range of activities including domestic tasks (72%), general care, such as assisting with mobility or giving medications (57%), emotional support (43%), intimate care (21%) and child care for siblings (7%). The following comments from young people indicate the range of caring tasks undertaken:

> Washing the dishes, drying the dishes, putting the washing out, just generally most things. (Naomi, age 16, quoted in Dearden and Becker 1998a, p.40)

> I make her [grandmother] breakfast, dinner and tea… I normally make a sandwich or something for lunch and leave it there and a Cuppa Soup, because then she's only got to boil the kettle. (Susie, age 18, quoted in Dearden and Becker 1998a, p.41)

> Giving her [mother] tablets, giving her injections…she didn't like using the commodes…but she did insist on 'I can get to the toilet' which frequently meant I would wake up with her screaming my name because she'd decided to make her own way from the bedroom, using banisters and rails to get to the toilet, and then half-way there she got dizzy and half fainted or whatever, and I'd have to support her and try to get her back to bed and basically I had problems lifting her. (Karen, age 20, quoted in Dearden and Becker 1998a, p.41)

> I'm used to it now…sometimes it's a bit awful when she's [mother] had an accident – a big accident – but apart from that we don't really see it like that. She wears pads and things… I just find it embarrassing when she's had a really big accident. (Marianne, age 14, quoted in Dearden and Becker 1998a, p.42)

> Well my mum has a language problem as well, so like, I would go around doing all the administrating work, dealing with bills and stuff like that. (Shazia, age 17, quoted in Dearden and Becker 1998a, p.43)

One of the major findings of both surveys was the high incidence of educational difficulties faced by young carers. Although this had been a feature of the earlier work, there was no evidence beforehand that it would be so widespread. However, in 1995 one in four of those young carers of compulsory school age were missing some school, while one in three were either missing school or in receipt of education welfare services or other educational support. The 1998 survey shows some improvements in young carers' situations, but 28 per cent continue to miss school or experience educational difficulties. Again, comments from young people indicate some of the educational difficulties they face:

> I skip school because of my mum. I've done it a few times because I'm worried about her. (Liam, age 12, quoted in Dearden and Becker 1995a, p.24)

> I just worry when I've got to go to school… I ring him [father] up at break and dinner to see how he is… I can't concentrate at school, even when I am there,

there's no point in going really. (Liz, age 15, quoted in Dearden and Becker 1995a, p.26)

I suppose really I missed out on a bit of education... I was worried about her [grandmother] basically...but it just got worse, basically I didn't go in for my fifth year at school... I must have gone in for about a week. (Susie, age 18, quoted in Dearden and Becker 1998a, p.45)

If she'd been ill through the night or whatever I'd go in late and things, because of having to wait for the home help to get here because I didn't want her to be on her own...[I'd miss] days and everything. And the school were kind of aware that mum was ill, because in a way they had to be, because you'd have to provide absent notes or whatever. But at the same time, they didn't – it wasn't like they offered for me to have extra lessons to make up on work I'd missed...they didn't really know how to help, but it just meant that I'd miss work and stuff and, obviously, you know, that was the worst period, the last two years of you being in school, you don't need to miss it. (Karen, age 20, quoted in Dearden and Becker 1998a, pp.45–46)

The impact of young carer research has been substantial. It has resulted in a great deal of media interest, partially stimulated by the powerful accounts of young people themselves. While media coverage has sometimes been less than helpful, portraying carers as saints or victims, it has done much to stimulate debate and raise awareness (Deacon 1999). By giving young carers a voice and enabling them to share their experiences, the research empowered them and helped them both as individuals and as a group to have their experiences acknowledged and validated.

Hearing the Voices: Informing Policy and Practice

It's [Young Carers Project] given me the chance to know who is in the same position as me, and for me to talk to someone that I know can relate to me, because they've either been through it or they're going through it. (Abigail, age 15, quoted in Dearden and Becker 1998a, p.54)

The accounts of young carers have been instrumental in raising awareness of their needs and in stimulating service provision. Organisations such as Carers National Association (CNA) have worked alongside young people to promote the development of support for them. In 1992 there were two designated support projects for young carers, by 1995 there were 37 (Dearden and Becker 1995b), and in 1998 there were over 100 (Aldridge and Becker 1998). Projects have developed as a result of research and wider public, professional and media interest and awareness. In turn, the projects have worked with and for young people to respond to their needs and to keep these needs on the wider social policy agenda.

The rapid expansion in the 1990s of designated support services for young carers has offered a further avenue for children's participation in service delivery. As representatives on project steering groups and committees, young people have been able to ensure that their needs are met in appropriate ways. Young carers' projects are child-centred while increasingly attempting to meet the needs of whole families. The YCRG has evaluated three such projects and young people have been interviewed to obtain their views regarding the effectiveness of a service designed to meet their needs. These evaluations demonstrate the value placed on projects by young people, parents and professionals (see e.g. Dearden and Becker 1996, 1998b; Newton and Becker 1998):

> They know what's going on. Projects like this have the whole, the general picture…they can understand what's going on and they've got the knowledge to be able to help. (Karen, age 19, quoted in Dearden and Becker 1996, p.42)

Furthermore, many local authorities and voluntary agencies have organised conferences intended to inform practitioners and policy makers about young carers' needs. Speakers from the YCRG, CNA and other carers' and children's organisations have spoken at these conferences, summarising the research findings and highlighting the issues. Young carers themselves have also been enabled to speak at such conferences and the combination of their accounts and the research findings and implications have been powerful tools in influencing both local and national policies.

In 1995 a letter was sent to all directors of social services informing them of their responsibilities to young carers (Social Services Inspectorate 1995). During 1995 and 1996 the Social Services Inspectorate (SSI) conducted fieldwork and ran a series of workshops which were attended by policy makers, practitioners, academics and young carers (DoH 1996a, 1996b). As a result of these initiatives young carers are now mentioned in all children's services plans. There is also an acknowledgement that they can be classified as children in need under section 17 of the Children Act of 1989 and can have their needs met via this piece of legislation.

With organisations such as CNA acting as brokers, young carers have met with government officials and have been able to influence legislation and policy. Their words have moved and influenced government ministers such as John Bowis (Junior Minister for Health when the SSI conducted its research); Malcolm Wicks (whose private member's bill resulted in the Carers (Recognition and Services) Act of 1995, the first piece of legislation specifically to mention young carers); and Paul Boateng (responsible for the National Strategy for Carers in 1999). Young carers are now entitled to an assessment of their own needs as *carers* under the Carers Act and as *children* under the Children Act. The National Carers Strategy (DoH 1999) includes a chapter devoted to them which highlights the importance of providing designated support services and of training practitioners to improve their knowledge and awareness.

While the situation remains far from perfect, recent policy initiatives are a step in the right direction and, although few young carers have thus far been assessed under any piece of legislation, assessment will provide an opportunity for their needs to be addressed. Our research (Dearden and Becker 1998a) suggests that 11 per cent of young carers have had an assessment and that the process of assessment is variable, ranging from poor (many young carers remaining unaware that they had been assessed even after the event) to excellent:

> I think it's [being assessed as a carer] just having someone to yourself, someone caring and spending time with you. They've got the time, sort of thing. Yes, that is very true, yes, very therapeutic... I can't stress how beneficial it's been, really. (Debbie, age 16, quoted in Dearden and Becker 1998a, p.65)

Despite the variability in the assessment process, young carers are often satisfied with the outcomes; often the introduction of, or increase in, home care services.

Many of the YCRG policy recommendations, based on the expressed needs and experiences of young carers themselves (Dearden and Becker 1998a) have now been incorporated into the National Carers Strategy. In the future, therefore, social care delivery should be more appropriate to the expressed needs of young carers and their families.

Conclusions

The work of the YCRG offers an example of how, by involving young people in research, hearing their voices and relating their stories, social research can influence both social policy and social care delivery. This has been particularly effective in highlighting the needs of a previously 'hidden' group and securing their involvement in policy and practice. Once research has highlighted a social issue, bringing it to the attention of the public, policy makers and practitioners, it becomes easier for young carers to have their voices heard and acknowledged. This has parallels in other areas of social research such as informal caring by adults and the experiences of children in local authority care. Social research can thus be both empowering and enabling and can ensure that those in need of professional support and services can participate in the policy process and the delivery of social care services which meet their own expressed needs.

Former young carers are acutely aware of how they were neglected by professionals and their stories should not be forgotten. With genuine user participation and involvement, children like Jimmy should never again experience the lack of appropriate professional support which leaves them vulnerable and neglected:

It's too late for me now. My dad died and I'm no longer a 'young carer', but for all those other kids out there who are in the same situation I was, then something should be done to help them. Not take them away from their mum and dad, but to help them care without worrying, without being frightened. (Jimmy, age 16, quoted in Aldridge and Becker 1993, p.81)

References

Aldridge, J. and Becker, S. (1993) *Children Who Care: Inside the World of Young Carers.* Loughborough: Young Carers Research Group, Loughborough University.

Aldridge, J. and Becker, S. (1994) *My Child, My Carer: The Parents' Perspective.* Loughborough: Young Carers Research Group, Loughborough University.

Aldridge, J. and Becker, S. (1996) 'Disability Rights and the Denial of Young Carers: The Dangers of Zero-Sum Arguments.' *Critical Social Policy 16,* 55–76.

Aldridge, J. and Becker, S. (1998) *The National Handbook of Young Carers Projects.* London: Carers National Association.

Becker, S., Aldridge, J. and Dearden, C. (1998) *Young Carers and their Families.* Oxford: Blackwell Science.

Bilsborrow, S. (1992) *'You grow up fast as well…' Young Carers on Merseyside.* Liverpool: Carers National Association, Personal Services Society and Barnardos.

Deacon, D. (1999) 'Old Hacks and Young Carers.' *The Journal of Young Carers Work 2,* 9–11.

Dearden, C. and Becker, S. (1995a) *Young Carers: The Facts.* Sutton: Reed Business Publishing.

Dearden, C. and Becker, S. (1995b) *The National Directory of Young Carers Projects and Initiatives.* Loughborough: Young Carers Research Group, Loughborough University.

Dearden, C. and Becker, S. (1996) *Young Carers at the Crossroads: An Evaluation of the Nottingham Young Carers Project.* Loughborough: Young Carers Research Group, Loughborough University.

Dearden, C. and Becker, S. (1998a) *Young Carers in the United Kingdom: A Profile.* London: Carers National Association.

Dearden, C. and Becker, S. (1998b) *Sheffield Young Carers Project: An Evaluation. Interim Report April 1997–September 1998.* Loughborough: Young Carers Research Group, Loughborough University.

Department of Health (1989) *Caring for People: Community Care in the Next Decade and Beyond.* London: HMSO.

Department of Health (1996a) *Young Carers: Something to Think About. Report of four SSI Workshops May–July 1995.* London: Department of Health.

Department of Health (1996b) *Young Carers: Making a Start. Report of the SSI Fieldwork Project on Families with Disability or Illness October 1995–January 1996.* London: Department of Health.

Department of Health (1999) *Caring about Carers: A National Strategy for Carers.* London: The Stationery Office.

Elliott, A. (1992) *Hidden Children: A Study of Ex-Young Carers of Parents with Mental Health Problems.* Leeds: City Council Mental Health Development Section.

Glaser, B.G. and Strauss, A.L. (1967) *The Discovery of Grounded Theory.* Chicago: Aldine.

Griffiths Report (1988) *Community Care: Agenda for Action.* London: HMSO.

Grimshaw, R. (1991) *Children of Parents with Parkinson's Disease: A Research Report for the Parkinson's Disease Society.* London: National Children's Bureau.

Imrie, J. and Coombes, Y. (1995) *No Time to Waste: The Scale and Dimensions of the Problem of Children Affected by HIV/AIDS in the United Kingdom.* Ilford: Barnardos.

Keith, L. and Morris, J. (1995) 'Easy Targets: A Disability Rights Perspective on the "Children as Carers" Debate.' *Critical Social Policy 44/45,* 36–57.

Landells, S. and Pritlove, J. (1994) *Young Carers of a Parent with Schizophrenia: A Leeds Survey.* Leeds: Leeds City Council, Department of Social Services.

Lindlof, T. R. (1995) *Qualitative Communication Research Methods.* Thousand Oaks, CA: Sage.

Mahon, A. and Higgins, J. (1995) '...*A Life of Our Own' Young Carers: An Evaluation of Three RHA Funded Projects in Merseyside.* Manchester: Health Services Management Unit, University of Manchester.

Newton, B. and Becker, S. (1998) *The Capital Carers: An Evaluation of Capital Carers Young Carers Project. An Interim Report Prepared for Capital Carers.* Loughborough: Young Carers Research Group, Loughborough University.

Olsen, R. (1996) 'Young Carers: Challenging the Facts and Politics of Research into Children and Caring.' *Disability and Society 11,* 1, 41–54.

O'Neill, A. (1988) *Young Carers: The Tameside Research.* Tameside: Tameside Metropolitan Borough Council.

Page, R. (1988) *Report on the Initial Survey Investigating the Number of Young Carers in Sandwell Secondary Schools.* Sandwell: Sandwell Metropolitan Borough Council.

Parker, G. (1992) 'Counting Care: Numbers and Types of Informal Carers.' In J. Twigg (ed) *Carers: Research and Practice.* London: HMSO.

Parker, G. (1994) *Where Next for Research on Carers?* Leicester: Nuffield Community Care Studies Centre, University of Leicester.

Parker, G. and Olsen, R. (1995) 'A Sideways Glance at Young Carers.' In *Young Carers: Something to Think About. Papers Presented at Four SSI Workshops May–July 1995.* London: Department of Health.

Segal, J. and Simkins, J. (1993) *My Mum Needs Me: Helping Children with Ill or Disabled Parents.* Harmondsworth: Penguin.

Social Services Inspectorate (1995) Letter to all Directors of Social Services, 28 April.

Tyler, A. (1990) 'Helping the children to cope...,' *Combat 37,* 16–20.

Walker, A. (1996) *Young Carers and Their Families: A Survey Carried out by the Social Survey Division of the Office for National Statistics on behalf of the Department of Health.* London: The Stationery Office.

White, P. (1989) 'Caring for the Caring.' *Young People Now,* June, 23.

CHAPTER 9

Older People as 'Participating Patients'

Rosemary Littlechild and Jon Glasby

Introduction

There is increasing recognition of the need for public participation in decision making concerning the nature and style of health services delivered to patients of the NHS (DoH 1997a). The NHS Executive (1996) summarised the reasons for giving this priority:

- Services are more likely to be effective if planned on the basis of needs identified with users

- Users of public services are themselves expecting and seeking to be involved in developing services

- Patients want more information about their health care

- Involving patients in their own care improves health outcomes and increases patient satisfaction

- As information improves about clinical effectiveness and outcomes, ways of communicating this to patients must be found, ensuring that the information reflects the patients' perspectives on the benefit of treatment.

The report *In the Public Interest* (NHS Executive, Institute of Health Service Management (IHSM), NHS Confederation 1998) recognises that there will barriers to overcome in developing a strategy for public participation in the NHS, including the need to develop the skills of health service professionals in working effectively in partnership with patients. It identifies four models of participation, stressing that there is no one 'right way' to achieve effective involvement but that the methods must be appropriately matched to the purpose and context of the consultation. The Health Secretary, Frank Dobson, announced in August 1998 that one way in which he intends to let patients have a voice is by commissioning the first large-scale national survey of patients' views and experiences of the NHS.

This trend for seeking users' views is replicated in the field of social care. Government guidance since the *Caring for People* White Paper (DoH 1989a) has stressed the centrality of carer and user involvement. A recent national review of social services concludes that the key to improving services is continuous effort to learn more from service users (Social Services Inspectorate/Audit Commission 1998). One of the targets in the social services assessment framework proposed in the White Paper *Modernising Social Services* (DoH 1998a) will be the quality of services from the perspective of users and carers. Means and Smith (1998) maintain that the rhetoric of user empowerment has given organisations of disabled people and service users some ammunition with local and central government to push for greater involvement. However, in reviewing the evidence from the last decade as to whether service users and carers generally have become more involved in planning their own care or in the development and monitoring of community care services, they conclude that the picture is less positive.

Barnes (1997) describes projects in which mental health users, people with learning disabilities and disabled people have organised themselves to be influential in having a say in the delivery of community care services. She asks, however, 'Is there a movement of older people?' (p.63). Evidence suggests that there are fewer initiatives involving older users in planning or evaluating services in the field of health or social care with some notable exceptions (see e.g. Barnes and Bennett 1998; Thornton and Tozer 1995a, 1995b).

This chapter describes how one project in south Birmingham did attempt to involve older people in the planning of services which might reduce emergency admissions to hospital. The project commissioned some research which used a radically different model to the usual quantitative approach to the issue, undertaking in-depth interviews with patients to gather *their* perceptions of their emergency admissions to hospital. The chapter describes the rationale for the research, the justification for the methodology, relevant ethical considerations, some of the findings and the implications for the delivery of health and social care services.

Background

The Emergency Hospital Admissions research project was commissioned by the Building Partnerships initiative, a joint venture between the Selly Park GP Commissioning Project (GPCP), Birmingham Social Services Department, the Southern Birmingham Community Health Trust and Birmingham Health Authority. The aim of Building Partnerships was to develop the co-ordinated commissioning of community-based services for the population of older people in the area. One of its main principles was that involving local people in decisions about commissioning would lead to better decision making and more responsive services.

A key priority was to reduce the number of emergency hospital admissions experienced by people aged 65 or over. As part of this process, a number of pilot schemes were set up, including a rapid response nursing team which sought to provide intensive nursing care in the home, increased domiciliary services and a late-afternoon assessment service to deal with borderline emergency admissions, referring those not deemed to require acute medical care to out-patient services or community hospital beds.

This local interest in emergency hospital admissions was mirrored by a national concern about the rise in emergency hospital admissions (Capewell 1996; Moore 1995; NHS Confederation 1997). Whilst most of the media interest has been focused on the crises that occur during the winter months, there is now evidence that these problems can occur at any time of the year (NHS Confederation 1997). In its report, *The Coming of Age* (1997), the Audit Commission drew attention to the vicious circle that leads to the increasing use of acute hospital beds by older people. It identified insufficient rehabilitation services and less money for preventative services as key factors in leading to admission or re-admission.

Specific policy measures to address some of these issues have included an additional £300 million allocated to the NHS to alleviate the pressure on health and social care services over the winter and a government circular *Better Services for Vulnerable People* requiring health and social services departments to co-ordinate relevant services through the production of joint investment plans (DoH 1997b).

It was against this background of national and local concern about rising hospital admissions of older people that the research was commissioned.

Aims of the research project

By investigating the social and medical factors which contribute to the emergency admission to hospital of older people from the GPCP population, the Selly Park Emergency Hospital Admissions project sought to identify those hospital admissions which might have been prevented and to analyse what alternative services or strategies could have been appropriate. It was anticipated that the findings of the study would inform the discussion about policies to reduce admissions for following years. The study was based on two key assumptions derived from local anecdotal evidence:

1. There are a significant number of isolated older people within the GPCP population whose hospital admissions are the result of social rather than medical factors and could therefore be prevented by alternative service provision.

2. Emergency admission to hospital represents a significant threshold for older people, prompting existing informal support to be replaced by formal support. Once this threshold has been crossed, informal support mechanisms begin to crumble, preventing the older person from returning home without extensive ongoing health and social services support.

To test these assumptions and to provide greater insight into the emergency hospital admission of older people, the present study sought to examine and analyse why older people had been admitted to hospital, whether they thought there might have been possible alternatives to admission, what kinds of services they received before admission and after discharge and how they perceived the whole experience.

Methodology

The admission and discharge of older people from hospital is a prime example of the convergence of primary health care, secondary health care and social care services. Despite the intention of the community care reforms to provide a 'seamless service' (Griffiths Report 1988), the evidence from the last decade suggests that this objective has not been achieved (Means and Smith 1998; Wistow 1995). During this time it is hospital discharge arrangements rather than admissions that have attracted the most attention from policy makers (DoH 1989b, 1994), professional bodies (British Geriatrics Society, Association of Directors of Social Services, Royal College of Nursing 1995) and researchers (e.g. Henwood et al. 1997; Henwood and Wistow 1994; Marks 1994; Neill and Williams 1992; Phillipson and Williams 1995).

Existing research on hospital admissions has a number of limitations. The appropriateness or otherwise of the initial hospital admission has received relatively little attention (Coast, Peters and Inglis 1996b). Instead many of the studies have concentrated upon the issue of inappropriate days of care and problems associated with delayed discharge (Victor et al. 1993). Early studies that did focus on hospital admission generally relied on professional opinion, with the researcher concerned deciding whether each admission was 'appropriate' or not (see e.g. Seymour and Pringle 1983; Stevens 1970). Such an approach has rightly been criticised for being too subjective (Coast et al. 1996b).

More recent studies on hospital admission have tended to focus upon the use of clinical review instruments, which are designed to provide objective criteria-based assessments of the appropriateness of hospital admissions and subsequent days of care. Examples used in recent UK studies include the Appropriateness Evaluation Protocol (AEP) (Audit Commission 1997; Smith et al. 1997; Tsang and Severs 1995), the Intensity-Severity-Discharge Review System with Adult Criteria (ISD-A) (Coast et al. 1995a, 1996a, 1996b) or the Oxford Bed Study Instrument (OBSI) (Victor and Khakoo 1994).

Although such clinical review instruments ensure a degree of objectivity and produce easily quantifiable data, there are five main limitations:

- The use of the OBSI to assess the appropriateness of hospital admission has been severely criticised (Coast et al. 1995b; Houghton 1995) and the ISD-A and AEP have been shown to overestimate the number of inappropriate admissions (Strumwasser et al. 1990)

- Such instruments fail to address the issue of *why* admissions judged 'inappropriate' were made

- Results take no account of the existence or availability of alternative service provision

- The instruments are applied retrospectively to the medical notes of each patient and therefore enjoy the benefit of hindsight

- Such an approach fails to consider the feelings or opinions of the individual patient and the professionals involved in his/her care.

For all these reasons, the Emergency Hospital Admissions research study adopted a more qualitative, user-centred methodology, collecting information from 52 patients (or the patient's main carer where appropriate) via semi-structured interviews in order to elicit a range of opinions on a wide variety of issues involving health and social care.

Ethics

Seeking to involve older service users in an evaluation of health and social service delivery raised three major ethical issues. First, it was necessary to recognise that every potential participant, by the very nature of the study, had recently been admitted to hospital as an emergency patient. Some may therefore still have been feeling unwell or have been experiencing a deterioration in their health or quality of life. It was important to ensure that they were not placed under undue pressure to take part in the study.

As a result, a system was established to protect the right to privacy of those who did not wish to be involved in the study. A letter was sent to potential participants asking them to telephone or write to the GPCP (in a prepaid envelope) if they were prepared to take part in the study. Only then were they contacted by telephone to arrange a convenient time for the interview to take place. Participants were given an exact time when the interviewer would visit and were shown a letter of introduction and an identity card with a photograph for security reasons.

A second ethical issue concerned the difficulty of engaging older people in detailed conversation about personal health issues. To prevent unnecessary embarrassment or breaches of privacy, the reasons for conducting the study and the purposes for which the information collected would be used were explained to every participant at the beginning of the interview and their contributions were anonymised. In addition, topics that participants did not want to discuss were dropped immediately. All participants spoke English as their first language and interviews were conducted in as sensitive and respectful a manner as possible. Whether or not a carer or family member was present was the decision of the older people themselves. Thirty people were interviewed alone, 20 were interviewed with a friend or family member and 2 people nominated their main carer to speak on their behalf.

A final consideration involved the role of the interviewer. Having visited service users in their homes, met their families and shared medical, personal and emotional experiences, the interviewer faced the risk of being 'pulled in' as an active participant in their lives. This was particularly the case with regard to three scenarios:

- Three participants took part in the study so that they could ask the interviewer to advocate on their behalf with service providers in cases where there was a dispute or an unresolved issue

- Some people were unsure whom to contact if their health deteriorated in the future, seeking advice from the interviewer about the nature of existing health and social service provision

- A minority of people confided in the researcher that they had experienced poor quality services, either before, during or after their admission to hospital.

In such situations, the interviewer felt a professional responsibility to advocate on behalf of those who expressed a desire for assistance. This involved providing up-to-date information to those who requested it and reporting back to the co-ordinators of Building Partnerships in order to rectify errors in current service provision and investigate allegations of poor service in the past. This resulted in a number of benefits for service users and led to three participants being referred to social services by the co-ordinators.

The research study can therefore be seen as a two-way process, gathering information about older people's experiences of emergency hospital admission on the one hand and providing practical support and assistance to those who requested it on the other.

Profile of the study group

Potential participants included people aged 65 and over who were registered with one of the GPCP practices and who had been admitted to the University Hospital Trust as emergency patients between December 1997 and March 1998 inclusive. Altogether, 250 people were eligible for the study and of these 59 died, moved or were too ill to participate. Of the remaining 191 people, 52 agreed to take part in the study (a response rate of 27%). There were 29 women and 23 men, a total of 20 aged between 65 and 74, 25 between 75 and 84 and 7 aged 85 years or over. The 52 people accounted for 63 emergency hospital admissions during the study period.

All 52 people were of white European origin. Nearly half (48%) defined themselves as fully independent, the remainder describing a spouse, children, formal carers or friends/neighbours as their main carers. Twenty-one people (40%) lived alone, 21 (40%) lived with their spouse only, 7 (13%) lived with other relatives and 3 (6%) lived in nursing or residential homes.

Findings – Challenging Images

Some findings from the study are presented below which illustrate the key themes expressed by the older people on their hospital admissions; sometimes these contrast sharply with the assumptions on which the research was based and with the media and public image of older people.

Assumptions underlying the study

Although local practitioners had suggested that many older people were being admitted to hospital for social reasons, the study found no evidence of this. On the contrary, every one of the 52 participants felt that their admissions had been caused by a medical emergency which required hospital treatment.

In the same way, the claim that hospital admission leads to a replacement of informal support by formal support was also shown to be inaccurate. On discharge, a number of people experienced changes but a significant proportion continued much the same as they had before. The most frequently mentioned change was greater informal support, and *nobody* experienced a reduction in informal support as a result of hospital admission.

Most importantly of all, however, the assumption that the study would identify practical policy measures to reduce the number of emergency admissions did not materialise. Although the study did reveal considerable scope for preventative work, this concept proved more complex than had been anticipated. Whilst all the participants felt that they had been admitted to hospital as a result of an immediate crisis in their medical condition, in 26 cases (41%) they felt that earlier action could have prevented the onset of the medical emergency which necessitated admission. For example:

> Mr D had heart trouble since a heart attack in 1994. Hospital staff debated whether to install a pacemaker, but decided against it. Mr D experienced four years of blackouts and ill-health before finally a pacemaker was installed after his emergency admission to hospital.

> Hospital staff told Mrs I that her second admission during the study period was caused by medication prescribed by her GP after her first admission.

Vitality of participants

Older people are often portrayed as a 'burden' on the resources of social services and the NHS and yet experience discrimination in health and other services (Age Concern 1998; Henwood 1990). There is no doubt that older people are major users of health and social services (Victor 1991) and that their health needs are often complex, straddling the boundaries of traditional service provision (Sidell 1995). However, the image of older people as frail and passive, dependent upon formal support services, was not borne out by this study.

Some participants, for whom this was one of a number of admissions in recent years, seemed frail and ill. The majority, for whom this was the first admission for many years, appeared healthy and active. For example:

> Mr B had trouble finding time to be interviewed. In the end he managed to meet the researcher just before his weekly darts match at a local social club. The week after the interview he and his wife were going to drive their caravan to Devon for a holiday. Mr B has been caravaning since 1965, but admits that he finds it hard work to drag the caravan from the back garden and attach it to the car since he is now 84.

Such vitality was reflected in a low level of service use, with 41 people (79%) using no community health or social services at all immediately prior to admission. At that time only one person was in direct contact with a social worker, although 11 people were receiving home care, day care or respite care and were therefore subject to review. In contrast, nearly two-thirds of the older people had seen or spoken to their GP on at least one occasion in the four weeks prior to their admission to hospital.

Routes to hospital

Although 34 (54%) of admissions were the result of a GP referral, many of the older people concerned had considered a range of alternatives before being admitted to hospital and their route there was often extremely complicated. Only two people dialled 999 direct, with the vast majority either contacting family members for advice or requesting an emergency visit from their GP. On a number of occasions, indeed, participants appeared reluctant to contact the emergency services directly. For example:

> One woman bruised her leg and fractured her elbow at a dance class, yet insisted that she was unhurt, returned home and only went to hospital on the advice of a neighbour. Even then, she refused to call an ambulance, choosing instead to walk to the nearest Accident and Emergency Department.

Although the study sought to define the older people's pathways to hospital in greater detail, this proved too complex to quantify. For example:

Mrs L fainted on the bus and had to be helped home by a passer-by. She consulted a neighbour, waited overnight and phoned her GP early the next morning. Her GP was unable to visit till after surgery, so Mrs L tried to walk to the practice. On arrival she fainted again and was helped onto the bed in the nurse's room. Her GP examined her, warned she may have a blood clot in her heart and tried to call an ambulance. Mrs L, however, wanted to collect some personal belongings from home and returned there against her GP's advice. En route she had to be helped home by some neighbours who themselves called an ambulance.

Patients' perception of admission, discharge and aftercare

Older people generally express high levels of satisfaction with services they receive (Wilson 1993) and indeed in this study, two-thirds of the emergency admissions were described as 'reassuring', for reasons such as the quality of hospital care, the availability of trained staff and a sense that someone was going to address their medical needs. Whilst in hospital, the vast majority of people were satisfied with their treatment, and many commented on the quality of care they received. For example: 'I don't think I could have got better treatment anywhere else. It was fantastic'; 'There's been so many complaints about the NHS recently and to be honest, I can't fault it at all.' Indeed, over one-third of the 52 participants reported that they had decided to take part in the present study specifically to counter negative stereotypes of the NHS, to express their satisfaction with their hospital stay or through gratitude for the help they had received.

However, 17 admissions were described as 'upsetting' for reasons such as fear of the unknown, physical pain, the trauma of leaving friends and family and waiting on hospital trolleys for long periods. Although not specifically asked, nine participants highlighted the fragmentation within and between the various health and social services they were receiving or had received in the past. Recurrent themes concerned difficulty in receiving home care on discharge, a lack of continuity and reliability among home carers and poor liaison between hospital and community services in general. For example:

> Mrs H was awaiting home care when she was re-admitted to hospital. After discharge she received a hospital home carer for two weeks, but had no contact with anyone after that finished. She had also been referred to the community dietician as she weighed just over four stone, yet the referral from hospital to community services appears to have been delayed or mishandled and Mrs H was left to rely on her daughter, herself disabled with a heart condition.

This fragmentation was exacerbated by the inaccessibility of certain services and a lack of knowledge about how to seek help in the community. A number of participants discussed with the researcher their difficulties in obtaining appropriate services. Others felt that they could manage at present, but were unsure whom to contact if they needed support in the future, or whether they would be entitled to help. As a result, several people sought advice from the researcher about the nature of existing service provision and the options available to them.

Information on medical condition

Of the 63 admissions, 36 (57%) were the result of known conditions. However, although almost all the participants could give a basic description of why they had been admitted to hospital, at least ten people were unsure as to a precise diagnosis or the exact nature of their condition. 'I don't know what was wrong with me exactly, I just know it was my chest' was a common response, as was the insistence that 'they didn't know what the matter with me was – or if they did they didn't tell me.'

Concerns for carers

A number of older people were concerned about what would happen if their carer, often an elderly spouse, became ill. This danger was also appreciated by the carers themselves, many of whom felt under pressure to remain as healthy as possible so that they could continue in their role as carer. For example:

> A 66-year-old man has been caring for his wife 24 hours per day since she had a stroke in 1994. Her condition has recently deteriorated following a second stroke and the amputation of her leg due to a gangrenous bedsore. He participated in the study specifically to highlight the burden of caring.

Discussion and Implications of Findings

The nature of the in-depth interviews conducted for this study meant that the older people provided a wealth of information and opinions on a wide range of issues. However, this discussion of the study as an example of patient involvement in research will focus on four key issues:

- research methodology
- outcomes for the older people
- implications for service developments
- implications for the practice and training of health care professionals.

Research methodology

This qualitative approach to gathering information about the nature of admissions of older people to hospital has indicated that the value of research into emergency hospital admissions, where data is of a quantitative nature only, is limited. Such statistics give no account of the immediate context in which people are admitted, the availability of other services or the complexity of people's routes to hospital. What has become apparent in this study is that whilst people said unanimously that their admissions were *appropriate* (i.e. they needed hospital treatment for a legitimate medical complaint), many were also able to identify another course of treatment that might have *prevented* their emergency hospital admission.

This distinction has been largely ignored in recent literature on inappropriate hospital admissions, where the power to define admissions as appropriate or not has been with the professionals or via a review instrument. In this study the older people themselves made their own definitions and the results revealed a subtle difference between inappropriate and preventable admissions.

The information gathered from the older people has also indicated that the two assumptions on which the study was based were largely unfounded. Although local practitioners had suggested that a significant number of older people were admitted to hospital for social reasons and that emergency admission prompted a replacement of informal by formal support, the study suggests that the opposite is true. Every participant was admitted for medical reasons and a significant number experienced greater informal support as the main change in their care arrangements after discharge.

Outcomes for the older people

Many initiatives involving services users have been set up to get feedback on existing services in order to make further improvements (Barnes and Walker 1996). However, for some older people such a long-term perspective on service development may not be appropriate and it is important that the process of participation is an end in itself as well as a means to improving services. Barnes and Walker (1996), in identifying the key principles that should underlie any attempt to empower older service users of health and social care services, argue that 'Empowerment should enable personal development as well as increasing influence over services' (p.381).

In this research study the initial intention was largely service-focused – to understand the circumstances leading to the admission to hospital of the older people in order to examine the scope for developing alternative services. However, there are indications that for some people the interview process was indeed an end in itself. Many people said quite spontaneously that they had wanted to have their views heard about the good treatment they had received in order to counteract the largely negative media reports of the NHS. Other people had not been satisfied with the services they were currently receiving and their interview with the researcher precipitated a re-examination of their circumstances. Knowingly, or unknowingly, they had used the researcher as an advocate on their behalf and as a result experienced an improvement in services. Others were given more information for future reference about existing health and social care provision.

Implications for service developments

Since the research was commissioned the government has announced its intention to legislate to make it easier for health and social services to work together (DoH 1998b). Following the publication of this research and the evaluation of a number of local 'winter pressures' projects, managers in health and social services in this authority have already identified four priority areas where service developments have, or will, take place:

- The majority of older people in the study came to the attention of health or social services only as a result of their emergency admissions. A jointly funded Healthy Alliance worker has been employed to work in a preventative capacity, identifying the needs of older people, *including* those who would not necessarily come into contact with many health and social services. She is therefore in an ideal position to deliver health promotion messages in the community.

- Over half the admissions in the study were as a result of known illnesses and many of the older people may have benefited from more advice about their condition and how to manage it. An appointment has been made from core health funding of a chronic obstructive pulmonary disease nurse who will identify people who are admitted to hospital with lung disease. Their needs will be assessed and their condition will continue to be monitored once they return to the community, with the intention of cutting down the number of re-admissions.

- The absence of social services involvement in the majority of cases in the study and the older people's perception of the fragmentation of services was of concern to the agencies. They are therefore proposing a further research project which would undertake an audit of services provided to older people in a particular area by health and social care agencies to identify where the gaps and overlaps might be. These perceptions would also be compared with the views of users themselves.

- Providing appropriate support to carers has been marked as the final priority area. To date a number of small local initiatives have been iden-tified, as yet linked by no coherent plan. The government's strategy 'Caring about Carers', launched in February 1999, should provide direc-tion and impetus to the development of a local policy.

Implications for the practice and training of health care professionals

> *When patients are well informed and are active participants in decision making about their own care and treatment, outcomes are improved. There are fewer complaints, greater satisfaction with health services and more appropriate use of services.* (our italics, NHS Executive, IHSM, NHS Confederation 1998, p.3)

The importance of clear communication and good information was a recurrent theme in this research study:

- There were examples of incidences where people were left confused about their care or positively discouraged from seeking information (Glasby 1999).

- Prior to admission the older people had considered their condition carefully and were reluctant to contact the emergency services directly. It appears that many people had internalised recent media reports of bed shortages and the inappropriate use of hospital services by older people. As one woman put it, 'I always feel like I'm wasting the doctor's time… I thought someone would need the bed more than me.'

- Although the study attempted to track the patients' routes to hospital, the information was too diverse to quantify. Older people in particular are likely to consult family or friends before taking action about their own health care (Rogers and Elliott 1997) and examples from the study showed that many of the patients arrived in hospital only after a complex sequence of events. General information about when to access emergency services is therefore crucial to ensure that older people do not *underuse* them.

- The question about how information is most appropriately delivered to older people is pertinent. In this study, the older people who were interviewed were not large consumers of health and social care services. The majority of people were not in contact with health or social care professionals in the community. The exception was their GP, whom two-thirds of the sample had spoken to in the month before their hospital admissions. This suggests that members of new primary care groups are key players in the dissemination of information which will help people make informed decisions about their own health care.

- There is recognition by the NHS Executive (NHS Executive 1996; NHS Executive, IHSM, NHS Confederation 1998) that the notion of partnership between health care professionals and patients will present some real barriers that have to be overcome. These include the attitude of some staff, a lack of skills and expertise, concern about the length of time taken to inform and consult patients thoroughly and expectations of creating more demanding patients. These will need to be addressed at both national and local level through professional and in-service training and the adoption of a strategy which will ensure that public participation is apparent and integrated in all areas of policy and practice.

Conclusion

This research was designed primarily to identify services that might prevent the emergency admissions of some older people to hospital. However, the rich qualitative data that was produced has meant that as a pilot study, it can contribute to a much wider debate about older people and their use of social and health care services.

It shows that older people can be willing and able participants in research studies. The relative neglect of attempts to seek their views and understand their perceptions of health care may be the result of an image of older people as passive recipients of services. Older people are often portrayed as being a drain on the resources of health and other services and yet the evidence suggests that they experience discrimination in many areas of service delivery (Age Concern 1998; McEwen 1990). In this study, although many of the participants were concerned that older people may be seen as using hospital services inappropriately, in reality they themselves used very few services, considered a range of alternatives before admission and were admitted for legitimate medical reasons. All too often the popular images of older people are based not on reality but on stereotypes and there is a risk that these images can become ingrained in professional beliefs and service provision.

This study has highlighted the importance of a qualitative perspective on what had previously been dominated by statistical analyses of hospital admissions. It shows clearly that an understanding of both the events prior to admission and of the factors that have influenced the ways that people manage their health *from the point of view of older people themselves* is important in planning appropriate services and designing preventative health promotion initiatives.

What the study lacks is a similarly detailed perspective from any health or social care workers. Further research might consider the encounters between older people and health and social care professionals to provide a more complete understanding of the factors which influence older people's beliefs and decisions about health care.

Acknowledgements

We are grateful to Conrad Parke, then Partnership Co-ordinator, Birmingham Social Services, Lucy Tye, then Project Officer, Selly Park GP Commissioning Project and Billy Foreman, Birmingham Health Authority, for their help in providing comments and information for this chapter.

References

Age Concern (1998) *Age Discrimination: Make it a Thing of the Past.* London: Age Concern England.

Audit Commission (1997) *The Coming of Age: Improving Care Services for Older People.* London: Audit Commission.

Barnes, M. (1997) *Care, Communities and Citizens.* Harlow: Longman.

Barnes, M. and Bennett, G. (1998) 'Frail Bodies, Courageous Voices: Older People Influencing Community Care.' *Health & Social Care in the Community 6,* 2, 102–111.

Barnes, M. and Walker, A. (1996) 'Consumerism versus Empowerment: A Principled Approach to the Involvement of Older Service Users.' *Policy and Politics 24,* 4, 375–393.

British Geriatrics Society, Association of Directors of Social Services, Royal College of Nursing (1995) *The Discharge of Elderly People from Hospital for Community Care.* London: British Geriatrics Society.

Capewell, S. (1996) 'The Continuing Rise in Emergency Admissions: Explanations and Responses Must be Properly Evaluated.' *British Medical Journal 312,* 991–992.

Coast, J., Inglis, A., Morgan, K., Gray, S., Kammerling, M. and Frankel, S. (1995a) 'The Hospital Admissions Study in England: Are There Alternatives to Emergency Hospital Admission?' *Journal of Epidemiology and Community Health 49,* 194–199.

Coast, J., Inglis, A., Frankel, S., Gray, S. and Peters, T. (1995b) 'Is Hospital the Right Place?' *Journal of Public Health Medicine 17,* 2, 239–240.

Coast, J., Inglis, A. and Frankel, S. (1996a) 'Alternatives to Hospital Care: What are They and Who Should Decide?' *British Medical Journal 312,* 162–166.

Coast, J., Peters, A. and Inglis, A. (1996b) 'Factors Associated with Inappropriate Emergency Hospital Admission in the UK.' *International Journal for Quality in Health Care 8,* 1, 31–39.

Department of Health (1989a) *Caring for People: Community Care in the Next Decade and Beyond.* London: HMSO.

Department of Health (1989b) *Discharge of Patients from Hospital.* Circular HC(89)5. London, HMSO.

Department of Health (1994) *Hospital Discharge Workbook: A Manual on Hospital Discharge Practice.* London: Department of Health.

Department of Health (1997a) *The New NHS: Modern, Dependable.* London: HMSO.

Department of Health (1997b) *Better Services for Vulnerable People.* Circular EL(97)62. London: HMSO.

Department of Health (1998a) *Modernising Social Services.* London: HMSO.

Department of Health (1998b) *Partnership in Action (New Opportunities for Joint Working between Health and Social Services).* London: HMSO.

Glasby, J. (1999) 'The Art of Conversation.' *Care: The Journal of Practice and Development 7,* 2, 20–26.

Griffiths Report (1988) *Community Care: An Agenda for Action.* London: HMSO.

Henwood, M. (1990) 'No Sense of Urgency: Age Discrimination in Health Care.' In E. McEwen (ed) *Age: The Unrecognised Discrimination.* London: Age Concern England.

Henwood, M., Hardy, B., Hudson, B. and Wistow, G. (1997) *Inter-Agency Collaboration: Hospital Discharge and Continuing Care Sub-Study – Final Report.* Leeds: Nuffield Institute for Health, Community Care Division.

Henwood, M. and Wistow, G. (1994) *Hospital Discharge and Community Care: Early Days.* Leeds: Nuffield Institute for Health, Community Care Division.

Houghton, A. (1995) 'Is Hospital the Right Place?' *Journal of Public Health Medicine 17,* 2, 239.

Marks, L. (1994) *Seamless Care or Patchwork Quilt? Discharging Patients from Acute Hospital Care* Research report 17. London: King's Fund Institute.

McEwen, E. (ed) (1990) *The Unrecognised Discrimination.* London: Age Concern.

Means, R. and Smith, R. (1998) *Community Care.* Second edition. Basingstoke: Macmillan.

Moore, W. (1995) *Emergency Admissions: The Management Challenge.* Birmingham: National Association of Health Authorities and Trusts.

Neill, J. and Williams, J. (1992) *Leaving Hospital: Elderly People and their Discharge to Community Care.* London: HMSO.

NHS Confederation (1997) *Tackling Emergency Admissions: Policy into Practice.* Birmingham: NHS Confederation.

NHS Executive (1996) *Patient Partnership: Building a Collaborative Strategy.* Leeds: NHS Executive.

NHS Executive, Institute of Health Service Management, NHS Confederation (1998) *In the Public Interest: Developing a Strategy for Public Participation in the NHS.* Wetherby: Department of Health.

Phillipson, J. and Williams, J. (1995) *Action on Hospital Discharge.* London: National Institute for Social Work.

Rogers, A. and Elliott, H. (1997) *Primary Care: Understanding Health Need and Demand.* Oxford: Radcliffe Medical Press.

Seymour, D. and Pringle, R. (1983) 'Surgical Emergencies in the Elderly: Can they be Prevented?' *Health Bulletin 41,* 3, 112–131.

Sidell, M. (1995) *Health in Old Age: Myth, Mystery and Management.* Buckingham: Open University Press.

Smith, H., Pryce, A., Carlisle, L., Jones, J., Scarpello, J. and Pantin, C. (1997) 'Appropriateness of Acute Medical Admissions and Length of Stay.' *Journal of the Royal College of Physicians of London 31,* 5, 527–532.

Social Services Inspectorate/Audit Commission (1998) *Getting the Best from Social Services: Learning the Lessons from Joint Reviews.* London: Audit Commission.

Stevens, R. (1970) 'Reasons for Admitting Patients to Geriatric Hospitals'. *Gerontologica Clinica 12,* 219–228.

Strumwasser, I., Paranjpe, N., Ronis, D., Share, D. and Sell, L. (1990) 'Reliability and Validity of Utilization Review Criteria.' *Medical Care 28,* 2, 95–111.

Thornton, P. and Tozer, R. (1995a) *Involving Older People in Planning and Evaluating Community Care: A Review of Initiatives.* York: Social Policy Research Unit, University of York.

Thornton, P. and Tozer, R. (1995b) *Having a Say in Change: Older People and Community Care.* York: Joseph Rowntree Foundation.

Tsang, P. and Severs, M. (1995) 'A Study of Appropriateness of Acute Geriatric Admissions and an Assessment of the Appropriateness Evaluation Protocol.' *Journal of the Royal College of Physicians of London 29,* 4, 311–314.

Victor, C., Nazareth, B., Hudson, M. and Fulop, N. (1993) 'The Inappropriate Use of Acute Hospital Beds in an Inner London District Health Authority.' *Health Trends 25,* 3, 94–97.

Victor, C. and Khakoo, A. (1994) 'Is Hospital the Right Place? A Survey of "Inappropriate" Admissions to an Inner London NHS Trust.' *Journal of Public Health Medicine 16,* 3, 286–290.

Wilson, G. (1993) 'Users and Providers: Perspectives on Community Care Services.' *Journal of Social Policy 22,* 507–527.

Wistow, G. (1995) 'Aspirations and Realities: Community Care at the Cross-Roads.' *Health and Social Care in the Community 3,* 4, 227–240.

CHAPTER 10

Working with Sickle Cell/ Thalassaemia Support Groups

Simon Dyson

Introduction

This chapter will report on the processes of research in working with support groups for sickle cell anaemia and beta-thalassaemia in conducting community-based surveys of knowledge of these two inherited blood conditions. The conditions have received little official recognition (Anionwu 1993; DoH 1993) and such relative neglect has left carers facing considerable challenges (Ahmad and Atkin 1996). The research aimed to find out what knowledge the communities had about the conditions. It aimed to question an equal number of those who were carriers for sickle cell or thalassaemia and those who were not. Knowledge was defined in a rather narrow technical sense (see Kerr, Cunningham-Burley and Amos 1998 for a criticism of this focus). The conditions primarily, although not exclusively, affect peoples of African-Caribbean and South Asian descent (Anionwu 1993). The research entailed support- group members of African-Caribbean descent and of South Asian descent interviewing members of minority ethnic groups in the community.

The respondents were drawn from a list of names and addresses of those tested for sickle cell and thalassaemia by the local hospital laboratory services. Following approval from the Medical Ethics Committee, and subject to the opportunity for the patient's GP to withdraw their client from the study, the lists were given to the author and in turn the groups. Half the respondents were carriers for the respective genetic condition and half were not carriers. Neither the author nor the interviewers were to know the carrier status of individual interviewees and the lists were merged into one in alphabetical order before being released to the author and interviewers. A more 'traditional' account of the results is given in Dyson (1997) and (2000), which discuss the technical knowledge the respective communities have of sickle cell and beta-thalassaemia. The interpretation of events in the research process has partly been made possible by three tape-recorded debriefing interviews of over an hour with five of the interviewers on the projects.

The chapter begins with an outline of the origins of the projects, emphasising the importance of the social and political context of research in setting the agenda, formulating the research question, and influencing the scope and timescale of the research and the attitudes of interviewers and respondents. These constraints are contrasted with certain ideals of anti-oppressive research contained in the literature.

The chapter then considers the consequences of involving service users as interviewers in the research process. A number of strengths and weaknesses in respect of this involvement are identified in respect of traditional conceptions of the quality of data such as reliability and validity.

The competing claims of empowerment and scientific truth to be the guiding value of social research are briefly discussed. It is argued that *both* researchers and communities of interest have skills relevant to the maximising of counterfactual critical reflection on the social world.

Finally, the outcomes of the projects for the service provision, for the interviewers and for the communities interviewed are reviewed. In conclusion it is suggested that claims to empower clients through the research process have been overstated and that critical social research constitutes a more circumspect ambition for researching with service users.

Project Origins

This section will examine the consequences of the particular origins of user involvement in the research. User involvement in the research process was not in this instance an initial value commitment but a pragmatic response to research that was already underway. The project was initiated by a junior doctor whilst completing her six months' training in public health. A senior public health doctor with responsibility for planning public health services had in turn suggested the project to her. The author in his role as a university lecturer was then approached in 1992 by the junior doctor, on the grounds that he had previous experience of conducting a community survey on thalassaemia (see Dyson, Davis and Rahman 1993b) and had developed a structured interview schedule for that purpose (Dyson, Davis and Rahman 1993a). A small amount of money was available from clinical audit funds to support the study. To this extent the author is testimony to the point made by Hammersley (1995) that conceptions of the researcher as powerful have been overstated, since what the author felt was responsibility for the research process, without the power.

The author approached the local self-help groups, with whom he had worked for nearly ten years, to ask if they were prepared to act as community interviewers on the project. In retrospect it is difficult to be clear about precise motivations but the following factors were influential to a greater or lesser extent.

1. The short time scale involved. There were only six further months during which a population that had been screened for sickle cell/thalassaemia would be available before the proposed appointment of a specialist nurse counsellor, and during which an audit of what was occurring in the absence of such a post could be conducted.

2. The fact that there was some money to support the community interviewers (£500 for each support group) to be paid from health authority clinical audit funds. Between 1986 and 1990 the author (as a health promotion worker then employed by the health authority) had worked with the two support groups in conducting training seminars for health workers, social workers, teachers and youth workers. The author and the respective groups had also organised community conferences for 40 and 110 people respectively in 1988. The support groups had themselves funded to the tune of £1,000 a postgraduate GP-training approved conference on sickle cell and thalassaemia for GPs, midwives and nurses and had provided a further £100 for a seminar for health authority decision-makers in 1990. Although the project entailed considerable work for the support groups, as we shall see, it did offer an opportunity to replenish the funds the groups had spent in health promotion initiatives – initiatives one might regard as properly the responsibility of the health authority itself.

3. The opportunity for a limited form of ethnic matching of interviewers and interviewees that using support-group members facilitated. Using support-group members also meant drawing upon people already relatively knowledgeable about sickle cell/thalassaemia.

4. Although the support-group members for thalassaemia were not trained interpreters, the ability of such interviewers to mix and match English, Gujarati and Hindustani (i.e. the spoken word of both Hindi and Urdu scripts) was a consideration. Whilst the importance of professional interpretation is usually held to be paramount (Ahmad, Kernohan and Baker 1989; Ahmad and Walker 1997), Atkin, Ahmad and Anionwu (1998) have found that the lack of condition-specific knowledge on the part of generic health service interpreters has led to clients experiencing difficulties in obtaining a good-quality service for sickle cell/thalassaemia. It was felt that there was no better group to uncover views on thalassaemia using several languages contingently than a group who have to represent themselves and their families as thalassaemia advocates as part of their everyday life in relating to English-speaking professionals, Gujarati-speaking relatives and Hindi/Urdu-speaking neighbours and priests.

5. The support groups themselves conceived of the process as a particular form of educational opportunity which, by surveying technical knowledge

of sickle cell/thalassaemia, facilitated a broader form of education that entailed respect for people with the conditions and their families.

6. The support groups wished to see the development of sickle cell/thalassaemia services in the locality, and in common with the author felt that the research was part of the process of consolidating the health authority's decision to appoint specialist nurse counsellors for sickle cell/thalassaemia.

Therefore, the genesis of the study differs from the anti-oppressive ideal delineated by Oliver (1992) in key respects:

1. Service users did not identify the 'research question'

2. The initial design as a questionnaire-survey was not negotiated with service users

3. The involvement of community members as data collectors was at least partially driven by considerations of minimising costs

4. The community members were only partially integrated into the analysis of data stage (at least from the point of view of the public health department)

5. The commissioners of the research did not specify in advance that they were prepared to instigate changes to services on the basis of the research findings. Neither did they specify in advance the nature or the extent of the dissemination of results that they were prepared to undertake.

It further differs from the observation of Humphries (1997) that reflexive researcher-centred accounts (rather than accounts written by interviewers or communities) still frame the researcher as the referent or norm.

On the other hand it is arguable that awaiting perfect conditions before intervening in the social world is itself a recipe for underpinning the *status quo*. To the best of my knowledge the decision to fund earlier conferences for the health authority and to take part in the research reported here represents the majority outcomes of self-help group discussions. In these discussions all acknowledged that the health authority should be doing more – funding specialist nurse counsellors many years before they actually did, funding health promotion initiatives themselves rather than relying on self-help group funds, funding research fully rather than relying on the goodwill of support groups as community interviewers. However, the strategy that prevailed in each instance was one of making voluntary group contributions, whether of time, money or both, in the hope of encouraging/cajoling the health authority into taking its responsibilities for sickle cell/thalassaemia service provision seriously. The alternative view, that in making such contributions the groups were inadvertently helping the health authority to escape its responsibilities to minority ethnic communities was strongly argued by some support-group members, but was not eventually upheld.

Effects of User Involvement in the Research Process

User involvement in researching the community knowledge of sickle cell/thalassaemia frequently had contradictory effects. In this section I examine issues concerned with gaining access to respondents; the quality of data obtained; the degree of mutuality between author and the community interviewers; and the degree of reciprocity between interviewers and respondents.

In terms of gaining access to respondents the utilization of service users as interviewers was crucial. Their behaviour stands in sharp contrast to the classic situations reported by Roth (1966) in which 'hired hand' researchers act in the time-honoured manner of many poorly paid workers at the bottom of organizational hierarchies and minimise effort, fabricate data and collaborate just long enough to deceive quality checks. The service users as researchers appeared to go to extraordinary lengths to secure community involvement, returning to an address five or six times to obtain the interview, for example.

Ten per cent (22) of addresses were missing from the original lists and a further 20 per cent (44) of addresses were different from the then separate Family Health Services Authority records against which addresses were cross-checked. Despite these difficulties the interviewers obtained a 50 per cent response rate across the sickle cell and thalassaemia projects (55 out of 104 for the sickle cell project and 55 out of 116 for the thalassaemia project). The allegedly 'poor response rate' was the sole reason given when an article on the research was rejected by a refereed journal. In retrospect perhaps a response rate of 71 per cent should have been claimed by the author (i.e. 110 out of the 154 potential respondents for whom even a potentially up-to-date address was available), since the failure was the quality of record keeping on the part of the service provider (specifically the various GPs and hospital departments requesting blood tests rather than the haematology department itself), not the service users as interviewers.

The interviewers also obtained new addresses not known to the service provider and followed these up on their own initiative. Where the named person was found, the new address was offered to the official register (although, interestingly these 'corrections' were declined by the service providers). The interviews were completed despite two of the sickle cell interviewers working 50 hours a week on shifts and others having child care responsibilities and worries, for example, about whether they could still complete the interview and collect their children from the mosque in time. A number mentioned the length of time they took to persuade respondents to take part. In doing this interviewers talked about calling on community solidarity ('unless we do this things will not get better for our community').

Four community interviewers took their own haemoglobinopathy cards stating their own carrier status and were prepared to discuss their own cases and families at considerable length in order to co-opt the interviewees. One interviewer reported returning to sit in her car for 40 minutes in order to let a potential respondent complete the viewing of her favourite television programme, before going back to complete the interview successfully. This enthusiasm also had its down side, as one sickle cell interviewer overstepped certain ethical boundaries by declaring himself a carrier when he knew he was not 'in order to make the respondent feel better'. In another complex example, another interviewer, whilst resisting the imputation of stigma for the thalassaemia in his family, was not above ascribing a different stigma of his own to a respondent. He continued to interview an elderly respondent (described as sickly and 'looking like' he had tuberculosis!) despite the perceived risk to himself of contracting that infectious disease.

In summary, user involvement in research may have benefits in terms of the *reliability* of research to the extent that users are prepared to report rather than hide variations in the procedures for collecting data between themselves and others, and between their process of involvement on different occasions. It may also have some advantages in *external validity* to the extent that they successfully co-opt greater proportions of respondents in communities who might conceivably resist 'traditional' research because they feel it to be exploitative.

I turn now to the relation of the interviewers to the quality or *internal validity* of data obtained. One of the principle advantages of service-user involvement with research appears to be that users can bring an insider's perspective to bear on the interpretation of data. This has methodological parallels to the power of the lay perspective (Stacey 1994) and to the notion of a 'key informant' in ethnographic research (Burgess 1984; Miles and Huberman 1994; Whyte 1984), though an uncritical adoption of an insider perspective has also been seen as a weakness of ethnography (Hammersley 1992). Four of the thalassaemia interviewers who took part in debriefing interviews with the author commented on the anxiety of those interviewed concerning being seen to know about a stigmatising condition. Some Hindu families who knew they had been tested for thalassaemia felt threatened by the very offer of an interview because they perceived it to undermine their test result which identified their family as 'clear' (i.e. as not being carriers for beta-thalassaemia). It is at least plausible, therefore, that some of the respondents may have underplayed their technical knowledge of the condition. Perhaps of more importance is that, unlike the Pakistani Moslem clients in other research on thalassaemia who are reported not to stigmatize the condition of thalassaemia, possibly owing to the practice of consanguinity (Darr 1990), here some clients of Indian Hindu descent did appear to stigmatise thalassaemia.

Once into the interview itself, the interviewers reported their perceptions of the influence of others present on the replies given. One example was given of a Gujarati mother-in-law who instructed her daughter-in-law that her answers to the multiple-choice questions of technical knowledge of beta-thalassaemia were 'don't know'. The daughter-in-law apparently suppressed her knowledge of the condition until the mother-in-law had left the room. At this point she was able to produce the haemoglobinopathy card (a card from the health service stating that her blood had been tested and her status as a carrier) – a card she had denied ever having seen when asked earlier in the interview.

At another interview, conducted jointly by a male and female interviewer married to each other, a Gujarati mother was reported to have been led in her replies by her husband, and allegedly colluded with professed ignorance of the issues, whilst simultaneously communicating concern by eye contact with the female interviewer. She also asked, whilst her husband was engaged in answering the telephone, for clarification as to whether the issue might affect her children (which of course it conceivably could). The female interviewer expressed the opinion that the mother had tested positive for beta-thalassaemia but had neither raised the subject with her husband nor had fully understood or investigated the implications of being a carrier. Here the fact that the interviewers and interviewees were married partners of the same ethnic origin was perhaps vital to facilitating this particular interpretation. On the other hand in certain circumstances people are more prepared to talk to outsiders to the community (Rhodes 1994), and the desirability and consequences of matching interviewers for ethnicity is something that must be judged contextually, and not programmatically read as a measure of the progressiveness of the research.

To summarise, service users as researchers may help estimate the correspondences of meanings between researcher and participants in the data at the several levels identified by Cicourel (1964). They can help clarify the *meanings of individual words* in some instances by sharing aspects of their technical knowledge. They can interpret *cultural significance of interactions,* noting for example when resistance to answering questions signifies a stigmatising of the condition of thalassaemia. And they can help convey the sense of *alternative realms of social significance* that an issue may hold for community members beyond any technical knowledge.

With respect to the levels of mutuality between research co-ordinator and community interviewers, there were again positives and negatives. On the positive side the interviewers themselves took control of decisions about who should interview whom, though this in turn had implications for the level of reciprocity between community interviewers and community respondents (discussed further below). Both the author and the community interviewers bore considerable costs associated with the project (travel, telephone, and meeting rooms that were unpaid, and time, which was underpaid). Though this was borne equally, the impact would not of course have been equal in terms of the overall level of income and point of the cycle of family life (such as the financial pressures of newborn children) of both the author and the interviewers.

However, the interviewers did express a variety of non-financial benefits that they felt they obtained from participation in the research. For one female Gujarati interviewer, interviewing, and indeed her overall involvement in thalassaemia politics, was explicitly viewed as the one legitimate reason by which she could publicly justify moving her daily activities beyond the domestic sphere. This seems to echo the controversial thesis that the realms of health and education represent an opportunity for some women to escape the patriarchal family at the expense of being co-opted by the state to police the population's health and educational behaviour (Donzelot 1979). Yet another female Gujarati interviewer felt that her involvement in the interviewing was part of her working through her own sense of isolation, an isolation that what Goffman (1968) called the 'courtesy stigma' of being the mother of an affected child had helped to create.

For a male Gujarati interviewer it was an opportunity not only to consolidate his knowledge about thalassaemia, but also to acquire interviewing skills which he said raised his self-esteem during a period of unemployment. Moreover, he felt he needed repeatedly to explain not only technical facts about thalassaemia, but also the personal experience of thalassaemia in the family that lay behind his own involvement in the research. He felt that as a consequence he was now more confident overall to represent himself to his community as the father of a child with thalassaemia.

On the other hand there were areas where reciprocity between the author and interviewers was poor. The author would have been insured as an employee of a university. As volunteers the interviewers were not insured. The author also gave insufficient thought to the issue of safety of female interviewers. One African-Caribbean interviewer said that she felt too intimidated to enter a tower block at night when a male voice answered the intercom, even though it was probably the male respondent who was due to be interviewed. Another was approached in the passageway by a male neighbour who wanted to know why she was looking for him and although he was entirely helpful, the incident unnerved her. Finally, one interviewer commented that in another paid interviewing job the issuing of identity cards and professional-looking clipboards to interviewers had made him feel valued – in stark contrast to the second-hand cardboard folders issued by the author in this study to save costs.

A less well-examined aspect of collaborative research is the degree to which community interviewers achieve a non-hierarchical relationship with their interviewees. It is important therefore to consider also the levels of mutuality between community interviewers and their community respondents in these projects.

One way in which greater access to data was obtained by the use of service-user interviewers concerns the relation of particular interviewers to particular respondents. In a small number of instances a name on the list was a person known to one or more members of the support group. The initial allocation of respondents to interview had been made by the author on the basis of allocating blocks of 10 or 20 from the alphabetical list to particular interviewers. The interviewers themselves contingently reallocated respondents not only on the basis of geographical proximity to their own address, but on occasions in relation to whether or not they knew the person concerned. Neither was such reallocation effected in the same manner on each occasion. On discovering that they knew the respondent, the interviewer proceeded in one of three ways:

1. The *interviewer* decided that they were the most appropriate person to conduct the interview and proceeded accordingly.

2. The *interviewer* decided that the respondent would prefer someone they did not know and passed the respondent on to another interviewer.

3. The *respondent* was contacted and (if willing to be interviewed at all) was asked whether they would prefer the interview to be conducted by the person they knew or a person they did not know.

Only in the third instance could one claim that a degree of choice over the terms of their inclusion in the research had been offered to the respondent.

The complexities of the relationship between the interviewers and the respondents are indicated by the following example. One male Moslem interviewer, interviewing a male Moslem he described as having 'traditional' and 'religious' views, found that the presence of the respondent's teenage daughters meant that clarification of the questions was possible with them in English as well as in Urdu with the father. From the point of view of the interviewer, the young women's role in helping the interviewer to gauge the extent to which their father had understood the questions became secondary to the fact that the interviewer felt that he was able to offer the daughters an opportunity to receive some information about thalassaemia. The daughters confirmed to him in English that this was an opportunity they wanted. The interviewer implied that the father may have wished to censor this information had it been self-consciously directed at the daughters rather than appearing to be incidental to their facilitation of the interview. Since the interviewer possibly contravened the spirit of the father's wishes but acceded to the expressed wishes of the daughters for technical information (albeit that the latter expressed need was itself socially constructed by the interview situation), it is difficult to argue that 'community' interests were served, since there were lines of cleavage in terms of gender, generation, disability and degree of religious orthodoxy. Claims that such a research process is empowering are difficult to sustain in the face of such complexity.

In this section we have examined the nature of the impact made by the participation in research of service users as interviewers. There are both pros and cons in terms of gaining access to respondents and in relation to the emerging quality of the data. There are also variable levels of reciprocity between author and interviewers on the one hand and between interviewers and community respondents on the other. The apparent tension between the pursuit of objective knowledge and empowering clients through research is, of course, a keenly contested arena, and one to which the chapter now turns.

Empowerment and Truth as Values in Research

Views on the possibility and desirability of social research empowering clients (e.g. Hammersley 1995; Humphries and Truman 1994; Oliver 1992) are complex and only a brief discussion is possible here.

Hammersley and Gomm (1997) have argued that a recognition that the production of research is dependent upon the social position of the researcher does not require that the researcher give up the aim of objectivity. They also propose that a research community is likely to be relatively more sceptical in examining truth claims (presumably than other geographical communities or communities of interest) where the primary objective of research is to avoid presenting as true that which is false. Hammersley (1995) has further indicated a belief that such terms of reference for research help to keep it relatively autonomous from the state and other political interests.

Romm (1997) has replied that Hammersley and Gomm do not consider views on knowledge construction which try to form relationships that do not privilege particular ways of accounting at the expense of others. Lather (1991) contends that research processes can make a difference to the lives of others by changing their conceptions of possibilities for seeing and acting. Romm (1997) therefore charges researchers with a responsibility to provide others with maximum opportunities to develop constructions and choices.

Meanwhile Humphries (1997) has argued that both objective truth-science and emancipatory research appeal to modern meta-narratives of emancipation and will-to-power. She follows Foucault (1993) in arguing that liberty is a practice that may only be exercised contextually, never possessed ahistorically, and she thereby also follows Gore (1993) and Troyna (1994) in contending that emancipation cannot be conferred by one group upon another.

Briefly, it seems to me that Hammersley's characterization of academic research communities has two major problems. One is that, as with natural science (Kuhn 1962) and genetic sciences (Kerr, Cunningham-Burley and Amos 1997), social science is shaped by social interests and not by evidence alone. Moreover, in the context of community understanding of genetic conditions, Kerr, Cunningham-Burley and Amos (1998) suggest that communities themselves can demonstrate knowledge of this social construction of scientific knowledge. The second is that Hammersley's conception of research communities is fundamentally elitist in the sense identified by Habermas (1978).

On the other hand, it occurs to me that in the concern to establish the criticism of scientific research for silencing alternative conceptions of knowledge, such alternatives silence, in turn, conceptions of knowledge that attempt to minimise bias in the senses identified by Hammersley and Gomm (1997). The keys to this impasse seem to lie in thinking about the division of labour and the democratization of social scientific research.

Hammersley's research communities are, of course, dependent upon a division of labour in society in which researchers have relatively more time, space and resources for mental labour than perhaps do others who feed, clothe and house researchers. The notion that anyone can become a researcher of their own lives might represent a democratisation of science, but as Hammersley (1995) has pointed out, the opportunity for extensive participation in research beyond the role of respondent may be experienced by some as an imposition. It might also, ironically, reduce the variety of conceptions of knowing which critics of Hammersley seem keen to facilitate.

It is possible to recast knowledge production as neither (exclusively) about the search for objective truth nor about emancipation of clients, but as an intervention in the social world with effects on researcher, clients and communities. Reflection on those effects is one mode of knowledge production. But such reflection could be critical in the sense of considering how things could be and not merely the way things are. In other words, such reflection could be counterfactual (Lukes 1974).

But such counterfactual reflection may be at its broadest if effected by researchers, client-interviewers and communities. This is because these three groups may have different particular skills and different social locations, possibly resulting in different types or outcomes of counterfactual thinking, not least a potentially different conception of the status and import of 'facts'. Graham (1976) cites the view of a community respondent that scientific evidence on smoking was 'only facts' and not grounded in real experiential knowledge. Similarly, Hill (1994) shows why medical 'facts' are unimportant in the lives of low-income families with sickle cell.

However, if one recognises that all people have skills they can bring to bear on problems (Mullender and Ward 1991) this must include academic researchers. Conversely, concerns that research preferences other than the search for knowledge may lead to avoidable errors (Hammersley and Gomm 1997) may be overstated. In this project the concern of the sickle cell group that 'results' should show that their community education had, over the years, been successful was a stated preference. The results in part were constituted by an estimate of what technical knowledge people had about sickle cell (see Dyson 1997). One interviewer commented that she was disappointed that, after years of community work on the part of the group, people still appeared to show little knowledge of sickle cell. This suggests a recognition that client-interviewers may share a preparedness with researchers to have their convictions challenged by the effects of research.

Outcomes of the Research

The outcomes were certainly complex and ambiguous. First, there is the impact on service provision to consider. This may be summarised as follows:

1. The decision by the health authority (belatedly) to appoint specialist nurses as counsellors for sickle cell and thalassaemia was legitimated by the research finding that in the absence of such specialist counsellors, generic health workers undertook little or no counselling of those found to be carriers.

2. The previous procedure of sending the haemoglobinopathy card (a card stating whether or not a patient is a carrier for either sickle cell or thalassaemia) to the GP was changed. The research showed that in such circumstances the card rarely reached the patient. The new procedure was to send the card to the specialist nurses who then offered the client a personal counselling session.

3. However, opportunistic screening of blood (testing blood from those identifiable as from a minority ethnic group when such blood samples were sent to the pathology laboratory for other reasons) continued. This meant a continuation of a policy (genetic testing unsolicited by the client) in contravention of suggested guidelines (Nuffield Council on Bioethics, 1993). It also represented one axis of the inherent contradiction in sickle cell/thalassaemia screening policy between reducing treatment costs and facilitating reproductive choice (Atkin and Ahmad 1998).

4. Moreover, for pregnant women at antenatal clinics, selective screening for sickle cell/thalassaemia continued; clients were selected for screening on the basis of presumed ethnicity, rather than explicitly offered the choice (see Dyson 1998).

Second, there is the impact on the interviewers. For a male interviewer, the father of a child with thalassaemia, the research gave confidence, interviewing skills and a platform to be an advocate for thalassaemia in the community. For members of the sickle cell support group, it provided a profile for the group within their communities. The research raised self-esteem in some interviewers. As we have already seen, for one Gujarati woman the research consolidated her expanded role beyond the domestic sphere. For another, it helped reduce the sense of isolation and perceived stigma associated with being the mother of a child with thalassaemia.

But here we enter the contradictory and complex nature of the impact. For although the mother of a child with beta-thalassaemia may regard it as a step forward to air the issue in a Gujarati Hindu community, many community members interviewed clearly did not. They did not wish their families to be 'tainted', even by the limited association resulting from being research subjects on a thalassaemia project.

This brings us to the third point, the outcomes for community respondents. Of course, neither the interviewers nor the communities are homogenous. The categories African-Caribbean and South Asian conflate, in the case of *both* interviewers and interviewees, important differences such as country of birth, religion, language, gender and age. As such their interests are neither always clear-cut nor unidirectional.

The research clearly raised anxieties in those who realised they were carriers for thalassaemia but had not been told or had not consciously faced the issues that this raised. This requires a defence of the research process, which may be stated as follows. The research draws attention to the fact that tests are carried out without specific permission and without pre-test explanations. The research process may thereby appear somewhat confrontational but is based on the supposition that communities would wish to know this was happening and/or would wish to know the implications. Contrary to health authority expectations, the research showed that such clients remained unaware of the test *and* of the result *and* of the implications of the result. The use of community interviewers at least permitted the distribution of an information leaflet and the opportunity for an elaborated explanation from those with personal experience of the conditions. What was certainly missing from the research was a more extensive context for the communities to express opinions on the processes of genetic testing – which in turn constitutes a future challenge for the author.

In this way it may be seen that most interviewers, many interviewees, and the author were challenged in unexpected ways. It is within the responses to these challenges that the possibility for change lies.

Conclusion

In this chapter I have considered the origins of a project involving community interviewers conducting research with members of a range of minority ethnic communities on their technical knowledge of sickle cell and thalassaemia. The decision to take part in less than ideal circumstances was itself a contested issue within the groups.

The effects of user involvement in research have been argued to be complex. There are both opportunities and the need for some caution in assessing their effect on the reliability and validity of the data. Contrary to accounts that claim that research empowers clients, here the levels of reciprocity between researcher and interviewers are acknowledged to be variable. Furthermore, the minority of service users who participate in research must themselves reciprocally assess the degree of mutuality they achieve with regard to clients who do not take part in the research.

It has been argued that it is not always clearly appropriate, in the pursuit of certain declared values, to defer to the face-value views of community members and abandon a critical perspective which asserts claims to knowledge counter to views expressed by community interviewers or community members. Community interviewers and/or community members may express views that the research co-ordinator may wish to challenge. This makes claims to empower clients through research difficult to sustain or indeed to regard as desirable. It may be that, following Troyna (1994) we need to draw a distinction between attempts to build an 'anti-oppressive research' and a 'critical social research'. The latter may be regarded as a more modest, more achievable and a less internally contradictory goal.

In one sense, if we conceive the question of evaluation to be one of the degree to which community interviewers and/or other community members were empowered, we would probably be left with some fairly tenuous claims that a limited range of skills, of dubious long-term value, had been imparted to some of the interviewers. The legitimacy of claims that those interviewed had been empowered would be still less. If, however, we recast the question so as not to ask whether there was any empowerment of users of the services, but what challenges were provoked by the research, then we may have more grounds for optimism.

References

Ahmad, W.I.U. and Atkin, K. (1996) 'Ethnicity and Caring for a Disabled Child: The Case of Sickle Cell or Thalassaemia.' *British Journal of Social Work 26*, 755–775.

Ahmad, W.I.U, Kernohan, E. and Baker, M. (1989) 'Patients' Choice of General Practitioner: Influence of Patients' Fluency in English and the Ethnicity and Sex of the Doctor.' *Journal of the Royal College of General Practitioners 39*, 153–155.

Ahmad, W.I.U. and Walker, R. (1997) 'Health and Social Care Needs of Asian Older People.' *Ageing and Society 17*, 141–165.

Anionwu, E.N. (1993) 'Sickle Cell and Thalassaemia: Community Experience and Official Response.' In W.I.U. Ahmad, (ed) *'Race' and Health in Contemporary Britain*. Buckingham: Open University Press.

Atkin, K. and Ahmad, W.I.U. (1998) 'Genetic Screening and Haemoglobinopathies: Ethics, Politics and Practice.' *Social Science and Medicine 46*, 3, 445–458.

Atkin, K., Ahmad, W.I.U. and Anionwu, E. (1998) 'Screening and Counselling for Sickle Cell Disorders and Thalassaemia: The Experience of Parents and Health Professionals.' *Social Science and Medicine 47*, 11, 1639–1651.

Burgess, R.G. (1984) *Field Research: A Sourcebook and Field Manual*. London: Allen and Unwin.

Cicourel, A.V. (1964) *Method and Measurement in Sociology*. London: Collier-Macmillan.

Darr, A. (1990) 'The Social Implications of Thalassaemia among Muslims of Pakistani origin in England: Family Experience and Service Delivery. Ph.D. thesis, University of London.

Department of Health (1993) *The Report of the Working Party of the Standing Medical Advisory Committee on Sickle Cell, Thalassaemia and Other Haemoglobinopathies*. London: HMSO.

Donzelot, J. (1979) *The Policing of Families*. London: Hutchinson.

Dyson, S. (1997) 'Knowledge of Sickle Cell in a Screened Population.' *Health and Social Care in the Community 5*, 2, 84–93.

Dyson, S. (1998) "Race", Ethnicity and Haemoglobin Disorders.' *Social Science and Medicine 47*, 1, 121–131.

Dyson, S. (2000) 'Knowledge of Beta-Thalassaemia in a Screened Population.' *Applied Community Studies* [forthcoming].

Dyson, S., Davis, V. and Rahman, R. (1993a) 'Thalassaemia: Establishing Basic Awareness.' *Health Visitor 66*, 10, 360–361.

Dyson, S., Davis, V. and Rahman, R. (1993b) 'Thalassaemia: Current Community Awareness in Manchester.' *Health Visitor 66*, 12, 447–448.

Foucault, M. (1993) 'Space, Power and Knowledge.' In S. During (ed) *The Cultural Studies Reader.* London: Routledge.

Goffman, E. (1968) *Stigma: Notes on the Management of a Spoiled Identity.* Harmondsworth: Penguin.

Gore, J. (1993) *The Struggle for Pedagogies.* London: Routledge.

Graham, H. (1976) 'Smoking in Pregnancy: The Attitude of Expectant Mothers.' *Social Science and Medicine 10*, 399–405.

Habermas, J. (1978) *Knowledge and Human Interests.* Second edition. London: Heinemann.

Hammersley, M. (1992) *What's Wrong with Ethnography?* London: Routledge.

Hammersley, M. (1995) *The Politics of Social Research.* London: Sage.

Hammersley, M. and Gomm, R. (1997) 'Bias in Social Research.' *Sociological Research Online 2*, 1. http://www.socresonline.org.uk/socresonline/2/1/2.html.

Hill, S.A. (1994) *Managing Sickle Cell Disease in Low Income Families.* Philadelphia: Temple University Press.

Humphries, B. (1997) 'From Critical Thought to Emancipatory Action: Contradictory Research Goals?' *Sociological Research Online 2*, 1. http://www.socresonline.org.uk/socresonline/2/1/3.html.

Humphries, B. and Truman, C. (1994) *Re-Thinking Social Research.* Aldershot: Avebury.

Kerr, A., Cunningham-Burley, S. and Amos, A. (1997) 'The New Genetics: Professionals' Discursive Boundaries.' *Sociological Review 45*, 2, 279–303.

Kerr, A., Cunningham-Burley, S. and Amos, A. (1998) 'The New Genetics and Health: Mobilizing Lay Expertise.' *Public Understanding of Science 7*, 41–60.

Kuhn, T.S. (1962) *The Structure of Scientific Revolutions.* Chicago: University of Chicago Press.

Lather, P. (1991) *Getting Smart: Feminist Research and Pedagogy with/in the Postmodern.* London: Routledge.

Lukes, S. (1974) *Power: A Radical View.* London: Macmillan.

Miles, M. and Huberman, A. (1994) *Qualitative Data Analysis.* Second edition. London: Sage.

Mullender, A. and Ward, D. (1991) *Self-Directed Groupwork: Users Taking Action for Empowerment.* London: Whiting and Birch.

Nuffield Council on Bioethics (1993) *Genetic Screening: Ethical Issues.* London: Nuffield Foundation.

Oliver, M. (1992) 'Changing the Social Relations of Research Production.' *Disability, Handicap and Society 7*, 2, 101–114.

Rhodes, P. (1994) 'Race-of-Interviewer Effects: A Brief Comment.' *Sociology 28*, 2, 547–558.

Romm, N. (1997) 'Becoming More Accountable.' *Sociological Research Online 2*, 3. http://www.socresonline.org.uk/socresonline/2/3/2.html.

Roth, J. (1966) 'Hired Hand Research.' In N. Denzin (ed) (1978) *Sociological Methods: A Sourcebook.* New York: McGraw-Hill.

Stacey, M. (1994) 'The Power of Lay Knowledge: A Personal View.' In J. Popay and G. Williams (eds) *Researching the People's Health.* London: Routledge.

Troyna, B. (1994) 'Blind Faith? Empowerment and Educational Research.' *International Studies in Sociology of Education 4,* 1, 3–24.

Whyte, W.F. (1984) *Learning from the Field: A Guide from Experience.* London: Sage.

CHAPTER 11

'Framing Our Own Questions'

Empowering Patients and Primary Health Care Workers
in the Planning of Primary Health Care Services

Angus McCabe and Liz Ross

In 1998 the Small Heath General Practitioner Commissioning Group (GPCG) tore up their provisional commissioning intentions with regard to mental health services in the area and completely redrafted their report to reflect and respond to user concerns. Focus groups facilitated by members of the two mental health service-user groups and involving local mental health service users had discussed their needs and come up with proposals that would help to address them. Members of the two groups then presented the findings from the focus groups to the GPCG. The rewritten commissioning intentions included a note that 'the Commissioning Plan on Mental Health has been informed in detail by user views' (Small Heath GPCG 1998).

The Context

Within primary health care as within other areas of health and social care there has been a developing emphasis on the involvement of the service user, the patient, in decisions that are made about services and service delivery.

The allocation of scarce resources has always been a controversial issue within the health services but, until recent policy and structural changes, decisions about allocation were largely confined to health practitioners and managers. Traditionally health care planning has depended almost entirely on epidemiological and statistical information to identify areas and extent of need which then in turn inform the planning of service provision. However, the introduction of an internal market and local decision making has opened the discussion about resource allocation to a wider public. This is particularly the case within the primary care setting, and a number of recent changes in organisation and policy have brought decision making and planning of local services into the community arena.

Indeed, within the National Health Service, recent policy and guidance documents have included reference, advice and direction on the participation of the public as a whole, not only patients or service users, in the planning, management and evaluation of health services at a local level (NHS Executive 1996, 1998a; NHS Management Executive 1992). Policy programmes, for example the Health Improvement Programme, the Primary Care Act Pilots and Health Action Zones, include requirements and opportunities for public participation in local planning. Within primary health care local public involvement has been integrated in the legislation and guidance surrounding the general practitioner commissioning process and in the primary care groups (PCGs) set up in 1999. There is, for instance, required lay representation on the primary care group boards.

Current guidance (NHS Executive 1998b) stresses that those charged with purchasing responsibilities for primary care should 'give greater voice and influence to the users of NHS services and their carers in their own care, the development and definitions of standards set for NHS services locally and the development of NHS policy both locally and nationally' (p.13).

Indeed, one of the key commitments given in a recent White Paper (DoH 1997) was 'to rebuild confidence in the NHS as a public service accountable to patients, open to the public and shaped by their views' (para 2.4).

Public participation in health care planning and service delivery, as well as a more active involvement, is perceived to have a range of benefits both for the NHS and for the service users. A recent publication (NHS Executive 1998a) stressed that both health and health care are improved by participation. The benefits to the NHS are perceived to be:

- restoration of public confidence
- improved outcomes for individual patients
- more appropriate use of health services
- potential for greater cost effectiveness
- contribution to problem resolution
- sharing with the public the responsibility for health care
- developing accountability in clinical governance. (p. 4)

And for the service users:

- better outcomes of treatment and care
- an enhanced sense of self-esteem and capacity to control their lives
- a more satisfying experience of using the health services
- more accessible, sensitive and responsive health services

- improved health

- a greater sense of ownership of the NHS.

It must be noted here that in the documentation and discussion there is an inconsistent use of the terms 'user', referring to people who use or who may use the health services, and 'public', referring to all citizens regardless of use. However, within the NHS all the public are potential service users. It is therefore perhaps most useful to distinguish between participation in decisions which are made about health and health services more generally, and those which relate to the use of a particular service or the treatment of a specific condition, for example, diabetes or mental health. Although the project described here is referred to as a user involvement project, participation in decisions about both general, that is local, health services and health needs, and specific areas, relating to particular conditions, were included.

There is also an apparently arbitrary use of the terms 'involvement' and 'participation'. Although the terms are used interchangeably we would suggest that where the public or service users can participate they have been involved *by* those who are the decision makers. In other words the planners, service providers and decision makers can decide to involve the public or service users and allow them to participate. Again, although the project focuses on the involving of the public in decision making, it also addresses the means through which they are able to participate.

With such high expectations of the benefits of user involvement, local participation is of particular importance: for the majority of the population the primary care services remain the first contact point with the NHS. It is at this level that the differing needs of local communities can be addressed through the purchasing of local services. With the introduction of first GP fundholding, then GP commissioning groups and now primary care groups, with responsibility for planning and purchasing local services, it is at this point that the public, rather than just patients, are best placed to have an input into the planning of services.

However, reconciling this very different approach to health care planning with more traditional methods and attempting to involve both professional and lay 'experts' in health decisions is fraught with difficulty if indeed it is to be more than ambiguous rhetoric. The interests of different professional groups may compete and professional interests may be in conflict with local needs, wants and aspirations. The very process of public consultation itself can, some fear, raise expectations on services which cannot be met. Separating social issues which impact on health, like housing conditions, unemployment and crime, from medical concerns and priorities can be problematic.

Models of Participation

Alongside a range of activities to involve patients there are now a growing number of both published accounts of these activities and guides for the health workers involved. It is clear that there are a range of approaches to public participation (Barnes 1997) involving patients and the wider public at different levels and different stages of the planning, service delivery and evaluation cycle. However, current research (Barnes and McIver, in press) indicates that for all the activity in this field, few initiatives are sustained in the longer term and even fewer operate at the strategic levels.

Developing a greater awareness of the different levels of participation is important if wide involvement in health care planning is to be meaningful for all participants and crucially, sustainable. To understand the nature of participation and the longer-term outcomes, the focus must include not only the techniques of public participation, but also the experience and the values of the participants of the process. It is not yet clear what facilitates or hinders public participation becoming an integral part of the decision-making process rather than a bolt-on, nor how the skills developed by all participants, members of the public, health care workers and planners can best be built on. Given the complex and changing nature of the NHS, lay people may feel that they lack sufficient information to engage in the debate on health priorities. A critical question for health planners is how participants in the health care planning process can make an informed contribution to it.

This raises questions too for researchers and those involved as 'user consultants'. To address the problematic aspects of involving service users in the planning we need also to identify the constraints raised by traditional approaches to social research. Put simply, if users are to participate in the planning process, they need also to be actively involved in the means by which the data, experience and knowledge of users is to be collected and interpreted. User involvement is itself a process rather than an output. The history of research within the health field is heavily influenced by positivistic methodologies, randomised controlled trials and research which is undertaken *on* patients rather than *with* patients. The expert knowledge of the service user is rarely acknowledged. Involving users in ways which empower them and produce the benefits outlined above includes ensuring that the process as well as the outcomes do not disempower those involved. Thus research approaches which encourage participation in themselves, where the research skills of both users and professionals are recognised and developed by the trained and experienced researchers, need to be considered.

A recent publication from the NHS Executive (1998a) identifies four approaches to public participation, which together it is suggested should make up the NHS strategy on user involvement. The four approaches are:

1. *Direct participation of users* — engaging user and voluntary groups in decision making at local and national levels and building partnerships at the individual level between the service provider and patient

2. *Informed views of citizens* — developing opportunities to engage with the informed views and experiences of citizens about health and health services

3. *Community development* — mobilising communities to become participants in both defining problems and developing solutions to health and health service issues

4. *Local scrutiny and accountability* — developing more effective systems for ensuring public scrutiny and public accountability at a local and national level. (p.7)

Whilst the focus of the work described here was on the development of a participating community (a 'community development' approach), elements of each of the other categories underpin the approach adopted, including opportunities for direct participation in the decision-making process, workshops which inform and enable participants to use information and experience to frame questions, and the publication of draft commissioning intentions for comment, challenge and review. It is with the questions raised about different models of participation, research approaches and the problematic aspects of user involvement in mind that we now turn to describe the User Involvement Project (UIP).

The User Involvement Project

The project was undertaken within the context of a pilot GP Commissioning Group in an inner city area of Birmingham between 1996 and 1998. The Small Heath GPCG has now been superseded by the primary care group as a result of the legislation which came into force in April 1999. However, the aims and objectives of the GPCG were a foretaste of those of the PCGs and there is much to be learnt from these pilot projects.

The Small Heath GPCG was a group consisting of all 63 GPs in the (then) constituency of Small Heath, who came together voluntarily:

- to ensure the purchase and commission of high-quality, cost-effective and clinically effective health care to their practice populations

- to improve patient access to health services both in the community and in hospital

- to reduce stress on GPs and their staff through co-operation between practices and centralisation of tasks where appropriate.

Small Heath is an inner city area with very high levels of deprivation and great cultural diversity. None of the GPs were fundholders. The GPCG had a written constitution and a project board. Funding from Birmingham Health Authority allowed it to employ two support officers. The group was formally constituted in April 1996 and covered a combined practice population of 110,000.

During the three years of the project the GPCG wrestled with the complex issues of involving users in the yearly production of its commissioning intentions. The UIP was set up alongside the GPCG and was commissioned from ENACT – a partnership between the Department of Social Policy and Social Work, University of Birmingham, Newtown/South Aston Health Action Area, and the Birmingham Settlement. The partnership between academics and practitioners enabled the UIP to draw on local community knowledge, expertise in community development techniques and social research, and the opportunities for education at the University. The UIP was initially funded for one year although delays meant that the project could not be started in time to inform the first year's commissioning intentions. Further funding was then sought for a second stage from the West Midlands Regional Health Authority. Again, the timing of funding meant that there were delays in the second stage getting underway, which resulted in some continuity gaps.

The UIP evolved in discussion with the GPCG. The 63 members of the GPCG lacked experience in involving service users but approached the project with a range of views from very enthusiastic, through those who were sceptical but thought it was worth trying, to those who did not expect any significant outcomes. It was recognised from the beginning of the project that it was to be a learning experience for all involved and one which would attempt to change attitudes amongst the various participants, GPs, other primary health care workers, service users and the local community. Members of the GPCG assisted in both shaping the work programme and identifying areas for user involvement in the commissioning process. Thus both the GPCG and the researchers shared an interest not only in the outputs and outcomes from the UIP but also in the process of user involvement itself.

The aims of the first stage of the UIP were:

- to review and report users' views on GP commissioning intentions for 1997/8, retrospectively

- to inform the GP commissioning processes for 1998/9

- to develop locally sustainable models for user involvement in GP commissioning in the future.

The project was set within an action research framework which emphasised both action and reflection within the process of involving the local public in the first year of commissioning. This recognised that there had been learning within both the GPCG itself and the UIP and built in opportunities for action and reflection on the part of the researchers and the GPCG.

STAGE 1 – AIMS	METHODS	FINDINGS	OUTCOMES
To gather a broad range of views on local perceptions of health issues and primary health care needs to inform the GPCG commissioning intentions for 1998/9 and to review intentions for 1997/8	• Generic focus groups facilitated by local community leaders in community languages • 'Talking about Health' workshops facilitated by Open University and Health Action Area • Focus groups and individual interviews on specific elements of commissioning intentions, e.g. health care needs of minority ethnic groups and users' views on specialist dermatology services • Focus group and information sessions with existing consultative groups, e.g. Community Health Councils	Generic focus groups • Primary health care needs were expressed in terms of social rather than medical priorities – e.g. poor housing, pollution, crime • Awareness of the range of primary health care services, other than GPs, was low • Language barriers hindered access to services • Little knowledge of the structure, role and basis of primary health care planning Examples of specific findings • For black African-Caribbean elders greater co-ordination between health and community care services was important, e.g. access to chiropody and physiotherapy in day centres • Ease of access to specialist dermatological services was a priority	The findings were only able to inform the commissioning process retrospectively. However, users' views were able to influence developments in the next round of commissioning, e.g. commissioning intentions for 1998/9 included • a proposal to set up a pilot community dermatological clinic provided by a local GP specialising in this area • primary care advocates to be appointed • role of nurse practitioner to be promoted. GPCG now more aware of the role and potential usefulness of involving local people and local groups; individuals now more aware of the work of the primary health care services and the GPCG

Figure 11.1. The first stage of the User Involvement Project

The first stage

With regard to the first two of these aims, the work undertaken by the project is described in Figure 11.1. This shows that a number of different methods for gathering data were used, and charts some of the outputs in terms of findings and the ways in which these findings impacted upon the commissioning intentions.

As can be seen from Figure 11.1, during the first stage the researchers addressed the aims of involving the local community in the GP commissioning process by collecting data themselves, running focus groups and enabling local community leaders to run focus groups in different languages. The groups addressed both generic topics, that is those relating to local health needs and services, and more specific topics, for instance leg ulcers and skin problems, with appropriate groups of local people. The findings and outcomes from these activities demonstrate some of the ways in which service users' views began to impact upon the decisions made by the GPCG.

A key theme arising from the initial stages of the UIP was the extent to which the NHS in general, and primary care in particular, remained something of a mystery to the general public. For the majority primary care was, and is, the GP, with low levels of awareness about the role of other professionals in the field (such as health visitors and community nurses). This raised a fundamental question. How could informed user debate be stimulated in a way which could, effectively, influence commissioning?

One strategy adopted was to offer three 'Talking about Health' workshops, run with tenants' organisations and a Bangladeshi women's group. These were jointly facilitated by members of the UIP team and the Open University. Workshops took the form of three days' participatory training addressing:

- issues impacting on local/community health
- health rights
- accessing services
- change in the NHS and its structures/service delivery
- the role of primary care teams.

Information-giving and discussion sessions were followed in the final day by a 'citizen jury' exercise in which participants questioned local GPs and other professionals, focusing on the match – or, indeed, mismatch – between community needs and service provision.

The 'Talking about Health' workshops produced a number of practical outcomes, including, in one area, the development of a needle exchange scheme. However, the shifts in attitude were perhaps even more important, particularly the extent to which the process increased understanding amongst the GPs of the role and potential of user involvement in informing commissioning plans.

In the words of one GP:

> I was frightened of doing it ['Talking about Health' workshop]. I thought it
> would be 'them and us' with everyone knocking the doctor. But it wasn't like
> that…it was more 'how can we work together to improve health and get a
> better service?'… The one thing I really learned was that it was okay to say no
> to people…but you had to explain clearly and reasonably why you were
> saying no. That has been a challenge.

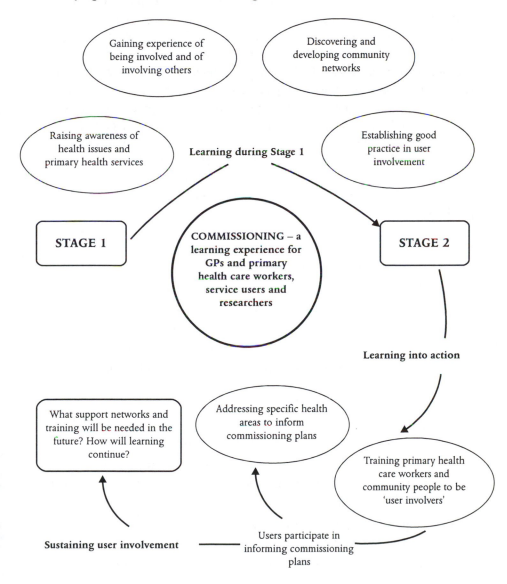

Figure 11.2. The learning process

In the words of another primary care worker:

> I was worried that [the workshops] would raise unrealistic expectations in the community. What happened was we found out how low people's expectations of health and other services are.

Learning and moving on to the second stage

Figure 11.1 (and Figure 11.3) inevitably give a rather flat, two-dimensional account of a project which was designed as a process as well as an out-come-orientated piece of action research. The third aim at the beginning of the project was to develop locally sustainable models for user involvement. To explore this it is necessary to look at the processes underlying the work in the first year and to demonstrate the learning about those processes that imbued the work of the second year. Figure 11.2 attempts to present the process in terms of the dimension and dynamic of participation in the project. The diagram centres on the concept of participatory learning about involvement in commissioning, and attempts to demonstrate the nature of involvement of all parties, that is the GPCG, the researchers, primary health care workers and community service users. Learning from the first stage can thus be identified under the following four headings:

RAISING AWARENESS OF HEALTH ISSUES AND PRIMARY HEALTH SERVICES:

- by running 'Talking about Health' workshops, attended by 75 local people
- by running focus groups involving different community groups on general health issues and local awareness of primary health care services
- by feeding back to the GPCG views from the focus groups and work-shops about local perceptions of health problems and services.

GAINING EXPERIENCE OF BEING INVOLVED AND INVOLVING OTHERS:

- by giving people opportunities to take part in focus groups and work-shops and experience involvement at first hand
- by facilitating involvement in focus groups and workshops by running groups in community languages, providing a crèche, including lunches and paying participants
- through ongoing dialogue with key members of the GPCG on the process of involving users
- through meetings between local groups and members of the GPCG.

DISCOVERING AND DEVELOPING COMMUNITY NETWORKS:

- by using the UIP team's experience in community development and community-based work

- by constructing a database of local organisations

- by involving local community leaders in running focus groups

- through the GPCG taking part in other locality-based participatory activities, e.g. setting up, with partner agencies, a locality action forum.

ESTABLISHING GOOD PRACTICE IN USER INVOLVEMENT:

- in the ways groups and workshops were organised at suitable times, in local venues and with appropriate community languages

- by taking account of cultural preferences and differences in bringing groups of people together

- by recognising the contribution of users by paying them

- by involving users in presenting findings to the GPCG

- by providing feedback to the local community on the outcomes of the user-involvement activities.

Towards the end of the first stage recommendations for the second stage were drawn up. With a view to developing a model of user involvement which would not be dependent on bringing in external researchers or consultants, but would rather embed locally maintained user involvement within the commissioning process, the researchers recommended that:

- the GPCG review its own learning about users informing commissioning

- the GPCG consider its role in relation to the broader locality planning system, particularly the locality action forum and the Single Regeneration Budget partnership

- both community members and primary health care workers be recognised as potential 'user involvers' and that training in social research and user involvement techniques should be developed.

Thus the aims of the second stage were:

- to enable the GPCG to produce a set of commissioning intentions for 1999/2000 which reflected the views of the Small Heath residents

- to provide a range of fora in which the Small Heath residents could be involved

- to train Small Heath residents and primary care team members to run focus groups and workshops across the constituency

STAGE 2 AIMS	METHODS	FINDINGS	OUTCOMES
To enable the views of users to inform the commissioning intentions around mental health, asthma and diabetes	Two focus groups with people with diabetes 23 individual interviews with asthma sufferers Two focus groups facilitated by mental health service users with other service users Focus groups on dermatology services	Examples from the mental health focus groups • GPs should have copies of mental health patients' care plans • An out-of-hours service providing telephone counselling and support staffed by a partnership between health care professionals and service users needed • Regular physical health checks for those with severe and enduring mental health problems needed 14 primary care workers attended the introductory session on user involvement	From mental health focus groups The commissioning plan on mental health was informed in detail by user views which were presented to the GPCG by service users. The Commissioning Intentions for 1999/2000 include proposals to work with the local Mental Health Trust to look at ways to establish access to an out-of-hours telephone counselling service and to ensure that all care plans of mental health patients are copied to their GP Mental health service users designed and facilitated focus groups and presented findings to GPCG
To develop a training and support programme to facilitate the establishment of a network of community organisations and primary health care workers able to involve users in the future	Half-day introduction to user involvement for primary health care workers Two-day in-depth training courses for members of community and primary health care workers	32 people from community and self-help groups and primary health care workers attended the two-day training course	

Figure 11.3. The second stage

- to develop the skills of individuals within the community and within primary care teams to facilitate user groups

- to run further 'Talking about Health' workshops and focus groups.

The second stage

Figure 11.3 summarises the activities of the second stage. We focus here on the third and fourth of the aims listed above and look in some depth at the training that was undertaken by the research team.

INTRODUCTORY TRAINING FOR PRIMARY HEALTH CARE WORKERS

A short course was offered to primary health care workers in the area and 14 attended for a half-day session. Here the emphasis was on introducing them to the key features of user involvement and good practice in the collection and interpretation of data was stressed. One focus was on the skills each worker already used within her work – the daily discussions with patients, the visits to their homes, facilitating group activities and discussions, recording case notes and organising health promotion activities. It is in these day-to-day tasks that primary care workers can themselves be researchers, gathering and interpreting data. Within the training sessions various ways of recording, organising data collection and collecting service-user opinions were discussed. The session finished with an opportunity to consider ways in which the findings might be presented to the GPCG and ways in which the GPCG could be made aware of the research resources they had in primary care workers.

IN-DEPTH COURSES

Two-day courses were advertised to primary care workers, community organisations and active members of the community. Called 'Different Voices: Getting Heard', the courses were free and a University certificate of attendance was presented to those completing the programme.

The course was itself a participatory learning experience, with the emphasis on the practical exercise of conducting a piece of research using a focus-group methodology. This approach was chosen because it enabled course participants to work through the whole research process in the two days and to experience all the stages of research.

Focus groups bring together people to take part in a time-limited and topic-focused discussion. The discussion is led by a facilitator, usually supported by a co-facilitator, and typically is designed to work towards the completion of a task. The task of the group may, for example, be to prioritise different service improvements, or to identify the most pressing needs of a group of service users. The members of the group may or may not know each other but they will have something in common which relates to the topic of discussion. They may, for example, all suffer from asthma or be mental health service users. Similarly, if the topic under discussion relates more generally to the health needs of a local community, then membership of that community would be their common characteristic.

A focus group is designed to enable the researcher to find out what groups, rather than individual people, think. Guided group discussion can enable people to develop and test out their views and ideas together. Group facilitators need to encourage discussion within the boundaries of the topic of interest, to manage the interaction between participants and to ensure that the task of the group is completed. Many of the skills associated with facilitating groups are already familiar to people who may have some experience with groupwork in the community, in self-help groups or in professional practice. Indeed we all have some experience of being part of a group. In some ways the focus group can be said to resemble the discussion around the family dinner table or over a drink in the pub. Furthermore, many of the skills associated with facilitating focus groups are transferable to undertaking semi-structured interviews and gathering data from documents (for example, case notes), and are in themselves then transferable to other areas of community life, such as taking part in meetings.

During the two-day course participants worked in small research groups, each with a topic to study. Each group planned a focus group, identifying questions, thinking about the process of the group discussion and designing a guide for the facilitator to use. The context of the focus group was also considered and each group developed a strategy for selecting potential participants and encouraging them to participate. Techniques for effective management of the discussion were shared, including for example, ways of encouraging everyone to take part and ways of ensuring that no one dominated the discussion. Towards the end of the course each group selected a facilitator and co-facilitator who then, bravely, facilitated a focus-group discussion with members from the other groups. The final session offered the opportunity to reflect on the experience of both facilitating and being part of a focus group before moving on to considering methods of gathering and interpreting the data collected from the groups and presenting it to the commissioning group.

Participants in the training programmes were encouraged to seek out opportunities to put their skills into practice and 'call-back' sessions were arranged for them to reflect together on their experiences. Few had the chance to involve other users within the limited time available but these occasions did enable people to keep in touch with each other, the project team and the GPCG.

MENTAL HEALTH SERVICE USERS
Focus Group Topic Guide

Purpose

To gather users' views on GP, primary and mental health services in Small Heath and identify ways in which they can be improved

1. Introduction
   All participants and facilitators introduce themselves and ground rules for the session are discussed:
   Confidentiality
   Everyone has an equal say
   Respect for each others' views
   Speak one at a time

2. Can you tell us about your experiences (both good and bad) of using your GP?
   PROMPTS – How aware are local GPs of the mental health services?
   Are local GPs involved in service users' care plans?

3. Can you tell us about your experiences (both good and bad) of using other primary care services – e.g. health visitors, chiropodists?
   PROMPTS – How aware are you of the range of primary health services available in the area?

4. Can you tell us about your experiences (both good and bad) of using mental health services?
   PROMPTS – Day care services
   Carer support
   Community psychiatric nurses
   Hospital services

5. Are there gaps in the current services?

6. How could the services currently available be improved or developed?
   (list on flip chart)
   GP services
   Other primary health services
   Mental health services

7. From the list of suggested improvements which are the most important?

8. How would you like to be involved in the planning of services in the future?

9. Anything else anyone wishes to say?

10. Thank you for taking part – explain what will happen – other focus groups being held, a report will be written and presented to GPCG, feedback to all who have taken part

Figure 11.4. Focus group topic guide

Putting participation into practice

We now turn back to the example with which we began this chapter, for it was in the field of mental health that the developmental processes, potential and outcomes of user involvement were best illustrated. This element of the project involved:

- training mental health service users in social research techniques

- service users designing a focus group topic guide (Figure 11.4), organis- ing and co-facilitating focus groups' sessions with 40 other service users

- users and the project team jointly drafting a report outlining user priori- ties for primary care (and specialist mental health) services

- users presenting these findings and recommendations for action to the members of GPCG charged with writing the mental health specific elements within the overall commissioning plan

- user-led follow-up contact with GPCG to ensure, wherever possible, that agreed action points were translated from commissioning intentions into service delivery.

The actual presentation and negotiation of a user-based set of commissioning intentions visibly influenced the local primary care plan. GPs literally ripped up their draft, containing somewhat generalised intentions, and replaced it with the highly specific objectives developed by service users. Further, over the past 18 months GPs have (despite the upheaval of the transition from commissioning to primary care group) aimed to shape their own and specialist service development within this mutually agreed framework.

Sustaining User Involvement

Within the two years of the UIP there was insufficient time to assess how far the third aim of establishing sustainable models of user involvement within the com- missioning process had been achieved. The demise of the GPCG and introduc- tion of primary care groups brought a change of boundaries and consumed much of the energies of the GPs in the area in the period immediately after the end of the project. Whether the learning of the participants in the UIP, including the GPs, will inform the development of the PCGs has yet to be seen, but it is useful here to highlight some of the learning points of the project which could inform a PCG that places an emphasis on user involvement.

This project emphasised the importance of user involvement being a learning experience for all participants and included training, dialogue, research and reflection. If local service users and primary health care workers are themselves to become researchers who can ask questions, interpret what they hear and contrib- ute to the planning process, then they need to begin to think of themselves as participant researchers, to recognise the research skills they have and to develop new skills which may in themselves be transferable to other parts of their lives.

The training offered to primary health care workers and service users built on these ideas. The training encouraged participants to work through the research process of exploring the area of interest, asking questions, designing a way of finding out more about the question areas, gathering and working with the data collected and presenting it to those who needed their findings to feed into the planning process. Furthermore, the training in itself brought together primary care workers from across the area, along with members of the local community. Links were established, common interests discovered and the potential for future work together was acknowledged. The training and support was valued by those who took part but support and further training must continue if these local involvers are to remain engaged with the planning process and if more local people are to be trained to replace those who move on.

The GPCG recognised that ongoing training and support would be necessary to sustain local involvers and that this would entail both financial and human resources, payment for local people, and time within their job specification for primary health care workers. Furthermore it was suggested that one member of the GPCG should have a particular responsibility and interest in involving users. How far this role can be taken on by the required lay member of the PCG board is yet to be seen.

Whilst this project was viewed as a positive experience by all the key stake-holders – and tangible outcomes were clearly identified – a note of caution should be sounded. Effecting change in large organisations can be difficult and time-consuming. Indeed, one GP described effecting change within the actual delivery of NHS services in the terms: 'It's about as easy as doing a three-point turn in an oil tanker.' That time-lag between intention and implementation can lead to disillusionment on the part of users participating in health care planning processes. This in turn makes the provision of regular, and ongoing, feedback, critical to ensuring sustained, and sustainable, public participation. Without this, scepticism (often misinterpreted as apathy) seeps in: 'We were consulted – but nothing ever changed.'

Perhaps the most significant outcome of the UIP was that GPs learnt that there was no one way of involving users, nor could a system simply be put in place which would continue to deliver without much maintenance. They and other primary health care workers are now aware of a range of different ways in which people can participate and primary care decision-makers can listen. If user involvement is to be embedded in the PCG planning process, both resources and commitment from all participants will be needed in the longer term.

References

Barnes, M. (1997) *The People's Health Service.* Research Paper No.2. Birmingham: Health Services Management Centre, University of Birmingham.

Barnes, M. and McIver, S. (1999) *Public Participation in Primary Care.* Research Report number 36. Birmingham: Health Services Management Centre, University of Birmingham.

Department of Health (1997) *The New NHS.* London: Department of Health.

NHS Executive (1996) *Patient Partnership: Building a Collaborative Strategy.* Leeds: NHS Executive.

NHS Executive (1998a) *In the Public Interest.* London: Department of Health.

NHS Executive (1998b) *Priorities and Planning Guidance for the NHS 1998/9.* London: Department of Health.

NHS Management Executive (1992) *Local Voice: The Views of Local People in Purchasing for Health.* London: Department of Health

Small Health General Practitioners Commissioning Group (1998) *Commissioning Intentions 1998–9.* Birmingham: West Midlands Health Authority.

CHAPTER 12

Policies of Neglect

Female Offenders and the Probation Service

Judith Rumgay

Introduction

Despite the thirst for incarceration characterising the British approach to the crime problem in recent years, it is still relatively easy to persuade the public of the inappropriateness of imprisoning large numbers of women. Perhaps it is a measure of this susceptibility in itself that the media, so frequently castigated for demonising women, has raised public consciousness on this issue. In 1996, for example, media exposure of the numbers of poor women being sentenced to terms of imprisonment for fine default facilitated invigoration of an intensive, if deplorably delayed, effort to reduce reliance on this sanction; the newly appointed Prisons Inspector aborted an inspection of Holloway women's prison in a widely reported display of outrage at the conditions he found on arrival; televised pictures of a woman shackled to male prison officers while in labour on a hospital maternity ward raised a storm of public disgust which forced a review of policies on restraint and supervision of females in custody.

Yet, despite widespread appreciation that institutional sanctions are frequently unjust, the female prison population has been rising alarmingly. Statistics for that same year revealed: 'Female prisoners increased in number by 14 per cent from an average 2,000 in 1995 to 2,300 in 1996. Male prisoners increased by an average 8 per cent' (Home Office 1997, p.1). The same report observed that the proportion of the female sentenced population aged under 21 had increased to 13 per cent by 1996, from a low point of 10 per cent in 1986. This escalating use of imprisonment has been visited predominantly on first and non-violent offenders (HM Chief Inspector of Prisons 1997).

Tough sentencing policies, designed almost entirely as responses to crimes which are typically male, and tightened discipline following spectacular security failures in male prisons (Learmont 1995; Woodcock 1994) have exerted a disproportionately harmful effect upon females. Perhaps this has arisen in part precisely because of the less serious nature of women's offending. There are always many more relatively minor offenders in the criminal justice system, representing the most common types of crime. Such offenders suffer acutely from the generalised impact of harsher penal policies originally aimed at the serious and recidivist criminal population. Paradoxically, therefore, female offenders have experienced the full weight of criminal sanctions amid a strong consensus that this is unnecessary.

In this context the probation service has had difficulty in defining its practice, since its favoured approaches to the provision of alternatives to custody appear to have failed to provide adequately for women. From the early 1980s, the probation service increasingly sought to target its interventions on high-tariff offenders. The aim of diversion from custody, with its concomitant goal of reducing numbers of first and relatively non-serious offenders on probation, became the policy driver of practice development. It also became an article of faith during this period that the imposition of intrusive measures, such as probation, upon first and minor offenders was unjustified: it widened the net of social control (Cohen 1985); and it forced offenders up tariff early in their offending careers, thus exhausting the community-based opportunities before diversion from custody was truly required (Thorpe et al. 1980; Walker, Farrington and Tucker 1981). Thus, the reportedly high numbers of women placed on probation for their first offence became an embarrassing, misguided and unwarranted intervention predicated on a response to personal need, rather than a measured sanction for their crimes (Buchanan, Collett and McMullan 1991; Worral 1981).

The probation service could be encouraged in this approach by the experience of juvenile justice, which bucked the trend of the 1980s for increasing use of custody. Not only did prosecutions of juveniles decrease, but those who were brought to court, despite being more serious and recidivist offenders, benefited from expanding recourse to the community-based disposals (Gelsthorpe and Morris 1994).

During the 1990s, in addition to the weight given to offence seriousness and criminal history, the probation service focused increasingly on questions of public safety and protection in its assessments of offenders and sentencing proposals to courts. This new element in the equation designed to demonstrate suitability for supervision has added to pressure to reject females as candidates for probation, because of their tendency to commit non-violent offences with a relatively low risk of recidivism and almost none at all of serious injury to members of the public.

Yet, while the probation service pursued a course which appeared, in its application to males, to decelerate the move up-tariff, female offenders have entered the prisons at a rate which is recognised to be inappropriate, unjust and even downright cruel in its effects. The service has been reluctant to acknowledge this problem, apparently confident that a policy which drives its interventions with male offenders must be the right policy for the times and, therefore, the right policy for women. Yet this perspective overlooks some inconvenient truths about the position of women in the criminal justice system.

First, the success of juvenile justice policy during the 1980s has been widely attributed to the multi-agency consensus which developed throughout that decade as to the utility of diversion from prosecution and custody (Gelsthorpe and Morris 1994; Pratt 1989). Reduced intrusiveness by the probation and social services was complemented by expansion in the work of other agencies, particularly police cautioning and voluntary-sector provision of community-based programmes. Whatever public sympathies there might have been for female offenders, they did not translate into an integrated multi-agency endeavour to accompany the probation service's drive to reduce the numbers of women subject to probation.

Second, perspectives on offence seriousness, risk and the place of probation on the sentencing tariff have been constructed around notions of characteristically male offending, particularly violence, sex and burglary. Yet these are not the offences for which women predominantly fill the prisons. In 1996, only 29 per cent of female prisoners on an average day were there for violent, sexual, burglary and robbery offences (Home Office 1997). Has the probation service's construction of the sentencing tariff failed female offenders, in ways that have helped to consign them to harsh and degrading incarceration, on the grounds that they are undeserving of the service's non-custodial opportunities?

This chapter explores the experience of an agency with a strong tradition of prescriptive practice, during a period of organisational introspection and policy transition. Its message concerns the struggle to hear clients' voices and to adopt their perspectives within such an environment.

Exploratory Practice in One Probation Service

In 1993, Hereford and Worcester Probation Service took a policy decision to create separate provision for female offenders under supervision, establishing a particular structure for service delivery. A groupwork programme was designed to introduce women to topics relevant to their offending and lifestyles, incorporating sessions on female crime, relationships, stress management, assertiveness, anger management, substance use, health and employment/training. Led by two female probation officers whose time was dedicated to developmental practice with women on probation, the programme was scheduled on one day per week, when transport, lunch and a crèche managed by volunteers were provided. It was enhanced by a serendipitous opportunity to use some redundant council premises as a centre for the exclusive purpose of delivering services to women. Female link officers, located in field teams, undertook the majority of direct individual work, liaised with the centre and advised their colleagues on provision. Focused staff investment, however, led in the longer term to recognition of issues which illuminated the predicament of women offenders in relation to their access to probation service provision. These issues, and their implications for service quality, will be explored in the following account of the project's experience.

The Role of Consultancy

The author was appointed as independent academic consultant to the women's programme in 1995, when separate provision had been in operation for two years. Planning for the contribution of consultancy took into account a number of staff concerns. Staff felt that their groupwork programme was well received by the women who attended it; the evaluative feedback collected from participants from every group was consistently positive. They thought, however, that the programme was underused owing to field officers' failure to refer and encourage women to attend. Moreover, recurrent challenges to the justification for separate provision arose within the service through the perception that it targeted low-tariff, low-risk offenders, whose supervising officers became enmeshed in a tangle of personal distress rather than focused on criminality. As a result of these organisational concerns, the role of consultancy became threefold: to examine the targeting of women offenders for probation through the medium of pre-sentence reports; to construct a profile of female offenders coming to the attention of the probation service; and to link this profile to broader research, thereby informing practice development.

The Targeting Controversy

To examine the probation service's dissatisfaction with its targeting of women for probation, a survey of the previous year's pre-sentence reports (hereafter PSRs) in female cases and their outcomes was carried out, involving 180 reports prepared in 1994 (Rumgay 1995).

Table 12.1 shows the frequency with which particular disposals were imposed by sentencers alongside the frequency with which they were proposed by report writers. Clearly, the preferred proposals coincided with their popularity as sentences in the courts, with standard probation (i.e. probation without additional requirements) being the most frequent proposal and outcome, followed by conditional discharge and community service. Nevertheless, officers proposed conditional discharge considerably more often than courts imposed it; they also worked to a shorter tariff in that they never proposed custodial sanctions and only one proposal for a combination order was made in the entire year. Thus, Table 12.1 does not reveal how often probation officers secured the outcome which they proposed in specific cases.

Table 12.1. Frequency of particular disposals as outcomes at court proposals in pre-sentence reports in 1994 (percentages in brackets)		
Disposal	Outcome	Proposal
Probation order standard	62 (34)	66 (37)*
Conditional discharge	37 (21)	55 (31)
Community service order	22 (12)	20 (11)
Fine	14 (8)	12 (7)
Probation order with requirement	12 (7)	19 (11)**
Custody	11 (6)	- (-)
Suspended sentence	9 (5)	- (-)
Combination order	8 (4)	1 (-)
Other	5 (3)	7 (4)
Total	180 (100)	180 (100)

*   Includes 1 supervision order
** Includes 1 supervision order with intensive programme requirement

Table 12.2 shows the 'concordance' between PSR proposals and the outcomes at court, i.e. the number of occasions on which the outcome in a particular case agreed with the report writer's proposal. Probation officers were more successful than otherwise in all categories of the proposals which they used, except for the combination order.

The enthusiasm for the conditional discharge suggested that officers were exercising tariff vigilance, seeking to push women down the scale where possible. These proposals included some adventurous successful arguments for conditional discharge, for example, in a case of deception involving £3500 and in two cases of drunk driving. The fact that officers appealed sparingly to extra requirements in probation orders also suggested active tariff attention, and reflected both the service's policy against forcing women onto programmes dominated by male interests, and preference for encouraging voluntary attendance at the women's groupwork programme. Overall, probation officers restricted appeals to extra requirements to cases in which they perceived little alternative.

Table 12.2 Frequency with which outcomes at court agreed
with and differed from proposals in pre-sentence reports
in 1994 (percentages in brackets)*

Proposal	Outcome		Total
	Agrees	Differs	
Probation order standard**	50 (76)	16 (24)	66 (100)
Community service order	13 (65)	7 (35)	20 (100)
Conditional discharge	33 (60)	22 (40)	55 (100)
Fine	7 (58)	5 (42)	12 (100)
Probation order with requirement***	10 (53)	9 (47)	19 (100)
Combination order	- (-)	1 (100)	1 (100)
Total	113 (65)	60 (35)	173 (100)

*   Figures exclude 7 pre-sentence reports with 'other' proposals and/or outcomes
**   Includes 1 supervision order
***   Includes 1 supervision order with intensive programme requirement

Of the 160 women for whom information was available, 60 (37%) were first
offenders. However, only eight first offenders were recommended for probation:
four were convicted of deception involving large sums of money over appreciable
periods of time; two had committed drink-driving offences involving both high
alcohol readings and aggravating features; one was convicted of a substantial
theft from an employer; and one of perverting the course of justice. Moreover,
what appeared as relatively trivial or first offences in the statistical information
collected within the service, often involved complex issues of seriousness. For
example, benefit fraud is commonly brought to court on the basis of one or two
'specimen' charges. Thus, statistical data recorded minor offences with a small
total value. Yet probation officers' proposals reflected appreciation that the court
was dealing with repeated offences, sometimes sustained over a substantial time,
amounting to large sums in total. Accumulation of such 'typical' female cases
contributed to the perception that the women targeted for probation were first,
minor and low-risk offenders, and should be disqualified from probation, while
obscuring problematic sentencing issues.

The profile of female offenders

To explore the alleged focus on personal distress at the expense of criminality, the PSR survey examined the offences for which the women were sentenced and the types of need to which report writers paid attention.

Table 12.3 Offences for which women were sentenced in 1994 (percentages in brackets)	
Offence	**Total**
Deception	51 (28)
Shoplifting	33 (18)
Other theft/handling	17 (9)
Total dishonesty	*101 (55)*
Personal violence	34 (19)
Excess alcohol	13 (7)
Burglary	6 (3)
Pervert justice	5 (3)
Drugs	5 (3)
Disqualified driving	4 (2)
Conspiracy	2 (1)
Arson	1 (0.5)
Blackmail	1 (0.5)
Threat to kill	1 (0.5)
Attempted robbery	1 (0.5)
Cruelty to animals	1 (0.5)
Criminal Damage	1 (0.5)
Offensive weapon	1 (0.5)
Public order	2 (1)
Road traffic	1 (0.5)
Total	180 (100)

OFFENDING

Table 12.3 shows that dishonesty accounted for over half of the offences for which the women were sentenced. The predominance of deception, the most common variety being benefit fraud, and shoplifting reflects research evidence that these are 'typical' female crimes (Hedderman and Hough 1994; Morris *et al.* 1994; Simon and Landis 1991). Probation officers related such offences to poverty and responsibility for family care in most cases. However, as we have seen, a connection with social deprivation does not prevent such offences from appearing serious to the courts.

NEEDS

After the almost universal poverty, five areas of need received particular attention in PSRs: psychological problems (38 cases, 21%); current or previous involvement in abusive partnerships (36 cases, 20%); child abuse survival (22 cases, 12%); alcohol problems (20 cases, 11%); and drug problems (18 cases, 10%). Since only explicit reference to abuse was counted, and non-specific accounts of 'difficult' or 'unhappy' childhoods or partnerships were rejected, these are probably underestimates of abuse histories.

Offence narratives frequently linked these areas of personal distress directly or indirectly to the women's criminality. For example, an excess alcohol and dangerous driving offence was committed in an attempt to escape from immediate domestic violence; seemingly uncontrolled aggression was displayed after a woman discovered her partner's abuse of her children, in an effort to prevent him from re-entering the house. In ten cases (6%), the offence was linked to a pressurised relationship with a male which was not said to include violence. For example, a partner's refusal of financial support or unpredictable absences often underlay benefit fraud; all cases of perverting justice were linked to intimidation by males.

Chronic psychological damage from abuse was also connected to offending. For example, in two cases, childhood trauma was linked to the development of obsessive-compulsive disorders which included shoplifting. Several women were rape victims; one woman's violence was an attempt to ward off further attack. Rare offences, such as arson and conspiracy, involved unique circumstances, usually compounded by complex psychological disturbance: a woman set fire to her flat in a suicide attempt, after first ensuring her child's safety.

Probation officers' proposals responded to these aspects of female offenders' lives. In two cases, community service was excluded because of the danger of exacerbating an abusive relationship. In two cases, the officer assisted the woman to a place of safety following an attack during the report preparation period. As implied by much research on female offenders (e.g. Baskin and Sommers 1998; Maher 1997), therefore, probation officers found themselves, in a very real sense, working with high-risk victims. This perspective challenges the common assumption that risk concerns only the degree to which predatory offenders threaten the safety of an innocent public.

The PSR survey thus revealed, first, that repetition, seriousness and risk were all observable in the offending of women, but were obscured by the application of measures of their presence derived from assumptions about typically male offences. Second, probation officers' involvement in areas of personal distress, commonly viewed as irrelevant to an offence focus, reflected connections drawn in the women's offence narratives. Third, the offences, needs and their interconnections characterising this group of women reflected research findings. Probation officers thus appeared not so much as trangressors of articulated policy as practitioners whose intensified exposure through the introduction of gender-separated provision sensitised them to these issues. Specialist and link officers received these observations with relief, having repeatedly claimed that their difficulties in formulating proposals and managing female offenders under supervision were misunderstood. One officer complained: 'They think if we refuse to work with them, these women will just go away. But they won't.'

A Model for Practice

The problem for practice development had been constructed as one of poor targeting and inappropriate focus, defined by the criteria applied to typically male offending. If, however, probation officers were neither inappropriately targeting minor offenders, nor involving themselves irrelevantly in personal distress, then the real challenge was to sensitise practice to the features of typically *female* offending. Assimilation of the PSR survey's observations was followed by a shift from defensive to pro-active practice. This involved developing strategies to enhance women's access to the service, particularly the groupwork programme, and articulating a rationale for gender-sensitive provision.

Enhancement of access

Attendance at the groupwork programme appeared in 46 of the supervision plans which supported proposals for probation. Of the 39 women for whom a probation order was actually made when groupwork formed part of the supervision plan, only 22 arrived at the programme. Reasons for non-arrival were unknown. Specialist staff believed they lacked influence over women's access to the centre. Two strategies in particular altered this predicament.

First, specialist staff reached out proactively to field teams, monitoring the imposition of probation orders, enquiring about supervision plans and exploring the potential contribution of groupwork participation. Regular meetings of specialist and link officers promoted open case discussion. Officers referring women accompanied them to the centre for a preliminary meeting with specialist staff, thereby engaging the women's interest and confidence.

Second, complementing the service's approach to its intensive programmes for male probationers, a book was produced to articulate its strategy for females (Hereford and Worcester Probation Service 1997). This initiative raised the visibility of a practice model which explicitly embraced separate provision, integration of individual and groupwork methods, and gender-sensitive responsivity.

Integration of services

The existence of an exclusive centre for the delivery of the groupwork programme facilitated investment in collaborative multi-agency effort. The overarch-
ing goal of 'normalisation' underpinned this aspect of practice: it enhanced
female offenders' access to community-based networks of support; and decreased
emphasis on the probation service as a focal resource for women whose social and
personal problems were shared by many non-offenders. Reducing emphasis on
the criminal justice base of the women's centre included, therefore, developing its
use as a community resource.

A specialist officer described three elements in the centre's development as a
community resource: provision of a space exclusively for women which was safe,
comfortable and enhanced their social and learning opportunities; development
of a focal point of networking and a forum for groups working with women; and
the offer of direct services for users, which included education, advice and the
probation groupwork programme. In pursuit of these themes, the centre accommodated a variety of community groups: sociology classes run by the college of
technology; the local women's refuge's support group for ex-residents, volunteer
training courses and management committee meetings; a voluntary agency which
offered direct support for families under stress and parenting skills courses; a
support agency for sexual abuse survivors offering counselling and volunteer
training; a sewing group of Muslim women; and female solicitors offering legal
advice.

While this is a very different approach from that of the conventional probation
centre offering offence-focused programmes exclusively for offenders, and therefore could appear peripheral to core provision, this integrative approach resolved
difficulties of locating women within the mainstream of the service's opportunities. Because of their typical offending patterns, women offenders were not
attractive candidates for conventional tariff-based provision. Because of their distinctive histories, it was inappropriate to force them onto programmes designed
for and dominated by males. Because of their particular needs, enhanced access to
community support networks represented empowerment. Precisely because of
the probation service's difficulty in locating these women in its core provision, it
became vital to connect them to their communities.

Introducing the user's voice

Staff collected programme evaluation questionnaires from women on completion
of each group. For the purposes of this chapter the questionnaires returned by
103 women, from 19 groups, were studied. The forms were not designed as
research instruments, but were used as 'process commentary' to inform adaptations to programme content and presentation. The most illuminating material
derives from the women's written comments in response to the invitation to

'please explain' after the required tick-box entry to each question, permitting some qualitative analysis of their collective remarks, which is offered here.

Most women had embarked on the programme with few expectations, at the behest of their probation officer or the court. Evaluations, however, were overwhelmingly positive. Women almost unanimously applauded the group's gender exclusivity, recording freedom of expression, mutuality of perspective and absence of discomfort and denigration which was associated with male presence:

> No male threats – able to discuss – not argue.
>
> Being able to speak openly without men to contradict what you say.
>
> Talk as equals – men always have to be top dog.
>
> We can say what we want without being put down.
>
> I could explain how I felt without people laughing or making sexist comments.

Women predominantly identified relationship as both the best and the most influential aspect of the programme. Group relationships were valued for fun, friendship, sharing of problems and experiences, self-validation and for providing a positive experience of helping others. The stimulation of helpful, interesting information and group discussion was also often cited as the best aspect, while some women mentioned specific sessions which they appreciated. Many comments identified influential programme features, almost invariably deriving from the relational group process: reduced stigma and isolation; increased confidence and self-esteem; enhanced self-identity and self-assertion; improved social skills and help-giving; altered criminal attitudes and behaviour; reduced stereotyping and greater appreciation of women's diversity; stimulation and learning; and increased readiness to seek help:

> I find myself more understanding towards people, give time out to listen and to help if I can.
>
> Because of listening to others' experiences I have learnt to put myself and my daughter first.
>
> I wouldn't have thought so many women from different walks of life would be on probation.
>
> More assertive, definitely not passive at all. Now I know the difference.
>
> I feel I don't have to do everything to please everyone in my life by being bullied.
>
> To be more open and honest about what I want.

Criticisms and suggestions for improving the programme were scarce. Many women declined to identify the worst part of the programme. Food quality was the most common complaint. Some disliked specific sessions. Relationship again featured strongly. The first session was the worst aspect for many, indicating anxieties about meeting other women and being shamed as offenders. For others, closure was problematic, incurring loss of relationship and return to the 'real world'. A few acknowledged difficulties in managing the group relationships.

Finding a slot to fit in which enables one to learn from others and also give.

Going home after talking about things.

Not being able to be accepted.

Although many women recorded enthusiasm for further programmes, they commonly declined to identify topics of interest. Some suggested developing topics of the existing programme; others wanted further opportunities to help other women. Few offered suggestions for new material. Responses collectively suggested that the desire to preserve a positive relational involvement was stronger than preferences for specific content:

It seems to lift me up.

Because you know you are not alone anymore.

The group has given me a lot of support so it would be nice to be able to give some back to someone else who needs it.

Anything.

Staff also used a range of tools for process feedback during the life of each group. For example, the 'Happy Chart' comprised a graph on which women marked their mood level in coloured ink as they left each session. Critical scrutiny of a topic's suitability and presentation followed observation that low moods were consistently recorded after particular sessions.

Hard Lessons to Learn

Staff defined problems in user participation, primarily in terms of resistance on the part of field officers, who controlled women's access to the groupwork programme. This is a common theme in the histories of local initiatives in the probation service, which, because of its particular agency function and its involuntary, often resistant client group, is more accustomed to defining the content of its service on behalf of targeted recipients than to engaging them directly in planning. Client shortages are commonly viewed as the result of staff inertia. Thus, energies are invested in improving *probation officer* participation, often at the expense of attention to user perspectives. Such an organisational focus was reinforced for specialist staff by the consistently high praise which women lavished on the programme. Several questions thus emerge from this experience.

What is the reality of user participation within a prescriptive agency tradition? How is agency resistance to be understood and managed? What is the future of pioneering local initiatives within an agency increasingly driven by broader political pressures?

Letting voiceless clients speak

Notwithstanding the probation service's commendable virtues of respect for and helpfulness to its clients (Mair and May 1997), it is not well known for direct involvement of offenders in development of provision. It is more likely to test its programme recipients for evidence that they have changed in prescribed ways than to open its service to the critical scrutiny of offenders. This experience, however, exposes users' difficulties in grappling with such an opportunity.

The shortage of criticisms and suggestions for improvement is open to interpretation. Possibly staff had grasped the needs and interests of their client group with exceptional perspicacity. Alternatively, perhaps these women were simply unused to articulating opinions. Many had learned that self-assertion was unwelcome, even dangerous within their relational 'real worlds'. Their lack of expectations reflected learned acceptance that others would define what was good for them. Positive self-validation, which was so strongly appreciated, was an unusual experience. But the very experience of personal validation during the groupwork process might inhibit the expression of criticism. What repayment for gains in self-worth and relational enjoyment would criticism represent to the staff who facilitated it? Might criticism 'spoil' the experience by implying that it had been less rewarding than participants felt it to be?

This is not to suggest that staff *lacked* responsive awareness, but rather to highlight the difficulty of progressing beyond applause for professional skill, to enable chronically muted women to contribute actively to service development. The use of process feedback tools perhaps reflects an intuitive grasp of this issue by staff, who attempted to monitor women's reactions when framed as subjective self-expression rather than objective programme evaluation. Adjustments to the programme followed process feedback. For example:

1. A session on debt management was abandoned. Women clearly disliked it, although their various reasons emerged gradually: they felt it was too confidential for group discussion; they were bored by the presentation; and they were distressed by the judgemental and patronising approach of guest speakers.

2. During early sessions on alcohol, women's comments suggested that this was not the only – or primary – substance problem. Relating this observation to a PSR survey finding, staff expanded the topic to include drugs.

3. A GCSE sociology course was introduced in response to women's asser-
tions that they wished to stay connected to the centre: 'We never thought
for a minute that these comments were about "working on their offending", but they did seem to be saying very clearly that the women wanted
to continue to work on something *in the same context* – women only,
women centred, child friendly, etc... that led us to negotiate with the
college and...that keeps us at it, despite the organisational horrors of
these classes' (Sheath 1999).

4. Women's curiosity about the support agency for abuse survivors occupy-
ing part of the premises suggested a need, amplified by evidence
emerging during groupwork discussions and the PSR survey. A specific
session was designed to enhance women's access to help, using the agency
workers to explore issues in self- and child protection.

5. Complaints about food quality stopped when staff dispensed with the
caterer and engaged the women collectively in meal preparation.

Clearly, staff felt required to interpret creatively the clues which women gave as to
their preferences. Nevertheless, efforts to draw out users' views and to develop
integrated practice remained encapsulated at the women's centre. Yet how *should*
the wider agency receive the news that dedicated resources had produced positive
relational experiences for over 100 offenders? Women's emphasis on the significance of relationship in the group process reflects the importance of relational
involvement for female psychological development, learning and rehabilitation
(Bandura 1997; Covington 1998; Gilligan 1988). Their attributions of liberation
to the group's gender-exclusivity are supported in research (Tannen 1992). Nevertheless, how powerful is a defence of practice based on appeals to the subtleties
of gender psychology, when advanced within an organisation under strong contemporary pressure to effect individual change by challenge, confrontation and
control? Paradoxically, current drives to improve evidence-based practice
(Underdown 1998) may further weaken attempts to increase minority participation:

> How do we actually identify the need to change? In the past, we have been
> able to sit round a table, Happy Chart in one hand, evaluations in another, and
> *experience* in mind, and have a discussion, make some decision, pilot
> something new. I doubt this will be enough in the brave new world of
> programmes – it's not scientific enough...neither does it rely on expert
> opinion... I suspect that whatever is designed...to identify needs will be male
> centred. (Sheath 1999)

Providing a validating agency environment

Despite the good intentions of individual practitioners, user participation will
never increase in a hostile agency environment. This experience demonstrated

that the policies and practices of an agency must be capable of responding to the needs of particular sub-groups of its clientele. This can only be accomplished through organisational willingness to accept as valid perspectives which contradict the assumptions informing provision for the majority. Senior management's endorsement of this gender-sensitive initiative and its practice implications was therefore vital.

Female offenders' failure to fit criteria for eligibility for service that were defined by typical male offence characteristics and supervision needs became a reason to reject them. In such an environment, a specialist officer described colleagues working defensively, to 'hide' their female caseload, in the belief that the wider agency denied the validity of their involvement. Link officers, located individually in field teams, were particularly vulnerable to criticism and erosions of their specialist time. Gender-sensitive practice developed through intuition and in isolation. Validation of the perspective through case analysis, linked to broader research and theory, provided the springboard to articulated and proactive practice. Yet specialist staff, to whom gender-sensitive perspectives and associated methodologies became familiar, were constantly surprised by the resistance of professional colleagues whose tasks remained dominated by male supervision. For example, transportation to the centre was seen by some to offer an unfair advantage to women in the absence of such provision for males. Specialist officers, however, observed that few male probationers were responsible for preparing their children for the day as well as themselves. From this perspective, transport equalised women's opportunity to meet programme requirements.

Table 12.4 Attendance at women's groupwork programme 1994–1999			
Year	Number of programmes	Women starting programme	Women completing programme**
1994	3	20	15 (75)
1995	4	51	31 (61)
1996	4	41	21 (51)
1997	3	39	27 (69)
1998	3	28	22 (78)
1999*	1	14	9 (64)

* As at April 1999
** Percentages in brackets

Sustaining the initiative

Table 12.4 shows some results of the endeavour from 1994 to 1999. The strategies for increasing participation in the groupwork programme reaped an immediate reward, which subsequently declined.

An initiative which embraces minority perspectives contradictory to those
informing interventions for the majority, is inherently fragile. The very existence
of such an enterprise becomes a focus of challenge at times when its host agency is
under pressure. When severe funding constraints necessitated radical organisational restructuring, the women's programme owed its survival to the continued
endorsement of the Chief Officer. Nevertheless, between 1996 and 1998, it was
specifically affected by altered mechanisms of line management, reduction of
dedicated specialist staff to one full-time officer and relocation in probation
service premises.

Efforts to secure the programme's future extended to attempts to integrate it
within broader fields of activity. The transition of one prison in the county from
male to female occupancy provided an opportunity to adapt the groupwork
programme for institutional presentation. While in principle this extended
opportunities for women to participate in a therapeutic groupwork programme,
in practice it also introduced the enterprise into a singularly hostile environment
(HM Chief Inspector of Prisons 1998; Roberts 1998). Later, inclusion in the
Home Office's Pathfinder initiative for the development of evidence-based
model projects necessitated detailed specification of the model of practice and
programme content.

The attention and energy demanded by these organisational adaptations to
insecurity may be related to falling participation in the groupwork programme in
so far as staff relied on the success of their earlier campaign. Clearly, however,
connection between elements of the supervision opportunities is maintained only
by sustained effort.

Adapting to an altered policy landscape

Britain's penal climate altered significantly following the Home Secretary's
announcement, during the previous Conservative government, that 'prison
works' (Howard 1993). Tables 12.5 and 12.6 reproduce part of the 1994 PSR
survey for reports prepared on women in 1998. The standard probation order
and conditional discharge have fallen dramatically in their proportionate use,
both as proposal and as outcome. Their popularity has been displaced by
increased focus on the intensified forms of supervision: attendance at the
women's groupwork programme, and other interventions such as substance
misuse treatment, have become more routinely coerced requirements. The use of
custody, however, has changed little. Concordance remains high, particularly for

forms of probation. These findings suggest a general trend up-tariff for female offenders into the more intrusive categories of supervision.

Table 12.5 Frequency of particular disposals as outcomes at court proposals in pre-sentence reports in 1998 (percentages in brackets)		
Disposal	Outcome	Proposal
Probation order standard	39 (23)	50 (30)
Probation order with requirement	27 (16)	30 (18)
Other	25 (15)	27 (16)*
Conditional discharge	22 (13)	22 (13)
Community service order	18 (11)	22 (13)
Combination order	16 (9)	10 (6)
Custody	13 (8)	- (-)
Fine	7 (4)	8 (5)
Suspended sentence	2 (1)	- (-)
Total	169 (100)	169 (100)

* Includes 10 without proposals

Table 12.6 Frequency with which outcomes at court agreed with and differed from proposals in pre-sentence reports in 1998 (percentages in brackets)			
Proposal	Outcome		Total
	Agrees	Differs	
Probation order with requirement	23 (77)	7 (23)*	30 (100)
Probation order standard	36 (72)	14 (28)	50 (100)
Conditional discharge	15 (68)	7 (32)	22 (100)
Fine	5 (62.5)	3 (37.5)	8 (100)
Community service order	13 (59)	9 (41)	22 (100)
Combination order	3 (30)	7 (70)**	10 (100)
Total	95 (67)	47 (33)	142 (100)***

*   Includes 1 proposal for probation order with 2 additional requirements, for which outcome is recorded as probation order with 1 additional requirement
**   Includes 4 proposals for combination order with additional requirement of attendance at the women's groupwork programme, for which outcome is recorded as combination order
*** Excludes 27 pre-sentence reports with 'other' proposals and/or outcomes

Of 153 offenders for whom information was available, only 88 (57.5%) had previous convictions. Table 12.7 shows the breakdown of offences for the total of 169 female offenders on whom PSRs were prepared in 1998. Dishonesty continues to represent the largest female contribution to crime, although the proportion of offences of deception has fallen. The proportion of violent offences has changed little. Increasing seriousness of female crime might be indicated by the involvement in supply of 12 (63%) of the 19 drug offenders. Offence narratives, however, revealed no convincing evidence of economic advancement through drug dealing, but criminality often arising within a complex web of drug-involved and oppressive relationships amid broader social and personal disadvantage.

Table 12.7 Offences for which women were sentenced in 1998 (percentages in brackets)	
Offence	**Total**
Deception	28 (16.5)
Other theft/handling	28 (16.5)
Shoplifting	22 (13)
Total dishonesty	*78 (46)*
Personal violence	32 (19)
Drugs	21 (12)
Excess alcohol	11 (7)
Disqualified driving	7 (6.5)
Arson	4 (2)
Burglary	3 (2)
Cruelty to child	3 (2)
Public order	3 (2)
Threat to kill	2 (1)
Pervert justice	1 (0.5)
Blackmail	1 (0.5)
Robbery	1 (0.5)
Criminal damage	1 (0.5)
Take without owner's consent	1 (0.5)
Total	180 (100)

In short, there is little evidence that the county's female offenders in 1998 were guilty of more serious offences, or that they posed a greater risk to public safety, than in 1994. Their treatment locally reflects national trends for rising imprisonment in tandem with the more intense forms of supervision, increasingly visited upon a less criminally experienced population of offenders (Home Office 1997). Thus, for female offenders in Hereford and Worcester, the price of a marginal rise in custody has been heavily intensified community-based intervention. Coercion, not participation, has gained emphasis in service delivery.

'Feeling More Able?'[1]

The decision to establish separate provision in this area forced into the open the difficulties of responding creatively to female offenders within the context of the probation service's modern sense of mission. These difficulties remain muted and unfocused where the predominance of male offenders swamps the client population and drives the forms of policy and practice which develop. Their deepest irony lies in the evolution of a policy framework in which the female offender, by the very nature of her less serious offending and lower public risk, has come to be regarded as undeserving of opportunities for rehabilitation. Equally, her status as offender disqualifies her from recognition as the victim with whom the probation service is most regularly and directly brought into contact. It is a distressing paradox that a service which has been engaged for some time in an effort to enhance its support for victims of crime, and which currently presents its mission in terms of public protection, should have come to perceive responsiveness to the real danger of victimisation experienced by many female offenders as an unwarranted reaction to a welfare problem. Poignantly, the female offender's isolation within local communities creates a situation in which the probation service may offer her only gateway to appropriate support networks.

Within a powerful organisational tradition of prescriptive practice, strengthened further by contemporary penal pressures, the user's voice is muted. The minority user's voice is weaker still, since to recognise its message demands the effort to engage with an alternative personal world, to locate need within a fully articulated organisational mission, to respond creatively and to sustain the vigour of that response.

Note

1   A woman wrote 'Feeling more able?' on her programme evaluation questionnaire when invited to comment on the assertiveness and anger management sessions.

Acknowledgements

I am indebted to Hereford and Worcester Probation Service for the inspiration behind this chapter, and permission to refer directly to their experience. I would particularly like to thank Jenny Roberts, Chief Probation Officer, Jim Farebrother, Senior Probation Officer, and Jan Sheath, Specialist Probation Officer Women's Centre for their assistance, interest and candid contributions.

References

Bandura, A. (1997) *Self-efficacy: The Exercise of Control*. New York: W.H. Freeman and Company.

Baskin, D.R. and Sommers, I.B. (1998) *Casualties of Community Disorder: Women's Careers in Violent Crime*. Boulder, CO: Westview Press.

Buchanan, J., Collett, S. and McMullan, P. (1991) 'Challenging Practice or Challenging Women? Female Offenders and Illicit Drug Use.' *Probation Journal 38*, 2, 56–62.

Cohen, S. (1985) *Visions of Social Control*. London: Polity Press.

Covington, S. (1998) 'The Relational Theory of Women's Psychological Development: Implications for the Criminal Justice System.' In R.T. Zaplin (ed) *Female Offenders: Critical Perspectives and Effective Interventions*. Gaithersburg, MD: Aspen.

Gelsthorpe, L. and Morris, A. (1994) 'Juvenile Justice 1945–1992.' In M. Maguire, R. Morgan and R. Reiner (eds) *The Oxford Handbook of Criminology*. Oxford: Oxford University Press.

Gilligan, C. (1998) 'Prologue: Adolescent Development Reconsidered.' In C. Gilligan, J.V. Ward and J.M. Taylor (eds) *Mapping the Moral Domain*. Cambridge, MA: Harvard University Press.

Hedderman, C. and Hough, M. (1994) *Does the Criminal Justice System Treat Men and Women Differently?* Research Findings No. 10. London: Home Office.

Hereford and Worcester Probation Service (1997) *Programme for Women Offenders*. Worcester: Hereford and Worcester Probation Service.

HM Chief Inspector of Prisons (1997) *Women in Prison: A Thematic Review*. London: Home Office.

HM Chief Inspector of Prisons (1998) *HM Prison Brockhill: Report of an Unannounced Short Inspection 7–9 July 1997*. London: Home Office.

Home Office (1997) *Prison Statistics England and Wales 1996*. Cm 3732. London: Home Office.

Home Office (1998) *Probation Statistics England and Wales 1997*. London: Home Office.

Howard, M. (1993) *Speech to the Conservative Party Conference*. London: Conservative Central Office.

Learmont, Sir J. (1995) *Review of Prison Security in England and Wales and the Escape from Parkhurst Prison on Tuesday 3rd January 1995*. Cm 3020. London: HMSO.

Maher, L. (1997) *Sexed Work: Gender, Race and Resistance in a Brooklyn Drug Market*. Oxford: Oxford University Press.

Mair, G. and May, C. (1997) *Offenders on Probation*. Home Office Research Study 167. London: Home Office.

Morris, A., Wilkinson, C., Tisi, A., Woodrow, J. and Rockley, A. (1994) *Managing the Needs of Female Prisoners*. London: Home Office.

Pratt, J. (1989) 'Corporatism: The Third Model of Juvenile Justice.' *British Journal of Criminology 29*, 3, 236–254.

Roberts, J. (1998) 'Redesigning Provision for Women Offenders.' Paper presented at Greater Manchester Probation Service, Hereford and Worcester Probation Service, University of

Liverpool and Association of Chief Officers of Probation 'What Works?' Conference, Manchester, 16–18 September.

Rumgay, J. (1995) 'Analysis of Pre-Sentence Reports on Women Offenders Prepared during 1994 by Hereford and Worcester Probation Service.' Unpublished Report to Hereford and Worcester Probation Service.

Sheath, J. (1999) Personal communication.

Simon, R.J. and Landis, J. (1991) *The Crimes Women Commit, the Punishments They Receive.* Lexington, MA: Lexington Books.

Tannen, D. (1992) *You Just Don't Understand: Women and Men in Conversation.* London: Virago Press.

Thorpe, D.H., Smith, D., Green, C.J. and Paley, J.H. (1980) *Out of Care: The Community Support of Juvenile Offenders.* London: Allen and Unwin.

Underdown, A. (1998) *Strategies for Effective Offender Supervision: Report of the 'HMIP What Works Project'.* London: Home Office.

Walker, N., Farrington, D.P. and Tucker, G. (1981) 'Reconviction Rates of Adult Males after Different Sentences.' *British Journal of Criminology 21,* 4, 357–360.

Woodcock, Sir J. (1994) *Report of the Enquiry into the Escape of Six Prisoners from the Special Security Unit at Whitemoor Prison, Cambridgeshire, on Friday 9th September 1994.* Cm 2741. London: HMSO.

Worrall, A. (1981) 'Out of Place: Female Offenders in Court.' *Probation Journal 28,* 3, 90–93.

CHAPTER 13

User Involvement, Community Care and Disability Research

Kathryn Ellis

As Hammersley (1995) observes, 'good research' used to be defined in terms of authenticity, but methodology textbooks now define good practice in terms of user involvement. What is signalled here is the contested nature of 'truth', and the power struggles involved in designing and conducting contemporary social research. The involvement of disabled people in community care research is no exception, and this chapter first examines the struggles of the disability movement to redefine 'disability' and the nature of appropriate policy responses. It is these new ways of knowing disability which inform debates amongst disability theorists about the potential for, and restrictions placed upon, disabled people's participation in community care and in policy- and practice-related research. In the light of cross-cutting power relations between service providers and users and between the researcher and the researched, the concluding section makes some suggestions about the type of methodology which may lead to meaningful involvement in research on the part of disabled people.

Disability Policies and Politics

Central to the critiques developed by disability theorists, as Hughes (1998) points out, is the role of medical ways of knowing the body and mind in marginalising disabled people from the able-bodied majority. By naturalising disability as 'individual sickness' or 'pathological condition' on the one hand and able-bodiedness as health and normality on the other, medicine has constructed disabled people as simultaneously deviant yet vulnerable and dependent. According to Priestley (1999), the 'culture of embodiment' dominating Western societies has linked the economic and social disadvantage experienced by disabled people to the impaired body, and characterised it as personal tragedy.

Drake's (1999) schema of disability policies can be used to demonstrate the ways in which the medico-welfare systems of industrial capitalism have reflected and reinforced dominant representations of disability. Three of the four successive but overlapping discourses within which he locates disability policies in Britain – segregation, compensation, integration and citizenship – have been shaped by medical orthodoxy. As Hughes (1998) argues, shifts in the institutionalised practices of welfare are congruent with changing knowledges of disability yet still retain common features, namely: the individualisation of disability in terms of individual pathology, a focus on the impairment rather than the person, and the location of power with the medical and allied professions.

In the nineteenth century, disability policies largely consisted of containing people with physical and cognitive impairments within the institutional apparatus of the Poor Law. At the same time, new discourses of humanitarianism found expression in organised philanthropy and legislation providing compensation for industrial accidents. During and after the First World War, the principle of compensating people for the individual tragedy of impairment became more fully established, with access to disablement benefits and services regulated by the medical profession. After the Second World War, there was a burgeoning of health and welfare services designed to integrate disabled people into the community, primarily through strategies of rehabilitation and normalisation.

Community care was framed within Drake's (1999) third dominant discourse of disability policies, reflecting aspirations to promote the integration of people with 'special needs' into ordinary life. As the unfortunate victims of individual circumstance, disabled people were to be treated benevolently rather than blamed for their situation. At the same time, their rehabilitation or integration was to be secured against a fixed notion of 'normality'. The underlying politics were those of service provision rather than social change, geared towards compensating individuals for and helping them adjust to, rather than transform, their experience of society (Braye and Preston-Shoot 1995). So far from achieving the social integration of people formerly confined to long-stay institutions, access to and delivery of community care came to constitute forms of administrative segregation in their reliance on definitions of disability as functional limitation and otherness (Priestley 1999).

The disability movement ushered in the fourth discourse framing disability policies: citizenship and rights. If disability is understood as a social construction then, as Gooding (1994) points out, its meaning can be transformed through social and political action. Central to the struggles of people with physical impairments over the past 25 years has been the construction of disability in a social model and the formation of organisations of disabled people. Campbell and Oliver (1996) trace the history of those struggles, pointing out that the formulation of a social critique of disability was part of a conscious strategy by people with physical impairments to develop a liberationist politics capable of countering oppressive models of disability. The social model, which identified the origins of disability in the socially constructed barriers of able-bodied society rather than bodily impairment, also gave disabled people the means of challenging internalised oppression and developing new ways of thinking and acting based on new understandings of the world (Brechin 1993). From the 1980s, the disability movement called for a shift in disability policies from 'charity to rights', reconstructing disabled people as citizens rather than dependent and needy individuals (Campbell and Oliver 1996).

The twin concepts of dependency and care lie at the heart of disability theorists' critiques of community care. Oliver (1991) suggests that traditional assumptions about the dependency of disabled people are open to challenge, as it is able-bodied professionals who consume by far the greatest part of the health and social services budget. The human condition is in any case characterised by interdependence rather than states of absolute dependency or independence. In order to counter medicalised definitions of 'independence' as the capacity to perform daily living tasks unaided, however, disability theorists have sought to redefine independence as people's ability to control the decisions and choices affecting their lives. According to Barnes, Mercer and Shakespeare (1999), community care is not delivered in ways which enable people to have control over their daily living activities, let alone play a role in wider society.

In contrast to civil rights and citizenship, disability theorists regard care as a form of compensation which serves to perpetuate hierarchical social relations by treating disabled people as needy and dependent. Moreover, given that services are generally only supplied directly to disabled people living alone, community care typically means dependence on family and friends (Barnes *et al.* 1999). Indeed the contemporary imperatives of welfare retrenchment have placed policies of supporting the informal carer at the centre of community care. Morris (1993) suggests that this emphasis on carers, and the failure to separate the needs and rights of carers from those of disabled people, threaten the autonomy and citizenship of the latter.

Universal citizenship hinges critically on anti-discrimination and equality legislation. Given the extent to which welfare policy and practices have compounded the marginalisation and oppression experienced by disabled people, however, their demands extend beyond equality legislation to embrace rights to, and control over, welfare provision (Oliver 1990). The user movement, which developed within and alongside the disability movement, sought to change the social relations of welfare production. Organisations such as People First and Survivors Speak Out challenged what Williams (1995) describes as 'the hierarchical relations between the providers and users of welfare services' (p.97).

Yet the legitimacy of the state as the arbiter of need and the main provider of services was called into question by the emergence of the new social movements (Pierson 1991). In the case of disability activists, the pattern of services developed by the traditional voluntary sector, and its underlying philosophy of charity, were also implicated in the social oppression of disabled people. Inspired by the independent living movement, local centres for independent/integrated living involved disabled people in the production of their own welfare. Moreover, the strategies and support services developed within them were based on an understanding of, and response to, the social causes of disability (Priestley 1999). By incorporating community development, skills training and arrangements for personal assistance adequate to support autonomy and choice, they provided a powerful alternative to traditional community-based services, such as day centres and social clubs.

Power, Empowerment and the Restructuring of Community Care

In a discussion of the 1990 National Health Service and Community Care Act (NHSCCA), Priestley (1999) points to areas of 'rhetorical convergence' between the emphasis in official guidelines on user involvement, autonomy, choice and needs-led provision on the one hand, and the philosophy of the independent living movement on the other. Yet, as Beresford (1988) argues, common references to choice and empowerment blur differing constructions of power. Within the ideology of consumerism underlying the NHSCCA, empowerment is effectively the buying power derived from exercising choice in the marketplace. For the user movement, the exercise of choice rests on first gaining power through involvement in decision making at both individual and collective levels.

At a collective level, the consumerist model of empowerment is limited both by a 'market research' model of consultation and by the capacity of disempowered groups to represent their interests (Braye and Preston-Shoot 1995). At most, disabled people are invited to provide 'feedback' according to a predetermined formula on how services might be refined, rather than to provide any fundamental challenge to the appropriateness of the response made (Drake 1999). Moreover, local authorities continue to rely on established networks of voluntary organisations in consultative exercises, many of which are organisations *for* rather than *of* disabled people (Barnes *et al.* 1999).

At an individual level, Braye and Preston-Shoot (1995) suggest that consumers are theoretically empowered through rights to information and redress, yet their ability to act autonomously is ultimately limited by the absence of any power of exit. Given that the majority of disabled people are on low incomes or are reliant on welfare payments, their choice is effectively limited to services chosen for them by the local authority social services department (Barnes *et al.* 1999). Services are paid for by the taxpayer, and the paying customers in the 'quasi-markets' of community care are the professionals who control the budgets rather than the consumer (Hugman 1998). To the extent that 'attempts to offer choice are met by users choosing more of the same', Braye and Preston-Shoot (1995, pp.109–110) suggest that internalised oppression may also constrain the exercise of consumer choice.

As Borsay (1990) points out, consumer sovereignty is also compromised where need outstrips supply because 'customers' have to accept whatever is available, irrespective of their expectations. Choice is therefore significantly restricted by a range of factors beyond the control of the consumer – eligibility criteria, limited budgets, a fixed menu of services and contracting arrangements based on the cost-efficiency imperative. Citizenship was interpreted by successive Conservative governments over the 1980s and 1990s in terms of the responsibilities of active citizenship, that is, remaining independent of the state by paying for one's own care or providing care for family members. Assessment and care management systems are therefore designed to target resources only on the most needy by managing access to, and use of, community care services. Access was made dependent on detailed assessments of individual needs and circumstances, including impairment-related functional limitations, family situation and financial resources (Barnes *et al.* 1999).

Nor does the NHSCCA do much to change a pre-existing patchwork of legislative measures governing social care which confers duties on local authorities to provide services rather than rights on individuals to receive them (Braye and Preston-Shoot 1995). Drake (1999) suggests that the language of user participation and involvement employed in contemporary community care is even weaker than that in the 1986 Disabled Persons Act which included procedural rights designed to enhance people's access to and involvement in the needs assessment process. Indeed, the 'quasi-consumerism' described by Hugman (1998) may actually obscure a strengthening of the hierarchical relations of welfare production, as the rights, needs and interests of different stakeholders in community care are reduced to a managerialist concern with meeting prescribed service standards.

Underlying debates about quality is the assumption that it is regulated by consumer choice, yet it is the purchasers rather than the consumers of community care who set the quality standards (Braye and Preston-Shoot 1995). In his study of the impact of new contracting procedures on services provided by a centre for integrated living, Priestley (1999) argues that the definition of quality standards within traditional discourses of tragedy, individualism and otherness means that service providers prioritise home-based care and judge quality in terms of the physical care afforded to individuals (see also Ellis 1999).

Nor is quality of service provision the same as quality of life, which is best defined as people receiving support to ensure that the one leads to the other (Braye and Preston-Shoot 1995). So far as disabled people's organisations are concerned, Priestley (1999) argues that quality of life depends on a level of autonomy that enables individuals to make the same choices in education, employment, personal relationships or community participation as any other citizen. Yet the type and level of services provided through statutory agencies are generally inadequate to support wider social integration, whilst 'ordinary choices' about how people use their time become commodified choices about the use of scarce financial resources.

Professional Power and Empowerment

The principles of anti-oppressive and anti-discriminatory practice, recently incorporated into social work, are also linked to the theories and techniques of empowerment (Hugman 1998). Macdonald (1999) suggests that the underlying structural analysis of inequality and need has shifted the traditional focus of social work away from the welfare of the client as a unique individual and away from interventions aimed at enhancing personal or psychological coping skills at the individual level. The extent to which social analyses have any significant impact on mainstream social work practice, however, is questionable (Seymour 1999). Moreover, Braye and Preston-Shoot (1995) argue that only anti-oppressive practice, which implies a fundamental change in the exploitative power structures and relationships that maintain inequality and oppression, challenges individual-ised models of disability and ageing and addresses the demands of the user movement for control, not just of services, but of individual lives.

Social work has historically centred on the regulation of individual confor-mity with dominant social norms in line with contemporary political ideologies (Macdonald 1999). In the restructuring of community care as 'productive', the familiar theme of social management has been reworked within managerialist discourse (Hadley and Clough 1996). By separating means from ends, managerialism promotes the effective and efficient production of services, with politicians, policy makers and managers taking control of the ends and assigning responsibility for the means to professionals (Hugman 1998). Assessment and care management systems have redefined social work as a series of technical tasks performed according to managerial specification and routinised professional decision making through the standardisation of front-line practice. The rights of the citizen are not to a specified outcome but to a fair and competent assessment to determine eligibility (Hugman 1998).

In their study of empowerment and community care, Stevenson and Parsloe (1993) suggest that social workers need to learn 'a new philosophy' and set of practices as a counterweight to 'bureaucratic over-regulation'. Yet Oliver (1991) is highly critical of the way in which organisations of disabled people have devel-oped ideas and practices such as empowerment and care management only to have them 'ripped off' by the welfare industry. Moreover, critics point out that the emergence of 'empowerment' as a new professional ethic has coincided with the stripping-back of social work to its social control functions. As such, professional empowerment arguably represents a largely defensive response to the threats to professional autonomy posed by welfare consumerism and managerialism. Baistow (1995), for example, suggests that empowerment may actually constitute a strategy of domination on the part of professionals and a means of extending their sphere of influence and regulatory powers within a reduced public sector.

In guidance to managers and practitioners on new community care arrangements, the Social Services Inspectorate (1991) recommended that professionals empower service users by using their skills to encourage participation and involvement. Jack (1995) argues that this is an example of the extent to which 'empowerment' frequently amounts to little more than enablement. Croft and Beresford (1995) similarly comment on the narrow focus of professional empowerment on personal empowerment. For them, professional empowerment represents a reworking of, rather than a retreat from, a social management role which consists in persuading people to take increased responsibility for managing their lives, relationships and circumstances in conformity with prevailing values and expectations and changing in accordance with professionally set goals and norms.

For disability theorists, therefore, empowerment as enablement is yet another form of paternalism which fails to extend beyond specialised and segregated 'care services' into mainstream services and opportunities in community life (Jack 1995). Moreover, it obscures the real sources of disadvantage and disempowerment and diverts attention away from claims for the rights of citizens to independence (Oliver 1992a). Within the disability movement, personal empowerment is understood as people gaining access to the support, skills and personal resources they require for self-organisation and participation to achieve wider social change (Croft and Beresford 1995). Empowerment is not a technical but a political activity, involving a struggle for power and control. Nor can empowerment be 'done' to disabled people, as power is gained only through collective struggle (Oliver 1991).

Disability Politics and Welfare Research

According to Hughes (1998), social scientific research is both part of the wider social construction of disability and open to critical interrogation as a way of knowing about social issues. Bury (1996) makes a similar point when he suggests that research is a field of struggle in which disability as oppression can be reproduced or resisted.

Barnes et al. (1999) argue that mainstream social research has been informed by policy and practice agendas designed to gather data on the service needs of disabled people in order to help them better cope with their 'personal tragedy' (p.213). For much of the post-war period, welfare policy has been dominated by a Fabian model of social administration rooted, in turn, in an Enlightenment representation of 'truth' as knowledge produced through the human capacity for rational thought. Social change in line with progressive political goals is brought about by scientifically planned interventions grounded in rational analyses of social problems. The predominantly quantitative form of positivist research deployed to uncover the necessary 'facts' is underpinned by a methodological individualism which has served to reinforce the individual model of disability (Oliver 1992b).

In his critique of the most recent national disability survey, Abberley (1992) illustrates the part that research conducted within this tradition plays in reproducing oppressive patterns of welfare provision and resource allocation. Conducted on behalf of the government by the Office of Population Censuses and Surveys in the 1980s (Martin, Meltzer and Elliott 1988; Martin and White 1988), the survey is based on a functional definition of disability that reflects ongoing government concerns with production, capacity for work and welfare. Claims to scientific objectivity legitimise the statistical representation of bodily impairment as the source of social and economic disadvantage, whilst the focus of interview questions on functional limitation serves to confirm disability as individual pathology to participants:

> The very process of isolated disabled people being asked this kind of individualised question by someone in authority can serve to disempower them, since it reproduces and reinforces, as it ostensibly asks 'neutral' questions, a personal tragedy view of disablement. (Abberley 1992, p.141)

Social research has therefore reinforced those meanings of disability deriving from administrative and medical categorisations – passivity, dependency, charity, otherness – that the disability movement set out to challenge and replace with more positive identities (Williams and Popay 1999). Even studies using interpretative methodologies, based on disabled people's own accounts, have tended to be conducted within the medical model with its in-built positivistic assumptions about disability as individual pathology (Oliver 1996a; Zarb 1992). Unsurprisingly, therefore, Oliver (1992b) argues that the paradigmatic shift from positivist to interpretative research failed to produce any significant improvements in the material conditions of disabled people's lives.

Although much contemporary policy research is based in positivistic rather than qualitative methodologies, its purpose is less obviously to base interventions on the rational analysis of social problems. As Hunter (1988) points out, policy developments over the 1980s were based on assumptions about the efficacy of particular policy solutions which were then legitimised in terms of management or organisational theory. Small (1996) maintains that many policy-related studies constitute forms of audit rather than research, in that they are designed to determine how effectively rationally planned interventions have been applied. Evidence is gathered against outcome-related criteria, derived in turn from the cost-benefit calculations of welfare-as-production (Shaw 1998; Small 1996; White 1998; Williams, Popay and Oakley 1999).

Many disability theorists argue that only emancipatory research can change the social relations of research production, taking issue with professional researchers from mainstream traditions on both epistemological and political grounds. Oliver (1996a) identifies the field of study occupied by emancipatory research as: 'the disablism ingrained in the individualistic consciousness and institutionalised practices of what is, ultimately, a disablist society' (p.143). Given its construction within the social model, the primary focus of emancipatory research is on 'the mechanisms and processes which influence people's understanding of disability, and the factors which inhibit disabled people's participation in the economic and social life of the community' (Barnes et al. 1999, pp.215–216). Researchers operating within this paradigm abandon claims to professional expertise based on detached objectivity and privileged knowledge (Brechin 1993) and commit to the struggles of the disability movement for self-empowerment and/or the removal of disabling barriers (Priestley 1999).

Emancipatory disability research represents a radical alternative to mainstream contributions not simply in its political standpoint but also in its methods (Barnes et al. 1999). Disabled people are treated as active participants in research exchanges rather than as passive objects to be studied (Oliver 1996a). Researchers place their knowledge and research skills at the disposal of disabled people and their organisations, acceding to them control over decisions about what should be researched as well as the means of research production and distribution (Barnes 1992; Oliver 1992b; Priestley 1999).

The realpolitik of participatory research proposed by Zarb (1992) offers a means of challenging disablist research agendas where research is sponsored by traditional research institutions and the social relations of research production are constrained by funders' interests and priorities. Researchers can help to change these material relations of research production by making their political stance explicit and resisting claims to objectivity. Participatory research also addresses the social relations of research, whereby steps are taken to ensure that disabled people and their organisations influence the research agenda and begin to take control of the process of research production. This in turn requires that researchers consult with, and make themselves directly accountable to, disabled people and their organisations at every stage of the research. At the same time, merely increasing participation and involvement can never add up to emancipatory research, which depends on ownership of the means of research production and distribution by the research participants rather than the researcher (Priestley 1999).

Doing Empowering Research with Disabled People

Debates about action research as a methodology mirror the epistemological and political challenges which emancipatory and participatory methodologies present to mainstream research traditions. As a methodology 'designed to change as well as study a situation' (Hedges 1985, p.72), Hart and Bond (1995) usefully distinguish between differing types of action research in health and social care in terms of the model of social change on which each rests. Over time, they argue, action research has shifted away from a consensus view of society and a scientific methodology towards a structural change and conflict model of society and a more qualitative and social constructionist methodology. Their typology therefore incorporates a range of assumptions about where change should be made, whom it is for and how it should be brought about.

Hart and Bond (1995) suggest that health and social care is currently dominated by 'professionalising' action research which inflects change interventions towards increases in professional control of the work situation. On the one hand, they suggest that this type of action research mirrors the principles of reflexive practice in its emphasis on an iterative process of investigation, intervention and evaluation. On the other, they acknowledge that the dominance of consumerist and managerialist discourses of welfare means that the professionalising type is also compatible with the current emphasis on evidence-based practice, cost-efficiency, accountability and consultation with user groups. In this they echo Hammersley's (1995) observation that 'scientific politics' has been reimported into some forms of action research. The instrumentalism of much contemporary policy research means that evaluations of professional practice tend to be designed to identify the adjustments required to ensure that practitioners perform effectively against predetermined outcomes.

Given this emphasis on technical expertise in measurement, Shaw (1998) styles the latter type of research 'empirical practice' and argues that it is non-participatory. So far as disability-related issues are concerned, Oliver (1996b) condemns all action research designed to inform policy development or improve professional practice as perpetuating the hierarchical relations of research production: 'Lacking in these approaches has been the involvement of disabled people in the research process as active participants rather than passive subjects' (p.36). The 'empowering' action research methodology described by Hart and Bond (1995), however, is based on a model of structural change and conflict which privileges the empowerment of oppressed groups as the objective of both the action and the research process. Chapter 6 in this volume provides a fuller account of the application of 'empowering' action research methodology in a collaborative project between a team of researchers and a group of disabled people.

Although the action is accorded a central place in empowering action research, it is nevertheless a methodology which proceeds on the basis of ways of knowing about a situation as well as ways of acting to change that situation. Reason (1988) suggests that 'co-operative inquiry', a form of research practice which has much in common with empowering action research, is underpinned by three types of knowing. All actors involved in this type of research properly engage in propositional knowing, or knowledge *about*; practical knowing, or knowledge *how to*; and experiential knowing, or knowledge *by encounter*. These three ways of knowing were integral to the action research project described in Chapter 6, the aim of which was to produce a disabled people's guide to accessing community care assessments.

Propositional knowing, according to Reason (1988), takes the form of ideas, propositions, theories. Practical knowledge, in contrast, takes the form of skills and abilities, and is formed in and for action rather than in and for reflection. Empowering action research into disability policies is necessarily predicated on the proposition that disability is socially created. What is sought as a result both of accomplishing the task set and engaging in the research process is a change in the dominant relations of research and welfare production and, ultimately, in the social relations of disability. In producing the guide, however, we found that a theoretical understanding of the politics of disability and disability research did not itself equip us to operate effectively within the group. The relations of research production had to be worked out between participants over a period of time in the light of the particular circumstances of the project.

Similarly, if the practical concerns of guide users were to be addressed, solutions had to be grounded in their understandings and experiences of the relations of welfare production. The guide therefore drew on material gathered in the wider research study of which the production of the guide formed part. In that study, both our interviews with disabled people about their experience of trying to gain access to services and our observations of front-line assessment practice had revealed the barriers which disabled people had to negotiate in order to access an assessment – not all of which could be simply read off policy and operational procedures – as well as some of the opportunities for maximising people's access to resources (Davis, Ellis and Rummery 1997).

Practical knowledge of front-line practice in community care is frequently obscured both by contemporary forms of research-as-audit and by overly deterministic accounts of disabling welfare production which obscure the agency of practitioners and users alike. Commentators have pointed to the correspondence between top-down managerialist rationality dominating welfare restructuring in the 1980s and 1990s and prevailing agendas and methodologies underlying research into quasi-markets (Cutler and Waine 1997); community care (Twigg 1997); and social work (Everitt 1998). According to Hammersley (1995), earlier fashions for qualitative methodologies in policy-related research were influenced by the view that policy making, implementation and professional practice were part of a political process rather than a set of technical procedures. Research attention was directed towards the perspectives and behaviour of the actors directly involved in policy implementation so as to illuminate the meaning of their actions and gain an understanding of interventions from the bottom up. To the extent that contemporary policy making is no longer research led, however, the concomitant risk of uncovering uncertainties and ambiguities is avoided (Pollitt *et al.* 1990).

Notwithstanding the importation of private sector techniques into new community care arrangements, Hugman (1998) argues that welfare services, unlike consumer goods, are produced at the point of consumption, partly in the heads of caring professionals. This can be linked to Lipsky's (1980) analysis of 'street-level bureaucracy' which suggests that the behaviour of front-line staff is governed as much by the local exigencies of everyday practice as by officially sanctioned objectives. Hudson (1989) maintains that street-level bureaucracy provides a useful basis for understanding the range of discretionary social welfare interventions affecting disabled people. Despite the top-down approach to the implementation of new community care arrangements, in common with the findings of our own study (Ellis, Davis and Rummery 1999), Priestley (1999) argues that discretion and relative autonomy provide considerable scope for street-level bureaucracy, particularly in relation to care management and assessment.

Understanding the practical concerns of disabled people in accessing community care therefore means moving beyond a propositional knowledge of policy, whether produced by government-sponsored research or critical theorists, to a practical knowledge of its implementation on the ground. In our own research, we discovered that the extent to which the front-line workers we observed used their discretion negatively or positively depended on such contingencies as levels of bombardment, the constructions of professional identity, disability and empowerment prevailing in different types of team, and the penetration of managerial specification or, alternatively, managerial support for more traditional forms of professional practice (Davis et al. 1997). Observation work, in particular, can reveal 'the complexity of the web of interests, ideologies and transactions that constitutes a community care assessment' (Stanley et al., p.78). Observation not only reveals 'the meanings and models of causation routinely attributed to events by social workers in their everyday encounters' (White 1998, p.155), but also serves to confound assumptions about the passivity of disabled people and carers by identifying their contribution to assessments (Stanley et al. 1998).

Reason (1998) argues that the third way of knowing, experiential knowledge, is gained by encounter with other members of the research group and the subject of the inquiry. In the guide project, we came to understand the centrality of group process and dynamics in the process of empowerment only in the course of several meetings with other participants. Hammersley (1995) suggests that the instrumental pursuit of emancipatory interests underpinning critical models of research can lead to a reification of democracy. Yet, as Greenwood, Whyte and Harkavig (1993) point out, participation is a process which can only be generated not imposed.

Moreover, the social model of disability on which the emancipatory paradigm is based has been critiqued, by feminist disability theorists in particular, for obscuring the experiential world of impairment. Based on a rigorous distinction between impairment and disability, the construction of disability in a social model fails to deal with the struggles and restrictions associated with impairment (Crow 1996; French 1993; Williams 1996). As Morris (1991) points out, the exclusion from the politics of disability of the subjective experience of physical or intellectual restrictions, of illness or of the fear of dying, mirrors wider gendered divisions between public troubles and private pain.

It is unsurprising, given the close intertwining of academic and political communities in disability studies, that calls for an embodied account of disability are challenged as potentially compromising hard-won gains. Campbell and Oliver (1996) defend the social model by pointing out that it was developed not as an all-encompassing social theory of disability but specifically as a political strategy for addressing oppressive institutions and practices. As such it must be used – and challenged – strategically, and not in ways which risk undermining past or potential gains. The need for constant vigilance is underlined by the way in which even anti-discrimination legislation, passed in Britain after years of struggle and action, attributed disadvantage to impairment and functional limitations (Chadwick 1996).

Yet Crow (1996) maintains that action against oppressive policy and practice would be all the more robust if the personal experiences of impairment were reclaimed, albeit simultaneously located within the wider social context. Experiential knowledge has the potential to take the social model 'beyond grand theory and into real life' (Crow 1996, p.223). Certainly many of the people we interviewed had chronic, often terminal, illnesses and bore testimony in their accounts to the oppressive impact of pain, depression and discomfort on their lives. They would arguably be best supported by interventions which respond to those experiences in ways informed by, but not limited to, a social analysis of disability. As Barnes *et al.* (1999) point out, critical analyses of the body may offer insights into the ambiguous relationship between the materiality of the body and its construction within social processes and institutions. The place of the body in social policy is also beginning to be examined, offering further avenues for the development of an embodied politics of ageing and disability (Ellis and Dean 1999; Twigg 2000).

Barnes *et al.* (1999) refer to 'the unprecedented politicization of disabled people' from the late 1960s and 1970s onwards (p.77), whilst Campbell and Oliver (1996) calculate that the British Council of Organisations of Disabled People represents 400,000 members through its organisational membership. Whereas organisations of disabled people can justifiably claim to represent the views of disabled people, the organisations' views, however, are not well represented amongst the majority of disabled people. The most powerful barrier to people joining the disability movement has been identified as the normalising effect of dominant discourses which divide people into the abnormal and the normal (Drake 1999). Yet a politics of resistance based exclusively on propositional knowledge may be unnecessarily alienating, failing to articulate fully with either the practical concerns of people who continue to have to rely on mainstream services or with their personal experience of living with impairment.

Conclusion

'Empowerment' and 'user involvement' in community care have passed into the vocabulary of both service provision and research activity. Yet disability theorists suggest that these terms serve to confirm disabling welfare identities of dependency and otherness rather than to address the aspirations of the disability movement for inclusive citizenship and rights. Indeed, given the dominance of consumerism and associated models of welfare-as-production, they are viewed less as the means of effecting any real shift in power relations than as strategies of incorporation and control.

This chapter has nevertheless argued that there are spaces for collaborative research in community care. The disability movement has posited the emancipatory research paradigm as the key means of countering the oppressive methodologies associated with mainstream research, yet much policy- and practice-related research is sponsored by traditional funding bodies. Based on the principles of participatory methodology, empowering action research has been identified as a means of working in partnership with disabled people and their organisations to tackle discriminatory forms of service provision (a fuller discussion is provided in Chapter 6).

It has also been argued that both the practice of empowerment and the achievement of empowering outcomes in action research depend on a shared understanding amongst participants of different forms of knowledge. Based on the principles and practice of independent living, the development of alternative models of delivering personal assistance by organisations of disabled people represent just such a synthesis of propositional, practical and experiental knowledges. Yet the majority of disabled people are depoliticised and continue to rely on community care services provided or funded by local authority social services departments. If the gap between 'grand theory' and lived reality is to be bridged, knowledges too have to be reworked in inclusionary ways.

What may be signalled here is a postmodernist acknowledgement of the provisionality and plurality of knowledges. As Small (1996) argues: 'If social research is to be influenced by postmodernism then plurality, contingency, local determinism, small narratives, reflexivity become important' (p.191). Grand narratives of citizenship, rights and democracy are necessary both to counter the universalising concepts of marketised welfare and to avoid a sterile relativity; yet they also require contextualisation if they are to be used strategically and effectively at the local level. The theory and practice of empowering action research arguably makes a modest contribution to this endeavour.

References

Abberley, P. (1992) 'Counting Us Out: A Discussion of the OPCS Disability Surveys.' *Disability, Handicap and Society* 7, 2, 139–155.

Baistow, K. (1995) 'Liberation and Regulation: Some Paradoxes of Empowerment.' *Critical Social Policy 14*, 3, 34–46.

Barnes, C. (1992) 'Qualitative Research: Valuable or Irrelevant?' *Disability, Handicap and Society* 7, 2, 115–124.

Barnes, C., Mercer, G. and Shakespeare, T. (1999) *Exploring Disability: A Sociological Introduction.* Cambridge: Polity Press.

Beresford, P. (1988) 'Consumer views: Data Collection or Democracy?' In I. Allen (ed) *Hearing the Voice of the Consumer.* London: Policy Studies Institute.

Borsay, A. (1990) 'Disability and Attitudes to Family Care in Britain: Towards a Sociological Perspective.' *Disability, Handicap and Society 5*, 2, 107–122.

Braye, S. and Preston-Shoot, M. (1995) *Empowering Practice in Social Care.* Buckingham: Open University Press.

Brechin, A. (1993) 'Sharing.' In P. Shakespeare, D. Atkinson and S. French (eds) *Reflecting on Research Practice: Issues in Health and Social Welfare.* Buckingham: Open University Press.

Bury, M. (1996) 'Defining and Researching Disability: Challenges and Responses.' In C. Barnes and G. Mercer (eds) *Exploring the Divide: Illness and Disability.* University of Leeds: The Disability Press.

Campbell, J. and Oliver, M. (1996) *Disability Politics: Understanding our Past, Changing our Future.* London: Routledge.

Chadwick, A. (1996) 'Knowledge, Power and the Disability Discrimination Bill.' *Disability and Society 11*, 1, 25–40.

Croft, S. and Beresford, P. (1995) 'Whose Empowerment? Equalising the Competing Discourses in Community Care.' In R. Jack (ed) *Empowerment in Community Care.* London: Chapman and Hall.

Crow, L. (1996) 'Including All of Our Lives: Renewing the Social Model of Disability.' In J. Morris (ed) *Encounters with Strangers: Feminism and Disability.* London: The Women's Press.

Cutler, T. and Waine, B. (1997) 'The Politics of Quasi-Markets: How Markets have been Analysed and How They Might be Analysed.' *Critical Social Policy 17*, 2, 3–26.

Davis, A., Ellis, K. and Rummery, K. (1997) *Access to Assessment: Perspectives of Practitioners, Disabled People and Carers. University of Bristol: Policy Press.*

Drake, R.F. (1999) *Understanding Disability Policies.* Basingstoke: Macmillan.

Ellis, K. (1999) 'The Care of the Body.' In K. Ellis and H. Dean (eds) *Social Policy and the Body: Transitions in Corporeal Discourse.* Basingstoke: Macmillan.

Ellis, K., Davis, A. and Rummery, K. (1999) 'Needs Assessment, "Street-Level Bureaucracy" and the New Community Care.' *Journal of Social Policy and Administration 33*, 3, 262–280.

Ellis, K. and Dean, H. (eds) (1999) *Social Policy and the Body: Transitions in Corporeal Discourse.* Basingstoke: Macmillan.

Everitt, A. (1998) 'Research and Development in Social Work.' In R. Adams, L. Dominelli and M. Payne (eds) *Social Work: Themes, Issues and Critical Debates.* Basingstoke: Macmillan.

French, S. (1993) 'Disability, Impairment or Something In-Between.' In J. Swain, V. Finkelstein, S. French and M. Oliver (eds) *Disabling Barriers – Enabling Environments.* London: Sage.

Gooding, C. (1994) *Disabling Lives, Enabling Acts: Disability Rights in Britain and America.* London: Pluto.

Hadley, R. and Clough, R. (1996) *Care in Chaos: Frustration and Challenge in Community Care.* London: Cassell.

Hammersley, M. (1995) *The Politics of Social Research.* London: Sage.

Hart, E. and Bond, M. (1995) *Action Research for Health and Social Care: A Guide to Practice.* Buckingham: Open University Press.

Hedges, A. (1985) 'Group Interviewing.' In R. Walker (ed) *Applied Qualitative Research.* Aldershot: Gower.

Hudson, B. (1989) 'Michael Lipsky and Street-Level Bureaucracy: A Neglected Perspective.' In L. Barton (ed) *Disability and Dependency.* London: Falmer Press.

Hughes, G. (1998) 'A Suitable Case for Treatment? Constructions of Disability.' In E. Saraga (ed) *Embodying the Social: Constructions of Difference.* London: Routledge.

Hugman, R. (1998) *Social Welfare and Social Value: The Role of Caring Professions.* Basingstoke: Macmillan.

Jack, R. (1995) 'Empowerment in Community Care.' In R. Jack (ed) *Empowerment in Community Care.* London: Chapman and Hall.

Lipsky, M. (1980) *Street Level Bureaucracy: Dilemmas of the Individual in Public Services.* New York: Russell Sage.

Macdonald, G. (1999) 'Social Work and its Evaluation: A Methodological Dilemma?' In F. Williams, J. Popay and A. Oakley (eds) *Welfare Research: A Critical Review.* London: UCL Press.

Martin, J., Meltzer, H. and Elliott, D. (1988) *The Prevalence of Disability among Adults.* London: HMSO.

Martin, J. and White, A. (1988) *The Financial Circumstances of Disabled Adults in Private Households.* London: HMSO.

Morris, J. (1991) *Pride Against Prejudice.* London: The Women's Press.

Morris, J. (1993) *Independent Lives? Community Care and Disabled People.* Basingstoke: Macmillan.

Oliver, M. (1990) *The Politics of Disability.* Basingstoke: Macmillan.

Oliver, M. (1991) 'Speaking Out: Disabled People and State Welfare.' In G. Dalley (ed) *Disability and Social Policy.* London: Policy Studies Institute.

Oliver, M. (1992a) 'Civil Rights and Citizenship – a Case of Disabling Welfare.' In T. Harding (ed) *Who Owns Welfare? Questions on the Social Services Agenda.* London: National Institute for Social Work.

Oliver, M. (1992b) 'Changing the Social Relations of Research Production?' *Disability, Handicap and Society* 7, 2, 101–114.

Oliver, M. (1996a) *Understanding Disability: From Theory to Practice.* Basingstoke: Macmillan.

Oliver, M. (1996b) 'A Sociology of Disability or a Disablist Sociology?' In L. Barton (ed) *Disability and Society: Emerging Issues and Insights.* Harlow: Longman.

Pierson, C. (1991) *Beyond the Welfare State?* Cambridge: Polity Press.

Pollitt, C., Harrison, S., Hunter, D. and Marnoch, G. (1990) 'No Hiding Place: On the Discomforts of Researching the Contemporary Policy Process.' *Journal of Social Policy 19,* 160–190.

Priestley, M. (1999) *Disability Politics and Community Care.* London: Jessica Kingsley Publishers.

Reason, P. (1988) 'Introduction.' In P. Reason (ed) *Human Inquiry in Action. Developments in New Paradigm Research.* London: Sage

Seymour, J. (1999) 'Constructs from the New Paradigm: An Exploration of Diverse Meanings.' In F. Williams, J. Popay and A. Oakley (eds) *Welfare Research: A Critical Review.* London: UCL Press.

Shaw, I. (1998) 'Practising Evaluation.' In J. Cheetham and M. Kazi (eds) *The Working of Social Work*. London: Jessica Kingsley Publishers.

Small, N. (1996) 'The Critical Welfare Agenda.' In N. Lunt and D. Coyle (eds) *Welfare and Policy: Research Agendas and Issues*. London: Taylor & Francis.

Social Services Inspectorate (1991) *Care Management and Assessment: Practitioners' Guide*. London: HMSO.

Stanley, N., Manthorpe, J., Bradley, G. and Alaszewski, A. (1998) 'Researching Community Care Assessments. A Pluralistic Approach.' In J. Cheetham and M. Kazi (eds) *The Working of Social Work*. London: Jessica Kingsley Publishers.

Stevenson, O. and Parsloe, P. (1993) *Empowerment and Community Care*. York: Joseph Rowntree Foundation.

Twigg, J. (1997) 'Deconstructing the Social Bath: Help with Bathing at Home for Older and Disabled People.' *Journal of Social Policy 26*, 2, 211–232.

Twigg, J. (2000) 'Social Policy and the Body.' In G. Lewis, G. Hughes and E. Saraga (eds) *Rethinking Social Policy*. Buckinghamshire: Open University Press.

White, S. (1998) 'Analysing the Content of Social Work. Applying the Lessons from Qualitative Research.' In J. Cheetham and M. Kazi (eds) *The Working of Social Work*. London: Jessica Kingsley Publishers.

Williams, F. (1995) 'Gender, "Race" and Class in British Welfare Policy.' In A. Cochrane and J. Clarke (eds) *Comparing Welfare States: Britain in an International Context*. London: Sage.

Williams, F. and Popay, J. (1999) 'Balancing Polarities: Developing a New Framework for Welfare Research.' In F. Williams, J. Popay and A. Oakley (eds) *Welfare Research: A Critical Review*. London: UCL Press.

Williams, F., Popay, J. and Oakley, A. (eds) (1999) *Welfare Research: A Critical Review*. London: UCL Press.

Williams, G. (1996) 'Representing Disability: Some Questions of Phenomenology and Politics.' In C. Barnes and G. Mercer (eds) *Exploring the Divide: Illness and Disability*. University of Leeds: The Disability Press.

Zarb, G. (1992) 'On the Road to Damascus: First Steps towards Changing the Relations of Disability Research Production.' *Disability, Handicap and Society 7*, 2, 125–131.

CHAPTER 14

Research Informing Practice

Some Concluding Remarks

Hazel Kemshall and Rosemary Littlechild

Introduction

In the opening chapter of this book Braye notes that 'terminology is less important than the intention behind the actions it describes' (p.9). For Braye the key to
such intentions is the commitment of the powerful to changing relationships of
exclusion and dependency. This book has brought together a collection of essays
which have explored the contribution of the research enterprise and the
researcher to the achievement of participation and involvement in a range of
social care organisations and settings. The chapters have explored the diverse
experiences and practices of researchers, and in particular the research strategies
used to transform the rhetoric of participation into reality. These strategies have
had varying degrees of success; see, for example, the contrasting experiences and
results of Fleming (Chapter 4) and Rumgay (Chapter 12). The chapters have
provided important insights into the mechanisms for promoting participation (for
example social action, Fleming; McCabe and Ross, Chapter 11; Ward, Chapter 3),
and on occasion insights into why participation is stymied (Dyson, Chapter 10;
Rumgay).

The contributors have also exemplified the differing approaches to participation in social care research, ranging from the emancipatory research paradigm of
social action (Ellis, Chapter 13; Ellis and Rummery, Chapter 6) to the collection
of user views within research parameters defined by statutory providers or
funders (Littlechild and Glasby, Chapter 9; Morris and Shepherd, Chapter 5;
Rogers, Chapter 7; Rumgay). Social action in particular exemplifies a radical
transformation of the relationship between researcher and researched, and in the
problem-solving approach emphasised by Fleming and also by Ward, the
outcomes of the research are not only owned by respondents but are directly
relevant to their needs. However, Rogers shows that even when an agency deter-
mines the nature of the initial research, a commitment to an action research
approach can guide the subsequent course and outcome of the project. Dearden

and Becker (Chapter 8) demonstrate how the very act of carrying out small-scale independent research can, over time, bring to the attention of practitioners and policy makers people whose needs were previously unknown or ignored, allowing their agenda to be addressed.

In contrast, Rumgay is presented with an agency-led definition of participation and with statutory limits on the levels of involvement service users can have in decision making. Rumgay's chapter highlights the significant difficulties involved in researching for participation and involvement in those agencies where service use is a matter of statutory compulsion, where involvement means greater compliance and take-up of 'relevant services', and participation means greater access to predefined services rather than partnership in decision making. In such situations, researchers are often confronted with the difficult issue of achieving a better match between user expectations and service provision. This can result in little long-term or radical change in patterns of service delivery or in levels of participation and involvement.

Morris and Shepherd too describe a service where families are compulsorily involved with an agency, but one which actively seeks their participation in the choice of services which are delivered to them. This chapter, as do others in the book (e.g. McCabe and Ross; Rogers; Dyson) clearly illustrates the varied commitment and enthusiasm amongst professionals to user involvement and participation.

In some cases researchers attempt to step outside the funder's remit and to reconstitute the research in order to prioritise respondents' views. Littlechild and Glasby demonstrate how it is possible to shift the perspective of agencies who have funded the research when the findings do not bear out the assumptions of professionals on which the research was based. However, such an approach is not without its difficulties, not least in terms of how findings may be received by funders and the expectations it raises amongst respondents.

The remainder of this concluding chapter reviews the contribution of research to the participation agenda, identifying possible limits and potential opportunities. To those researchers embarking on participatory research, it offers some pointers for good practice in the field and identifies issues for consideration in research training and teaching.

The Contribution of Research to the Participation Agenda: Limits and Potential

Limits

Shaw has stressed the notion of 'just inquiry' carried out in the spirit of mutuality and within a commitment to social justice (Chapter 2). Such research has an unashamed commitment to 'political action and social transformation' (Shaw p.29). Research methods located within the emancipatory research model have been seen as central to participation. However, Barnes (1992a) has argued that their success is constrained by their context of use, which includes power relations between researcher and researched; researcher or funder control of dissemination and funds; the costs of research; and the location of research within traditional and hierarchical institutions such as universities. Barnes (1992a) concludes that the success of emancipatory research is dependent upon the 'integrity of the researcher and their willingness to challenge the institutions which control research' (p.123).

Such challenges are not always easy within academic career structures linked to funded research (Barnes 1996), or within the parameters of research specifications set by those who commission the work. Allen (1992), in a project designed to investigate and enhance resident involvement in a therapeutic community, found that whilst agreement could be established about the key aims of the community, differences in decision making, and in levels of responsibility and power, persisted. Whilst specific changes were achieved, changing the culture of the community proved more intractable. Allen's study highlights the issue of structural and contextual constraints upon change, and the very real limitations on research as a vehicle for achieving participation.

Such constraints can also be mirrored in the conduct of research. As Cornwall and Jewkes (1995) express it, '"participation" is rapidly becoming a catch-all concept' (p.1668), encompassing 'top-down' research with minimal participation and involvement of respondents, to social action research which facilitates respondents in defining and seeking solutions to their own problems. This book mirrors this continuum, and the links between research strategies which are genuinely participative and subsequent sustained organisational commitment to the participation of users are well made in the chapters by Ellis and Rummery, Fleming, McCabe and Ross, and Shaw. As Cornwall and Jewkes (1995) following Rifkin (1990) note, genuine participation involves more than just taking part; it involves 'activeness, choice and the possibilities of that choice being effected' (p.1668). The chapters in this collection illustrate varying levels of activeness both in the research process and in organisational life by users of services, differing opportunities of choice, and differing levels of power to implement such choices. For Cornwall and Jewkes (1995) a key differential on this participation continuum is by whom and for whom the research question is formulated, and by whom and for whom the research findings are used. This is not simply an issue of the imposed constraints of funders or the limits often inherent in contract research; it is also an issue of academic commitment to participatory research strategies.

Biggs (1989) has argued that 'shallow' participation is characterised by contractual arrangements between researchers and respondents in which the latter are processed either willingly or with some degree of compulsion (for example they are using the service being investigated) into a predefined research inquiry. This may on occasion progress to more consultative inquiries in which the opinions of respondents are sought, but recommendations and subsequent actions are largely researcher- and funder-led. 'Deep' participation is characterised by increasingly collaborative arrangements in which local people and /or respondents work jointly with researchers on academically defined projects, for example as interviewers. The final participatory level is 'collegiate', with researcher and researched working together in a process of mutual learning and problem solving in which respondents control the research process and the outcomes of research.

However, as Cornwall and Jewkes (1995) and others (Hart and Bond 1995) suggest, this is not a neat and tidy process. As the chapters in this collection illustrate, differing levels of participation may occur at differing stages of the research process, or, as Dyson's chapter shows, efforts at collaboration may have unintended and on occasion disappointing results. The collegiate level of participation as exemplified by social action is rarely achieved, although the work of Fleming illustrates that it is possible to pursue genuinely participative research from within the academic community, as commissioned research with clear accountability to funders, and in difficult social and economic conditions. Ellis and Rummery show how their research team was committed to taking the lead from disabled participants in the project, even though this meant undertaking recommendations which ran counter to their own values and views. However, ultimately, they define their project as participatory rather than emanicipatory because of their primary accountability to their funding body.

The difficulties and challenges of participatory research for academic researchers have been well documented (Barnes 1992b, 1996; Bury 1996; Cornwall and Jewkes 1995; Richardson 1997; Shakespeare 1996), not least the higher costs involved, the extensive effort to achieve and support collaborative systems of working, and the difficulties in balancing the various competing needs and expectations of respondents, local communities, professionals and funders. The capacity of participatory research truly to engage and empower the poorest and most marginalised in society has also been doubted (Kaseje, Sempebwa and Spencer 1987; Morley, Rohde and Williams 1983).

The current context of academic research also presents challenges to researchers. The increasingly programme-led orientation of much academic funding (for example by the various research councils), whilst stressing greater inclusion and relevance to users (Rappert 1997), still excludes many local and marginalised communities from the research agenda (Oliver and Barnes 1997). As Rappert (1997) expresses it, the notion of user is itself contested, because in the context of research council funding, users can mean 'industry, charities, universities, local authorities and other public bodies, government departments and independent public bodies' (para 2.5). The participation agendas of government departments and local statutory agencies may not coincide with those of local communities or service users, and the claims to knowledge of both experts and local people may be disputed (Wynne 1982, 1989).

In particular, traditional positivistic understandings of research methodologies and service evaluation present distinct criteria for academic credibility and rigour which can serve to marginalise or devalue participatory research (Cornwall and Jewkes 1995; Everitt and Hardiker 1996; Stone and Priestley 1996). Stone and Priestley (1996) acknowledge that there are contradictions in 'surrendering control and maintaining personal and academic integrity' (p.715). However, this is not to assume that it cannot be done.

Potential

Research validity can be achieved in participatory research and the qualitative methodologies it relies upon (Barnes 1992a; Hart and Bond 1995) Whilst critics have dismissed it as subject to researcher bias and accountable to lay knowledge rather than the peer review of academic experts (Ellis in this book), participatory research can achieve credibility and rigour. Silverman (1993) has refuted the notion that the canons of scientific validity are necessarily free from defect, or are indeed appropriate to qualitative research methods. Science as an activity has increasingly come under scrutiny (Barnes and Edge 1982; Fleck 1979; Kuhn 1970; Lakatos 1978; Latour 1987; Latour and Woolgar 1986). Whilst the notion of objective, authoritative scientific expertise 'has deep roots in the history of science' (Horlick-Jones 1998, p.84) it has been heavily critiqued. Horlick-Jones (1998) has shown that scientific canons do not translate into practice and that improvisation and context play an important role in actual practice. By presenting the 'contrasting findings about carcinogenicity or toxicology of chemicals in Britain and the United States', Horlick-Jones (1998, p.81) illustrates the use of heuristic devices in the process of scientific deduction. Lakatos (1978) has illustrated similar patterns in scientific hypothesis testing; Latour and Woolgar (1986) have demonstrated how laboratory practices themselves create order out of disorder; and Wynne has drawn similar conclusions about the rationality of science (Wynne 1989, 1996).

From this social constructivist epistemology, claims to knowledge and the grounds upon which they are based are more important than claims to objective truth (Jasanoff 1996; Wynne 1996). However, this is not a recipe for arbitrary imposition of meaning by the researcher or rampant subjectivism. Fielding and Fielding (1986) have argued that researchers must demonstrate sufficient 'warrant for their inferences' (p.12) by considering the plausibility and credibility of the knowledge-claims they are making (Hammersley 1990; Silverman 1993) whilst also prioritising respondents' views. Stanley (1990) has argued that lay person and researcher share the documentary method of interpretation, and that those researched are the best judges of the applicability and validity of the explanatory model offered. Bloor (1978) following Frake (1964) has suggested that it is also possible to test such explanations through 'structured respondent validation' in which the participants' responses are predicted in their actual situations of use and then tested through predicted responses in hypothetical cases.

Minichiello *et al.* (1990) argue that validity is also achieved through the researcher 'staying close to the empirical world in order to ensure a close fit between the data and what people say and do' (p. 209). Constant cross-checking of the data and testing of hypotheses against negative cases is the hallmark of the inductive analytical method best epitomised by grounded theory techniques of data collection and analysis (Glaser and Strauss 1967). Silverman (1985) has argued that whilst the 'accounts' of respondents are not to be assessed for either their accuracy or bias, they are considered to be real.

Key features of participatory research are the deliberate prioritisation of hidden or marginalised accounts (see for example the discussions by Ellis and Ellis and Rummery in this book on disabled people's participation, and Dearden and Becker's portrayal of young carers' stories); how these accounts may differ from official accounts (Davis, Ellis and Rummery 1997); and how accounts come to count and thereby gain legitimacy and power (Giddens 1991; Wynne 1982). Within such research, openness and reflexivity about the nature of the research enterprise, how research decisions are made, and the position of both researcher and respondents are essential. The subjectivities of researcher and respondent positions need not be problematic if they are explicitly stated and the perspectival nature of the enterprise is acknowledged (Humphries 1999; Minichiello *et al.* 1990). Part of such reflexivity and openness is the sharing of research hypotheses and outcomes with research participants during which research questions, hypotheses and findings may be revised (Kemshall 1998; Stone and Priestley 1996). Whilst some see this accounting as a potential threat (Stone and Priestley 1996), and others argue that researchers should have analytical autonomy (Shakespeare 1996), researchers such as Fleming have illustrated in this book how collaboration, participant accounting and academic rigour can be combined. Similarly, McCabe and Ross show how their project, whilst having specific objectives, was also designed as a process whose outcome was determined by the way in which the researchers engaged with the service users.

Stone and Priestley (1996) have argued for an emancipatory epistemology in which respondents are posed as the 'true knowers', in contrast to the positivist epistemology in which the expertise of researchers is prioritised. This does not mean that research expertise must be denigrated; rather, it must be used in collaboration with respondent and so-called lay knowledge. Wynne (1989), for example, in a study of sheep farming post-Chernobyl, found that Ministry of Agriculture experts had miscalculated levels of radiation contamination because they lacked local knowledge about soil types – knowledge typically held by local farmers. As Stone and Priestley express it (1996), academic rigour is crucial, as is research expertise, but 'this should not be taken as a green light to assume knowledge of the needs, feelings and conceptualisations of other research participants' (p.713).

Good Practice in Researching User Involvement and Participation

Shaw has suggested the notion of 'just inquiry' as a guiding principle for research in this area, and in essence this is a practical application of Stone and Priestly's (1996) emancipatory epistemology. However, in practical terms what might this mean for research inquiry?

Initially it will require greater openness from researchers about their position, and critical reflection upon the place of their research inquiry within Biggs's (1989) participation typology. At very least this may prompt rather more critical scrutiny of research tenders and the intentions of funders than may currently be the case. Within the real constraints of academic life, it may also enable the renegotiation of research tenders and contracts towards greater participation (for example Littlechild and Glasby in this book), or the pursuit of contracts from an explicit political stance such as social action. This suggests that at the point of bidding and negotiating contracts researchers should consider:

- the framing of the research: is it shallow or deep participation, contractual or collegiate?

- the distribution of power and control within the research enterprise

- the understanding and commitment to participation and involvement held by those commissioning the research

- the relationship and forms of accountability the researcher will have to those commissioning the research and to those who participate in the research

- the level of commitment to the dissemination and implementation of recommendations for change.

In the design and conduct of research, researchers will not only have to consider whether participation is shallow or deep, but the types of mechanisms and processes required to facilitate and sustain participation over the long term. This suggests that attention to the following is imperative:

- the type of participation sought and why; who is to participate, how and why?

- how participation from hidden or marginalised groups can be actively sought and maintained

- how the differing interests and expectations of those participating can be balanced and if appropriate reconciled

- the mechanisms to facilitate 'activeness' and the likelihood of respondents' control over implementation

- the appropriate combination of research expertise and respondent knowledge

- ownership, use and publication of research material

- the mechanisms to support change over the long term, particularly once the research inquiry has ceased

- systems to monitor, evaluate and account for long-term change once the researcher has left the field.

Implications for the research curriculum

There are also implications for research training and teaching. Traditional curricula have tended to emphasise competence in research methodologies and familiarity with the key research traditions. There has been less attention to the social and political role of the researcher (Barnes 1996; Broad 1994; Humphries 1994) or to the transformational potential of the research process itself. With the emergence of an emancipatory epistemology, research teaching will be required to consider the implications of 'just inquiry' and the radical research agenda of paradigms such as social action.

Ellermann (1998) in an article on social work teaching has argued that curricula should reflect the contingency and competing nature of contemporary discourses and assist students in locating both themselves and such discourses within particular social and historical contexts. Ellermann (1998) contends that professionals who are critically self-conscious about the discourses within which they operate are also likely to be reflective practitioners and within this context, reflective researchers (p. 53). Such reflection is essential in a context in which researchers will be confronted with differing constructions of reality and competing claims to truth. In this situation it is imperative for researchers to be open to new ways of knowing, and critically to evaluate claims to truth. In such an approach the value and power base of differing discourses can be more clearly identified. Ellermann (1998) argues that educators including researchers should adopt 'positions of uncertainty' 'in order to develop understandings of the world that are historically, temporally and culturally specific as well as comparative' (p.42).

Research positions would then be characterised by 'deconstruction and self-questioning' (Ellermann 1998, p.43). This need not result in 'epistemological relativism' (Jasanoff 1996, p. 393). For Jasanoff (1996) the essential task is to make connections between ways of knowing and the institutions, practices, cultural beliefs, and material resources which sustain these ways of knowing. In this sense, explanations of the world, including those of the researcher, are intrinsically politicised. For Jasanoff (1996) this legitimates and characterises the researcher's enterprise as an attempt to 'render more visible the connections and unseen patterns that modern societies have taken pains to conceal' (p.413); or as Wright Mills (1970) expressed it, 'the transformation of "private troubles" into public issues'.

References

Allen, P. (1992) 'User Involvement in a Therapeutic Community.' *Therapeutic Communities: The International Journal for Therapeutic Supportive Organisations 1*, 34, 253–263.

Barnes, C. (1992a) 'Qualitative Research: Valuable or Irrelevant?' *Disability, Handicap and Society* 7, 2, 115–124.

Barnes, C. (1992b) 'Day Care on the Move: Learning from a Participative Action Research Project at a Day Centre for People with Learning Difficulties.' *British Journal of Social Work* 27, 6, 951–958.

Barnes, C. (1996) 'Disability and the Myth of the Independent Researcher.' *Disability, Handicap and Society 7*, 2, 115–124.

Barnes, B. and Edge, D. (eds) (1982) *Science in Context.* Milton Keynes: Open University.

Biggs, S. (1989) *Resource-Poor Farmer Participation in Research: A Synthesis of Experiences from Nine National Agricultural Research Systems.* OFCOR Comparative Study Paper 3. The Hague: International Service for National Agricultural Research.

Bloor, M. (1978) 'On the Analysis of Observational Data: A Discussion of the Worth and Uses of Inductive Techniques and Respondent Validation.' *Sociology 12*, 3, 545–557.

Broad, B. (1994) 'Anti-Discriminatory Practitioner Social Work Research: Some Basic Problems and Possible Remedies.' In B. Humphries and C. Truman (eds) *Re-thinking Social Research.* Aldershot: Avebury.

Bury, M. (1996) 'Disability and the Myth of the Independent Researcher: A Reply'. *Disability and Society 11*, 1, 111–113.

Cornwall, A. and Jewkes, R. (1995) 'What is Participatory Research?' *Social Science and Medicine 41*, 2, 1667–1676.

Davis, A., Ellis, K. and Rummery, K. (1997) *Access to Assessment: Perspectives of Practitioners, Disabled People and Carers.* University of Bristol: Polity Press.

Ellermann, A. (1998) 'Can Discourse Analysis Enable Reflective Social Work Practice?' *Social Work Education 17*, 1, 35–44.

Everitt, A. and Hardiker, P. (1996) *Evaluating for Good Practice.* London: Macmillan.

Fielding, N. and Fielding, J. (1986) *Linking Data.* London: Sage.

Fleck, L. (1979) *Genesis and Development of a Scientific Fact.* Chicago: Chicago University Press.

Frake, C. (1964) 'Notes on Queries in Ethnography.' *American Anthropologist 66*, 132–145.

Giddens, A. (1991) *Modernity and Self Identity.* Oxford: Polity Press in association with Blackwell Publishers.

Glaser, B. and Strauss, A. (1967) *Grounded Theory.* Chicago: Aldine.

Hammersley, M. (1990) *Reading Ethnographic Research: A Critical Guide.* London: Longman.

Hart, E. and Bond, M. (1995) *Action Research for Health and Social Care: A Guide to Practice.* Buckingham: Open University Press.

Horlick-Jones, T. (1998) 'Meaning and Contextualisation in Risk Assessment.' *Reliability Engineering and System Safety 59*, 79–89.

Humphries, B. (1994) 'Empowerment and Social Research: Elements for an Analytical Framework.' In B. Humphries and C. Truman (eds) *Rethinking Social Research.* Aldershot: Avebury.

Humphries, B. (1999) 'Feminist Evaluation.' In I. Shaw and J. Lishman (eds) *Evaluation and Social Work Practice.* London: Sage.

Jasanoff, S. (1996) 'Beyond Epistemology: Relativism and Engagement in the Politics of Science.' *Social Studies of Science 26,* 393–418.

Kaseje, D.C.O., Sempebwa, E.K.N. and Spencer, H.C. (1987) 'Community Leadership and Participation in Saradidi, Kenya. Rural Health Development Programme.' *Annual Tropical Medicine Parasite 81,* 46.

Kemshall, H. (1998) *Risk in Probation Practice.* Aldershot: Ashgate.

Kuhn, T.S. (1970) *The Structure of Scientific Revolutions.* Chicago: Chicago University Press.

Lakatos, I. (1978) *The Methodology of Scientific Research Programme.* Philosophical Papers, vol. 1, edited by J. Worrall and G. Currie. Cambridge: Cambridge University Press.

Latour, B. (1987) *Science in Action.* Milton Keynes: Open University Press.

Latour, B. and Woolgar, S. (1986) *Laboratory Life: The Construction of Scientific Facts.* Princeton, NJ: Princeton University Press.

Minichiello, V., Aroni, R., Timewell, E. and Alexander, L. (1990) *In-Depth Interviewing: Researching People.* Cheshire, Melbourne: Longman.

Morley, D., Rohde, J. and Williams, G. (1983) *Practising Health for All.* Oxford: Oxford University Press.

Oliver, M. and Barnes, C. (1997) 'All We are Saying is Give Disabled Researchers a Chance.' *Disability and Society 12,* 5, 811–813.

Rappert, B. (1997) 'Users and Social Science Research: Policy, Problems and Possibilities.' *Sociological Research Online 2,* 3, 131–143.

Richardson, M. (1997) 'Participatory Research Methods: People with Learning Disabilities'. *British Journal of Nursing 6,* 19, 1114–1121.

Rifkin, S.B. (1990) *Community Participation in MCH/FP Programmes: An Analysis Based on Case Study Material.* Geneva: World Health Organization.

Shakespeare, T. (1996) 'Rules of Engagement: Doing Disability Research.' *Disability and Society 11,* 1, 115–119.

Silverman, D. (1985) *Qualitative Methodology and Sociology.* Aldershot: Gower.

Silverman, D. (1993) *Interpreting Qualitative Data: Methods for Analysing Talk, Text and Interaction.* London: Sage.

Stanley, L. (1990) 'Doing Ethnography, Writing Ethnography: A Comment on Hammersley.' *Sociology 24,* 4, 617–627.

Stone, E. and Priestley, M. (1996) 'Parasites, Pawns and Partners: Disability Research and the Role of Non-Disabled Researchers.' *British Journal of Sociology 47,* 4, 699–716.

Wright Mills, C. (1970) *The Sociological Imagination.* Harmondsworth: Penguin.

Wynne, B. (1982) *Rationality and Ritual: The Windscale Inquiry and Nuclear Decisions in Britain.* The British Society for the History of Science 168.

Wynne, B. (1989) 'Sheep Farming after Chernobyl.' *Environment 31,* 11–15, 33–39.

Wynne, B. (1996) 'May the Sheep Safely Graze? A Reflexive View of the Expert–Lay Knowledge Divide.' In S. Lash, B. Szerszynski, and B. Wynne (eds) *Risk, Environment and Modernity.* London: Sage.

The Contributors

Saul Becker is the Director of the Young Carers Research Group and a Senior Lecturer in Social Policy at Loughborough University. He has also worked as a senior welfare rights officer, a social worker and as a researcher. He has published extensively on informal care, community care, social security, poverty and social work. His most recent books include: *Responding to Poverty: The Politics of Cash and Care* (Longman, 1997); *Young Carers and their Families* (Blackwell Science, 1998); *Young Carers in the UK* (Carers National Association, 1998); and *We're in this Together: Conversations with Families in Caring Relationships* (Carers National Association, 1999).

Suzy Braye is a Reader in Social Work at Staffordshire University. She has previously worked in local authority social services as a social work practitioner, trainer and manager in both adult and children's services. She teaches and has published on social work law, community care policy and the organisational context of social work. She is engaged in evaluative research on services for children in need and support systems for carers.

Chris Dearden is a Research Fellow in the Young Carers Research Group at Loughborough University. She previously worked as a nurse. She has been involved in research into community care, carers' and young carers' issues for several years. Recent publications include *Young Carers: The Facts* (Reed Business Publishing, 1995); *Young Carers in the UK* (Carers National Association, 1998); and *Young Carers and their Families* (Blackwell Science, 1998).

Simon Dyson is currently a Principal Lecturer in Health Studies at De Montfort University, Leicester. He is author of *Mental Handicap: Dilemmas of Parent–Professional Relationships* (Croom Helm, 1987). He has worked with self-help groups for sickle cell and thalassaemia for the last 14 years and his current research interests are the social aspects of sickle cell/thalassaemia.

Kathryn Ellis is a Senior Lecturer in Social Policy at the University of Luton. Before taking up a career in higher education she worked for several years in the voluntary sector. She has a particular interest in disability politics, particularly community care, an area in which she has previously worked, published and conducted research. Her most recent book is *Social Policy and the Body: Transitions in Corporeal Discourse* published by Macmillan (1999).

Jennie Fleming is a Research Fellow based in the Centre for Social Action at De Montfort University. Prior to this she worked for many years as a youth worker, community worker and social worker. Since 1991 she has worked in partnership with youth workers, social workers and academics in Russia and Ukraine. She has also published work on the social action approach to research and practice.

Jon Glasby is a social worker and a research student at the University of Birmingham. His research and publication interests include community care, work with older people, social history, local government finance, and the interface between health and social services.

Hazel Kemshall is Professor of Community and Criminal Justice at De Montfort University. She was previously a probation officer, manager and trainer before entering academia. Her research interests include quality in service delivery, evaluating services, effective practice, and risk assessment and risk management. She has completed research for the Economic and Social Research Council, the Home Office, and the Scottish Office, particularly in the areas of risk, criminal justice and penal policy. She has published extensively in these areas, including (with J. Pritchard) in the 'Good Practice' Series (Jessica Kingsley Publishers, 1996–1999). Her most recent book is *Risk in Probation Practice* (Ashgate, 1998). She is currently evaluating multi-agency public protection panels (with Cardiff University) in a project funded by the Home Office Policing Unit.

Rosemary Littlechild is a Lecturer in Social Work at the University of Birmingham. She is a qualified social worker and has worked in local authority social services departments as a social worker, staff development officer and project officer for the implementation of the NHS and Community Care Act 1990. Her current research, publication and training interests are in community care, work with older people, and user and carer involvement in the planning and delivery of health and social care services.

Angus McCabe is currently a Research Fellow in the Department of Social Policy and Social Work at the University of Birmingham. His background is in community development and training in both inner city and rural settings. Over the past four years he has been involved in developing public participation initiatives in primary health care planning and evaluating participatory approaches to drug interventions with young people. Recent publications include: *Community Networks in Urban Regeneration* (Policy Press, 1996); *Networks and Partnerships: A Development and Evaluation Manual* (York Press, 1997); and *Framing the Debate: Crime and Public Health* (Public Health Alliance, 1997).

Kate Morris is a qualified social worker and lectures in social work with children and families in the Department of Social Policy and Social Work at the University of Birmingham. She has substantial professional experience as a practitioner and manager, and as an advocate for service users. Her research and writing interests centre on the involvement of children and their families in the design and delivery of child welfare services. She also has an active role in the development of post qualifying education and training for social workers.

Helen Rogers is a Research Fellow in the Department of Social Policy and Social Work at the University of Birmingham. Prior to this she worked as a social worker and manager in the field of mental health, substance misuse and HIV. More recently she has worked as a quality assurance manager in a National Health trust. Her current research is concerned with inter-agency partnership working in mental health.

Liz Ross is a lecturer in the Department of Social Policy and Social Work at the University of Birmingham. She is a sociologist with a postgraduate qualification in research methods. She has a particular interest in community development and social care services, and the participation of community members, service users and providers in research and evaluation. This interest is reflected both in her teaching on postgraduate programmes and in her research. Recent examples of her research include: an investigation of the experiences of adult survivors of child abuse, the impact of community care legislation on services provided by the Catholic Church, and the action research on the GP commissioning process described in this volume. She is currently working on an evaluation of the Human City Neighbourhood Project.

Judith Rumgay, a former probation officer, was probation tutor for the postgraduate social work programme at London School of Economics for several years. Currently, as Senior Lecturer in Social Policy in the Department of Social Policy, London School of Economics, her teaching mainly focuses on the areas of psychology and crime, and rehabilitation of offenders. Her research interests and publications concern the probation service, drug- and alcohol-related crime, and women offenders. She is the author of *Crime, Punishment and the Drinking Offender* (Macmillan 1998), and has recently completed an account of partnership programmes for substance-misusing offenders (*The Addicted Offender*, Macmillan, 2000).

Kirstein Rummery is a Research Fellow at the National Primary Care Research and Development Centre at the University of Manchester, having previously worked as a social policy researcher at the universities of Kent and Birmingham and as a residential social worker in Kent. She is currently working on a programme of research looking at the effect of inter-agency partnerships on disabled and older people's citizenship status.

Ian Shaw qualified as a social worker in the UK and worked for several years as a probation officer. He is currently an academic at the University of Cardiff and has previously researched service user-patient satisfaction, participation in social work and primary care, and on the principles and theories of assessing service-user satisfaction. He is currently researching in the field of social exclusion (in particular homelessness), supported housing, day care, and young people's involvement in prostitution. He has written widely on practitioner research and evaluation methodology, and is involved in computer-assisted learning software for social work. His recent books include *Evaluation and Social Work Practice* (with Joyce Lishman, 1999), and *Qualitative Evaluation* (1999), both published by Sage.

Carmel Shepherd qualified as a social worker in both the UK and Israel. She has substantial experience as a social worker and a manager in services to children and their families. She currently acts as a Guardian ad Litem for the Inner London Panel of GALs. She also acts as an independent investigating officer for complaints about services. She has a particular interest in family involvement in social work practice, and in the involvement of service users to achieve high-quality services.

Dave Ward is Professor of Social and Community Studies at De Montfort University, Leicester. He has researched and published extensively in the areas of empowerment, participation and social action. In developing his ideas about empowerment and user participation he has worked closely with colleagues in the Centre for Social Action at the University. The Centre promotes and undertakes practice, training and research within the framework advocated in his chapter.

Subject Index

access 112
  enhancement of 201
accountability and local scrutiny
  179
ACPC (Area Child Protection
  Committee) 93
action research
  for development of children's
    services in Ukraine 65–81
  blocks and difficulties
    76–8
      different approaches
        78
      lack of cultural
        awareness 77
      language 76–7
      situation in Ukraine
        77–8
  de-institutionalisation of
    child care project 68–9
  empowerment research
    70–2
  evaluation from viewpoint
    of Ukrainian partners
    74–6
      perceptions of
        involvement and
        participation 75
  future: continuing
    development of
    empowerment 79
  learning together 79–80
  methodology 69–7
  outcomes 73–4
  partnership between East
    and West 67–8
  responsibility 75–6
  setting research agenda
    72–3
  situation in Ukraine 66–7
  value of international
    partnerships 76
  empowering 99–100
  as empowerment: an
    evaluation 105–9
active citizenship 48

admission, patients' perception
  of 151–2
advocacy and support 112
AEP (Appropriateness
  Evaluation Protocol) 146
aftercare, patients' perception of
  151–2
Afro-Caribbeans 159, 166, 171
AIDS 131
All Ukrainian Committee of
  Children's Rights 65
alternative realms of social
  significance 165
Alzheimer's Disease Society 121
Appropriateness Evaluation
  Protocol (AEP) 146
Area Child Protection
  Committee (ACPC) 93
Audit Commission 145
Australia 32
authoritarian values of work in
  groups 52

Bangladeshis 182
Birmingham 144, 179
  Health Authority 144, 180
  Settlement 180
  Social Services Department
    144
black and minority ethnic
  groups 14, 24
Boateng, Paul 139
Bowis, John 139
Britain 15, 31, 65, 69, 78, 79,
  237
British Council of Organisations
  of Disabled People 227
Building Partnerships initiative
  144, 148

Cabinet of Ministers 74
carers
  concerns for 152
  do carers see themselves as
    carers? 113
  of older people with mental
    health problems:
    adapting to organisational
      change 123–4
    developing a relationship
      125
    developing strategies for
      collaborative working
      with 111–27

identifying hurdles and
  barriers 112–15
implementing changes 126
lessons learnt from projects
  123–6
project 115–23
  organisational
    context 115–16
  stage 1: outcomes of
    evaluation 119;
    valuating services –
    the process
    117–19
  stage 2:
    psycho-educational
    sessions with carers
    of people affected
    by dementia
    120–2
  stage 3: closing the
    gap 122–3
statutory bodies and cultural
  change 112–13
stress and strain among
  114–15
understanding demands on
  carers 124–5
Carers National Association
  (CNA) 138, 139
Carers (Recognition and
  Services) Act 1995 119,
  139
'Caring about Carers'
Caring for People White Paper
  143
case studies 73
Centre for Social Action (CSA),
  De Montfort University 54,
  58, 65, 69, 70, 76, 79
change(s)
  cultural, and statutory bodies
    112–13
  implementing 126
  initiatives for 23–5
Charter Mark 116
Chernobyl 238
child care 49
  project, de-institutionalisation
    of 68–9
childhood 23
child protection 14, 15
  family group conferences in
    85–6
  family involvement in 83–96

Child Protection Register 86, 90
children
  listening to 135–8
  services in Ukraine, action research for development of 65–81
  sexual abuse of 14
Children Act 1989 13, 14, 15, 48, 130, 139
Children's Service Plans 83
clarity and appropriateness of information 112
citizen action and control 20, 45
citizens, informed views of 179
citizenship 219
collaboration 54
collective control 49
collective participation 45
Commissioning Plan on Mental Health 175
Commissions for Care Standards 15
commitment 113
Community and Mental Health Services NHS Trust, Shropshire 115
community care
  power, empowerment and restructuring of 218–20
  user involvement and disability research 215–31
Community Care (Direct Payments) Act 1996 13
community development 179
Community Development and Community Care Action Research Project 46
community mental health nurses 123
community networks, discovering and developing 185
confidentiality 41
conscientisation 55, 56
consultancy, role of 196–201
consultation 20
consumerism 18, 45
context and constraints, understanding 54
covert inquiry 41
critical incident analysis 72

cultural awareness, lack of 77
cultural change and statutory bodies 112–13
cultural significance of interactions 165
culture of embodiment 215
Debbie (age 16) 140
de-institutionalisation of child care project 68–9
delegated power 20
demands on carers, understanding 124–5
dementia, psycho-educational sessions with carers of people affected by 120–2
democratic model of participation 18
democratic values in groupwork 52
De Montfort University 65, 68
Department of Health 86, 88, 129
dialogue 55
'Different Voices: Getting Heard' 187
direct observation 72
direct participation of users 179
disability
  politics
    and policies 215–18
    and welfare research 221–3
  power, empowerment and restructuring of community care 218–20
  research
    doing empowering research with disabled people 223–8
    politics of 98–9
    user involvement, community care and 215–31
  social model of 17
  training 74
disabled people 14, 144
  guide to access community care assessments, production of 97–110
    action research as empowerment: an evaluation 105–9
    empowering action research 99–100

politics of disability research 98–9
  producing the guide 101–5
    establishing purposes of guide 101–3
    setting up guide panel 101
    translating principles into practice 103–5
  professional power and empowerment 220–1
Disabled Persons (Services, Consultation and Representation) Act 1986 13, 219
discharge, patients' perception of 151–2
disposals 197, 209
Dobson, Frank 143

East and West, partnership between 67–8
Eastern Europe 67
East London Somali group 58
economy 46
effectiveness 46
efficiency 46
emancipatory research 105
embodiment, culture of 215
Emergency Hospitals Admissions research project 144, 145, 147
empowerment 31, 49–52
  action research as: an evaluation 105–9
  of action research 99–100
  contested notion of 20–1
  continuing development of 79
  participatory inquiry for 34–7
  and professional power 220–1
  research 70–2
  of research with disabled people 223–8
  and restructuring of community care 218–20
  and respect and mutuality in practice inquiry 33–41
  and truth as values in research 168–9
ENACT 180
encounter, group 52
enfranchisement 48

Enlightenment 221
equality of opportunity 55
ethics 147–9
ethnography 42
Europe 53
European Convention on
    Human Rights and
    Fundamental Freedoms 15
European Foster Care
    Conference 74
European Union 58
evaluation/evaluating
    of action research as
        empowerment 105–9
    in practice 37–40
    and research for service users
        29–44
    for social justice 40–1
external validity 164

Fabian Society 221
families 14
family group conferences
    (FGCs) 83–96
    in child protection 85–6
    criteria for referrals to 87
    overview 83–5
Family Health Services
    Authority 163
family involvement in child
    protection 83–96
    family experiences 90–2
    Haringey project 86–8
    issues and dilemmas 92–4
    professionals' views 89–90
    research 88–9
    ways forward 94–5
Family Right Groups (FRG) 86
female offenders and probation
    service 193–213
    exploratory practice in one
        probation service 195–6
    feeling more able? 211
    model for practice 201–4
        enhancement of access 201
        integration of services 202
        introducing user's voice
            202–4
    problems with user
        involvement 204–11
        adapting to changes in
            policy 208–11
        letting voiceless clients
            speak 205–6

providing validating agency
    environment 206–7
    sustaining initiative 208
    role of consultancy 196–201
    profile of female offenders
        199–201
        needs 200–1
        offending 199–200
    targeting controversy
        196–8
feminist research 29, 31, 35, 40,
    41
First World War 216
focus group(s) 38, 73
    topic guide 189

General Household Survey
    1985 129
Gillick v. West Norfolk and
    Wisbech Area Health
    Authority [1986] AC112
    14
GPCG (Small Health General
    Practitioner
    Commissioning Group)
    175, 179, 180, 182, 184,
    185, 186, 188, 189, 190,
    191
GP Commissioning Group 179
GPCP (Selly Park GP
    Commissioning Project)
    144, 145, 147, 148
GPs 122, 150, 151, 155, 159,
    161, 163, 177, 179, 182,
    183, 186, 189, 190, 191
group encounter 52
groups 45
groupwork 52–3
    and empowerment 49–52
    and participation and
        partnership 47–9
    shifting to work in groups 52
    and social action 54–60
    user involvement 46–7
    as vehicle for user
        participation 45–64
Gujarati 164, 165, 166, 170

Haringey project 86–8
Haringey Social Services and
    Area Child Protection
    Committee 83
Health Action Zones 176

Health Improvement
    Programme 176
health issues and primary health
    services, raising awareness
    of 184
Healthy Alliance 154
Hereford and Worcester
    Probation Service 195
Hindi 161
Hindus 164, 170
HIV 131
hospital, routes of older people
    to 150–1
Human Rights Act 1998 15
Hungary 74
Huntington's disease 131

imposition 41
individualistic values of work in
    groups 52
individual participation 45
information, clarity and
    appropriateness of 112
informed consent 41
informed views of citizens 179
informing 20
initiatives for change 23–5
integration of services 202
Intensity-Severity-Discharge
    Review System with Adult
    Criteria (ISD-A) 146
interactions, cultural significance
    of 165
internal validity 164
international partnerships, value
    of 76
inter-professional learning 42

Jimmy (age 16) 141
Joseph Rowntree Foundation 46
justice-based commitments
    within research 41

knowledge
    tacit 30
    test 121
Kyiv 69, 72, 73, 74, 76

ladder model of participation 47
language 76–7
learning disability 23, 144
learning process 183
legal and policy mandates
    13–15

local scrutiny and accountability 179

male sex abusers 52
managerialism 22, 53
mandates
  legal and policy 13–15
  professional 16–17
  user 17–18
manipulation 20
market research 106
meanings of individual words 165
medical condition of older people, information on 152
Medical Ethics Committee 159
Mental Health Act 1983 13
  Code of Practice 13
Mental Health NHS Trust 186
  Shropshire 115
mental health problems 23, 131
methodological practice 32
methodology 37
midwives 161
MIND 115
minority ethnic groups 14, 24
Moslems 167, 202
mothers, working-class 40
multiple sclerosis 131
mutuality, respect and empowerment in practice inquiry 33–41

National Carers Strategy (1999) 139, 140
National Health Service see NHS
National Health Service and Community Care ACT (NHSCCA) 1990 13, 97, 218, 219
National Schizophrenia Fellowship 115
National Strategy for Carers in 1999 139
neo-Marxism 40
New Right 45, 47
Newtown/South Aston Health Action Area 180
New Zealand 83
NHS 143, 145, 150, 151, 153, 176, 177, 178, 182, 191
NHSCCA see National Health Service and Community Care ACT 1990

normalisation 48
North America 32
nurses 161

OBSI see Oxford Bed Study Instrument
Odessa 69, 72, 73, 74, 75, 76
offences by women 199, 210
offenders, female, and probation service 193–213
Office of Population Censuses and Surveys 222
old age 23
older people as 'participating patients' 143–58
  aims of research project 145–6
  background 144–6
  discussion and implications of findings 152–6
  implications for service developments 154
  implications for practice and training of health care professionals 155–6
  research methodology 152–3
  ethics 147–9
  findings 149–52
    assumptions underlying study 149
    concern for carers 152
    information on medical condition 152
    patients' perception of admission, discharge and aftercare 151–2
    routes to hospital 150–1
    vitality of participants 150
  methodology 146–7
  outcomes for 153–4
  profile of study group 148–9
Older People's Directorate of Mental Health NHS Trust, Shropshire 115, 116, 117, 119, 120, 122, 124, 126
Open University 182
opportunity, equality of 55
organisational change, adapting to 123–4
organisational politics 22
Oxford Bed Study Instrument (OBSI) 146

panel meetings 108
Parkinson's disease 131
'participating patients', older people as 143–58
participation
  agenda, contribution of research to 234–9
  limits 234–7
  potential 237–9
  democratic model of 18
  good practice in researching user involvement and 239–41
  implications for research curriculum 240–1
  initiatives for change 23–5
  and involvement in social care 9–25
  models of 18–21, 178–9
    contested notion of empowerment 20–1
    degrees or levels of participation 20
    purposes of participation 18–19
  and partnership 47–9
  perceptions of involvement and 75
  researching for 233–42
  rights of 54
  therapeutic model of 19
  why not participation? 21–3
    organisational politics 22
    professional politics 23
  why participation? 13–18
    legal and policy mandates 13–15
    professional mandates 16–17
    user mandates 17–18
participatory inquiry for empowerment 34–7
participatory reflective inquiry 30
partnership(s) 20, 54
  between East and West 67–8
  and participation 47–9
  value of international 76
patients and primary health care workers in planning primary health care services 175–92
  context 175–7
  models of participation 178–9

putting participating into
    practice 190
sustaining user involvement
    190–1
user involvement project
    179–90
    first stage 182–4
        discovering and
            developing
            community
            networks 185
        establishing good
            practice in user
            involvement 185–7
        gaining experience of
            being involved and
            involving others
            184
        learning and moving
            on to second stage
            184–7
        raising awareness of
            health issues and
            primary health
            services 184
    second stage 187–9
        focus group topic
            guide 189
        in-depth courses
            187–8
        introductory training
            for primary health
            care workers 187
patients' perception of
    admission, discharge and
    aftercare 151–2
PCGs (primary care groups)
    176, 179, 190, 191
People First 217
perceptions of involvement and
    participation 75
placation 20
politics
    of disability 215–18
    of disability research 98–9
    organisational 22
    of poverty 59
    into practice 97–110
    professional 23
Poor Law 216
poverty 59
power, empowerment and
    restructuring of community
    care 218–20

practice, reflective 33
practice inquiry, mutuality,
    respect and empowerment
    in 33–41
pre-sentence reports see PSRs
Primary Care Act Pilots 176
primary care groups (PCGs)
    176, 179
primary health care workers and
    patients in planning
    primary health care
services, empowering 175–92
probation officers 204
probation service
    exploratory practice in 195–6
    and female offenders
    193–213
problematisation 55
process 60, 107
professional mandates 16–17
professional power and
    empowerment 220–1
PSRs (pre-sentence reports)
    196, 197, 200, 201, 205
psycho-educational sessions
    with carers of people
    affected by dementia
    120–2
puzzle-solving 103

qualitative evaluating in practice,
    methods for 37
quality of participation 45
questionnaires 73

R v. Gloucestershire County
    Council, ex parte Barry
    [1997] 2 All ER 1 22
Race Equality Council 58
reflective evaluating 30
reflective practice 33
reflexivity 30
relative stress scale 121
reliability of research 164
research
    contribution of, to
        participation agenda
        234–9
    limits 234–7
    potential 237–9
    curriculum, implications for
        240–1
    with disabled people 223–8

into disability, politics of
    98–9
empowerment 70–2
empowerment and truth as
    values in 168–9
and evaluation for service
    users 29–44
    mutuality, respect and
        empowerment in
        practice inquiry 33–41
    evaluating in practice
        37–40
    evaluating for social
        justice 40–1
    participatory inquiry
        for empowerment
        34–7
    reflective practice 33
    questions – and answers?
        41–2
on family involvement in
    child protection 88–9
feminist 29, 31, 35, 40, 41
good practice in researching
    user involvement and
    participation 239–41
-minded practitioner 57
for participation 233–42
reliability of 164
setting agenda 72–3
into welfare, and disability
    politics 221–3
respect, mutuality and
    empowerment in practice
    inquiry 33–41
rights of participation 54
routes of older people to
    hospital 150–1

Scotland 46
Second World War 216
self-actualisation 21
self-advocacy 23
self-help 20
Selly Park Emergency Hospital
    Admission Project 144,
    145, 147
Selly Park GP Commissioning
    Project (GPCP) 144, 145,
    147, 148
sensory impairment, people with
    14
service users, research and
    evaluation for 29–44

sexual abuse
of children 14
survivors 202
sexuality 59
Shelton Hospital 115
sickle cell/thalassaemia support
groups, working with
159–74
effects of user involvement in
research process 163–7
empowerment and truth as
values in research 168–9
outcomes of research 170–1
project origins 160–2
simulations 39
Small Heath 185
General Practitioner
Commissioning Group see
GPCG
social action 54–60
social care, participation and
involvement in 9–25
social justice, evaluating for
40–1
social model of disability 17
Social Services Inspectorate
(SSI) 139, 221
social significance, alternative
realms of 165
sociological imagination 60
Somali community in East
London 58
South Asians 159, 171
Southern Birmingham
Community Health Trust
144
Soviet Union 66
stakeholding 48
statistical data 73
statutory bodies and cultural
change 112–13
stigma 47
stress and strain among carers of
older people with mental
health
problems 114–15
support and advocacy 112
Survivors Speak Out 217
SWOT analysis 73

tacit knowledge 30
'Talking about Health'
workshops 182, 183, 184,
187

targeting controversy 196–8
thalassaemia/sickle cell support
groups, working with
159–74
therapeutic model of
participation 19
therapy 20
Third Way 60
Third World development
research 31
timing 113
training 69
transformative capacity of
groups 52
truth and empowerment as
values in research 168–9

UIP (User Involvement Project)
179, 180, 182, 185, 189,
190, 191
first stage 181–4
second stage 184–9
Ukraine
action research for
development of children's
services in 65–81
situation in 66–7
Ukrainian Foster Care
Association 79
Ukrainian Institute of Social
Research (ISR) 65, 69 79
understanding context and
constraints 54
Unicef Ukraine 65, 66, 79
United Kingdom 15, 31, 53,
70, 79, 83, 94
post-1997 Labour
government 53
United Nations Convention on
the Rights of the Child
1989 15, 65–6, 130
United States 32, 59, 237
University Hospital Trust 148
University of Birmingham
Department of Social Policy
and Social Work 180
University of Sheffield 83, 86,
88
Urdu 161, 167
user
involvement 46–7
community care and
disability research
215–31

good practice in
researching 239–41
implications for
research curriculum
240–1
mandates 17–18
participation, groupwork as
vehicle for 45–64
User Involvement Project see
UIP

validation 206–7
validity
external 164
internal 164
valuing others' skills 54

welfare research and disability
politics 221
West Midlands Regional Health
Authority 180
Wheelchair User's Group 115
Wicks, Malcolm 139
women
groupwork 207
offences by 199, 210
offenders and probation
service 193–213
working-class mothers 40
work in groups and groupwork
52

young carers, meeting needs of
129–42
'hidden' problem 130–5
informing policy and practice
138–40
listening to children 135–8
Young Carers Research Group
(YCRG) 131, 132–5, 138,
139
youth offenders 54

zero sum perceptions of
empowerment 51

Name Index

Abberley, P. 222
Acker, J. 35, 36
Adams, R. 20, 45, 49, 50, 56
Age Concern 150, 156
Ahmad, W.I.U. 159, 161, 170
Ahmed, B. 55
Aldridge, J. 129, 130, 131, 132, 134, 135, 136, 138, 141
Allen, P. 235
Amos, A. 159, 168
Anionwu, E.N 159, 161
Antonova-Turckenko, A. 80
Archbold, P.G. 113
Argyris 30
Arnfred, S. 68
Arnstein, S. 20, 47
Association of Directors of Social Services 146
Atkin, K. 113, 159, 161, 170
Aubrey, J. 67, 74, 80
Audit Commission 144, 145, 146

Badham, B. 70
Baistow, K. 50, 51, 220
Baker, M. 161
Bandura, A. 206
Barker, I. 17, 18
Barnard, S. 85
Barnes, C. 217, 218, 219, 221, 223, 227, 235, 236, 237, 240
Barnes, M. 11, 17, 19, 36–7, 98, 111, 113, 144, 153, 178
Barry, K. 35
Barry, M. 51, 58, 59
Baskin, D.R. 200
Becker, S. 129–42, 234, 238
Bentzon, A. 68
Beresford, B. 23
Beresford, P. 18, 19, 20, 24, 31, 45, 46, 47, 57, 218, 221
Bewley, C. 14, 112
Biggs, S. 23, 235, 239
Bilsborrow, S. 131
Binns, C. 12

Biss, D. 15
Blakeney, J. 14
Bloor, M. 42, 238
Bond, M. 99, 100, 101, 102, 106, 223, 224, 236, 237
Borsay, A. 219
Boulton, I. 80
Bowl, R. 17, 19
Braithwaite, V.A. 114
Branford, S. 59
Braye, S. 9–28, 49, 51, 216, 218, 219, 220
Brechin, A. 106, 223
Breton, M. 50, 54
British Geriatrics Society 146
British Youth Council 61
Britton, P.G. 114
Broad, B. 240
Brown, A. 53, 54
Bullock, R. 93
Buchanan, J. 194
Burdge, C. 80
Burgess, R.G. 164
Bury, M. 221, 236
Butler, S. 58, 59

Campbell, B. 48
Campbell, J. 216, 217, 227
Capewell, S. 145
Carpenter, J. 16
Cemlyn, S. 66
Centre for Social Action 58
Chadwick, A. 227
Cicourel, A.V. 165
Clough, R. 220
Coast, J. 146
Cohen, S. 194
Collett, S. 194
Community Development Foundation 61
Coombes, Y. 131
Coombs, M. 14
Corby, B. 14
Cornwall, A. 235, 236, 237
Covington, S. 206
Cox, M. 48
Cowburn, M. 52
Crepaz-Keay, D. 12
Cress-Welsing, F. 55
Croft, S. 18, 20, 24, 45, 46, 47, 221
Crosby, G. 14
Crow, G. 10, 85, 86, 89, 90, 92, 96

Crow, L. 227
Cunningham-Burley, S. 159, 168
Cutler, T. 225

Darr, A. 164
Davies, A 58
Davis, A. 36, 97, 107, 108, 225, 226, 238
Davis, K. 50, 70
Davis, V. 160
Deacon, D. 138
Dean, H. 227
Dearden, C. 129–42, 233, 238
DETR (Department for the Environment, Transport and the Regions) 12
Dobash, R. 39
DoH (Department of Health) 12, 13, 14, 15, 16, 19, 20, 22, 46, 48, 83, 85, 95, 119, 130, 139, 143, 144, 145, 146, 154, 159, 176
Donzelot, J. 166
Douglas, T. 53
Drake, R.F. 215, 216, 218, 227
Dullea, K. 31, 57
Dunkle, R. 113
Dyson, S. 58, 159–74, 233, 234, 236

Eadie, T. 70
Eagles, J.N. 114
Edge, D. 237
Edwards, M. 31
Eisner 30
Ellermann, A. 240
Elliott, A. 131
Elliott, D. 222
Elliott, H. 155
Ellis, K. 97–110, 215, 225, 226, 227, 233, 237, 238
England, H. 31, 33
Erikson, E. 30, 33
Esseveld, J. 35
Evans, C. 11, 31
Evans, M. 55, 57
Everitt, A. 7, 12, 13, 19, 31, 57, 98, 225, 237
Exworthy, M. 22

Family Rights Group 85
Farrington, D.P. 194
Faulkner, D. 46

Feuerstein, M. 71
Fielding, J. 237
Fielding, N. 237
Finch, J. 40
Fisher, M. 20, 31, 36
Fitzpatrick, S. 47
Fleck, L. 237
Fleming, J. 54, 57, 58, 65–81, 233
Flynn, R. 22
Fook, J. 31, 32
Forbes, J. 19
Foucault, M. 50, 51, 168
Frake, C. 238
Freire, P. 55, 56, 59, 70
French, S. 227
Fuller, R. 7

Garbach, P. 114
Gardiner, C. 80
Gaster, L. 111, 112
Gelsthorpe, L. 194, 195
Gibbs, A. 38
Giddens, A. 60, 238
Gilbert, K. 67
Gilhooly, ML.M. 114
Gilleard, C.J. 114
Gilligan, C. 206
Gilroy, P. 55
Glasby, J. 143–58, 233, 239
Glaser, B.G. 132, 238
Glendinning, C. 14, 112
Goffman, E 166
Gomm, R. 168, 169
Gooding, C. 216
Gore, J. 168
Gould, N. 31, 57
Graham, H. 71, 169
Greene, J.G. 114, 121
Greenwood 226
Griffiths Report 130, 146
Grimshaw, R. 131
Guba, E. 29

Habermas, J. 168
Hadley, R. 220
Halford, S. 22
Hallet, C. 47
Hammersley, M. 49, 100, 160, 164, 168, 169, 215, 224, 225, 226, 237
Hardiker, P. 7, 31, 237
Harding, T. 14, 22
Harkavig, ? 226

Harrison, M. 58, 80
Hart, E. 99, 100, 101, 102, 106, 223, 224, 236, 237
Hastings, A. 47
Hedderman, C. 200
Hedges, A. 106
Henwood, M. 146, 150
Hereford and Worcester Probation Service 201
Heron 30, 31
Higgins, J. 129
Hill, S.A. 169
HM Chief Inspectorate of Prisons 193, 208
Hodgkin, R. 15
Hollis, C. 80
Holman, B. 31
Home Office 15, 193, 195, 211
Hough, M. 200
Houghton, A. 146
House, E. 33, 40–1
Howard, M. 208
Hoyes, L. 112
Huberman, A. 164
Hudson, B. 226
Hughes, G. 215, 216, 221
Hugman, R. 16, 109, 218, 220, 226
Humphries, B. 31, 45, 57, 59, 161, 168, 238, 240
Hunter 222

Imrie, J. 131
Inglis, A. 146
Institute of Health Service Management (IHSM) 143, 155
Ivanova, I. 80

Jack, R. 221
Jackson, S. 20, 84, 85, 93
Jakobsson, G. 54
James, T. 55
Jarrett, R. 38
Jasanoff, S. 237, 240
Jayaratne, T. 60
Jerrom, B. 114
Jewkes, R. 235, 236, 237
Jones, J. 71

Kaseje, D.C.O. 236
Keenan, E. 74
Kemshall, H. 238
Kernohan, E. 161

Kerr, A. 159, 168
Keith, L. 134
Khakoo, A. 146
Kidd, R. 51, 56
Kintrea, K. 47
Kitzinger, J. 38
Komarova, N. 74, 80
Konopka 52
Kuhn, T.S. 168, 237
Kumar, K. 51, 56
Kurland, R. 52

Lakatos, I. 237
Landells, S. 131
Landis, J. 200
Lather, P. 31, 35, 168
Latour, B. 237
Layder, D. 59
Learmont, Sir J. 193
Lee, K. 54
Le Richie, P. 32
Levin, E. 114
Lewis, A. 15
Lincoln, Y. 29
Lindlof, T.R. 133
Lindsay, T. 45
Lipsky, M. 226
Lishman, J. 32
Little, M. 93
Littlechild, R. 14, 143–58, 233, 234, 239
Lorde, A. 49–50
Lovelock, R. 14
Lukes, S. 50, 51, 169
Lupton, C. 85

McCabe, A. 175–92, 233, 234, 238
Macdonald, G. 220
McEwen, E. 156
McGee, J. 48, 49
McIver, S. 178
McMullan, P. 194
Maher, L. 200
Mahon, A. 129
Mair, G. 205
Marks, L. 146
Marsden, D. 67
Marsh, P. 10, 83, 85, 86, 89, 90, 92, 96
Martens, M. 34, 35
Martin, J. 222
Martin, L. 111, 112
May, C. 205

Means, R. 144, 146
Meltzer, H. 222
Mercer, G. 217
Mertens, D. 31
Mian, I. 114
Mikkelsen, B. 67, 71, 78
Miles, M. 164
Miller, J. 34, 35
Millham, S. 93
Minichiello, V. 238
Mistry, T. 52
Modi, P. 52
Moore, W. 145
Morley, D. 236
Morris, A. 194, 195, 200
Morris, J. 11, 15, 17, 98, 134, 217, 227
Morris, K. 83–96, 233, 234
Morris, L.W. 114
Morris, R.G. 114
Motenko, A.K. 114
Mullender, A. 19, 31, 45, 49, 51, 52, 54, 55, 57, 70, 71, 169
Munford, R. 32
Murray, C. 60

Naboka, S. 80
National Institute for Social Work 53
Neill, J. 146
Newton, B. 139
NHS Confederation 143, 145, 155
NHS Executive 143, 155, 176, 178
NHS Management Executive 176
NHS Training Directorate 12
Nuffield Council on Bioethics 170

Oakley, A. 222
Oakley, P. 67
O'Brien, J. 12
Oliver, M. 55, 98, 105, 161, 168, 216, 217, 220, 221, 222, 223, 224, 227, 236
Olsen, R. 134
O'Neill, A. 129, 131

Page, R. 50, 51, 131
Parker, G. 129, 134
Parsloe, P. 220

Parton, N. 49
Pateman, C. 20
Patton, M. 71
Payne, M. 20, 54
Pearlin, L. 114
Peck, E. 17, 18
Perring, C. 113
Pesha, I. 80
Petch, A. 7
Peters, A. 146
Petrova, N. 80
Phillipson, J. 146
Pierson, C. 217
Pierson, J. 20, 49, 65
Pithouse, A. 45
Plumb, A. 18, 21
Pollitt, C. 225
Popay, J. 222
Popple, K. 45
Potts, M. 83
Powell, J. 14
Pratt, J. 195
Preston-Shoot, M. 14, 16, 18, 23, 24, 49, 51, 216, 218, 219, 220
Priestley, M. 215, 216, 218, 219, 223, 226, 237, 238, 239
Pringle, R. 146
Pritchard, C. 48
Pritlove, J. 131

Rahman, R. 160
Rapoport, R. 97
Rappert, B. 236
Rawls, J. 40
Reason, P. 30, 31, 106, 224, 225, 226
Rees, S. 20, 21, 50, 51
Rhodes, P. 165
Richardson, A. 47
Richardson, M. 236
Rifkin, S.B. 235
Roberts, J. 208
Rogers, A. 155
Rogers, H. 111–27, 233, 234
Rohde, J. 236
Romm, N. 168
Ross, L. 175–92, 233, 234, 238
Roth, J. 163
Royal College of Nursing 146
Rukanyake, N.G. 114
Rumgay, J. 193–213, 233, 234

Rummery, K. 97–110, 225, 226, 233, 238

Salabaj, N. 80
Salmon, R. 52
Sanders, J. 32
Sashidharan, S. 19
Sbaraini, S. 16
Scally, M. 45
Schon, D. 30
Scottish Community Development Centre 47
Sedgwick, A. 14
Seeley, M. 80
Segal, J. 131
Sempebwa, E.K.N. 236
Severs, M. 146
Seymour, D. 146
Seymour, J. 220
Shakespeare, T. 217, 236, 238
Shaw, A. 42
Shaw, I. 7, 29–44, 46, 222, 224, 234
Sheath, J. 206
Shemmings, D. 15
Shepherd, C. 83–96, 233, 234
Silverman, D. 71, 237, 238
Simkins, J. 131
Simon, R.J. 200
Sinclair, I. 114
Small, N. 222, 228
Small Health General Practitioners Commissioning Group 175
Smith, H. 146
Smith, K. 83
Smith, R. 144, 146
Smoliy, V. 66
Social Services Inspectorate 139, 144, 221
Sommers, I.B. 200
Spencer, H.C. 236
SSI 14
Stacey, M. 164
Stake, R. 29
Stanley, L. 237
Stanley, N. 226
Staples, L. 49, 70
Steshenko, V. 66
Stevens, R. 146
Stevenson, O. 220
Stewart, A. 60
Stewart, J. 112
Stoker, G. 112

Stone, E. 237, 238, 239
Strauss, A.L. 132, 238
Stringer, E.T. 116, 125
Strumwasser, I. 146
Svyatnenko, A. 80
Swall-Yarrington, M. 85

TACIS 67
Tannen, D. 206
Tanner, K. 32
Taylor, G. 57, 59
Taylor, I. 31
Thoburn, J. 15, 20, 83
Thomas, C. 113
Thomas, M. 20, 49, 65
Thompson, A. 45
Thompson, N. 21
Thornton, P. 144
Thorpe, D.H. 194
Todd, P.A. 114
Tozer, R. 144
Treu, H-E. 54
Troyna, B. 168, 172
Trueman, C. 57, 59
Truman, C. 31, 168
Tsang, P. 146
Tucker, G. 194
Tunnard, J. 20, 86
Turner, M. 39
Twigg, J. 113, 124, 225, 227
Tyler, A. 131

Ukrainian Institute of Social
    Research 67
Underdown, A. 206
Unicef 66, 80

Valentyuk, N. 80
Vdovenko, T. 66
Victor, C. 146, 150
Volynets, L. 74, 80

Waine, B. 225
Walker, A. 129, 153
Walker, N. 194
Walker, R. 161
Walsh, K. 112
Ward, D. 45–64, 71, 80, 169,
    233
Ward, H. 20
Ward, S. 19
Wasoff, F. 39
Waterhouse, L. 48, 49
Wattley, R. 71

Weiss, C. 32
White, A. 222
White, P. 130
White, S. 226
Whitmore, E. 34
Whyte, W.F. 30, 164, 226
Wiffen, J. 83, 85
Williams, F. 217, 222
Williams, G. 227, 236
Williams, J. 146
Williamson, H. 45, 54, 58
Willow, C. 15
Wilson, C. 74
Wilson, E. 12
Wilson, G. 151
Wistow, G. 11, 17, 19, 36–7,
    111, 146
Woodcock, Sir J. 193
Woolgar, S. 237
Worrall, A. 194
Wright Mills, C. 49, 60, 241
Wynne, B. 237, 238

Yakabova, Y. 80
Yakoba, Y. 74
Yaramenko, a. 80
Young, K. 49, 56

Zarb, G. 98, 99, 222, 223
Zarit, M. 114
Zarit, S.H. 114
Zimmerman, W. 39